THE CHINESE REVOLUTION IN HISTORICAL PERSPECTIVE

THE CHINESE REVOLUTION IN HISTORICAL PERSPECTIVE

John E. Schrecker

New York
Westport, Connecticut
London

Library of Congress Cataloging-in-Publication Data

Schrecker, John E.
The Chinese revolution in historical perspective / John E.
Schrecker.
p. cm.
Includes bibliographical references and index.
ISBN 0–275–93646–5 (pbk. : alk. paper)
1. Revolutions—China—History. 2. China—History—19th century.
3. China—History—20th century. 4. China—Intellectual life.
5. China—Politics and government. 6. China—Social conditions.
I. Title.
DS740.2.S33 1991b
951—dc20 90–40901

A hardcover edition of *The Chinese Revolution in Historical Perspective* is
available from the Greenwood Press imprint of Greenwood Publishing Group, Inc.
(Contributions to the Study of World History, 19; ISBN 0–313–27485–1)

Library of Congress Catalog Card Number: 90–40901
ISBN: 0–275–93646–5

First published in 1991

Praeger Publishers, One Madison Avenue, New York, NY 10010
An imprint of Greenwood Publishing Group, Inc.

Printed in the United States of America

The paper used in this book complies with the
Permanent Paper Standard issued by the National
Information Standards Organization (Z39.48–1984).

10 9 8 7 6 5 4 3 2 1

Copyright Acknowledgments

The author and publisher gratefully acknowledge the use of material:

Extracts taken from *The Analects of Confucius* by Arthur Waley, reproduced by kind permission of Unwin Hyman Ltd. Copyright 1938.

Vincent Y. C. Shih, *The Taiping Ideology*. Seattle: University of Washington Press, 1967. Reprinted courtesy of the University of Washington Press.

William Theodore de Bary et al., *Sources of Chinese Tradition*. 2 Vols. Copyright © 1960. Columbia University Press, New York. Used by permission.

Wang Yangming, *Instructions for Practical Living and Other Neo-Confucian Writings*. Tr. with notes and commentaries by Chang Wing-tsit. Copyright © 1963. Columbia University Press, New York. Used by permission.

Fung Yu-lan, *A History of Chinese Philosophy*. Tr. by Derk Bodde. 2 Vols. Princeton: Princeton University Press, 1958. Reprinted courtesy of Princeton University Press.

D. C. Lau, tr. *Mencius*. Copyright © 1970. Penguin Classics, London. Used by permission.

In memory of my father, Karl Steiner, and
my stepfather, Franz Schrecker

If names are not rectified, then what is expressed will not be in accord with truth. If what is expressed is not in accord with truth then practical affairs cannot be carried to success.

The *Analects* of Confucius
Bk.13. Ch. 3.

Contents

Preface

This book is primarily concerned with two interrelated issues in the study of Chinese history and, in particular, in the understanding of the past two hundred years. The first of these issues is how to conceptualize and evaluate what has occurred in China in the nineteenth and twentieth centuries. It is widely agreed that this period has been an era of revolution, but the character and success of that revolution remain perennial and important questions. The second issue is how this revolution relates to the long and often misunderstood period that preceded it. This question is crucial in the study of any revolution and of the modern era anywhere in the world. It has been a particularly complex topic in the study of China because the West and Western ideas played a crucial role in the revolutionary process, and this role has tended to obscure China's indigenous background from both participants and historians.

As I began working on these issues, I also found that the effort to relate modern China to her past and, in this sense, to de-emphasize Western points of view, was leading me to an approach that might, in addition, make some contribution to addressing another long-felt concern of China specialists: the fact that material on China is still peripheral to Western historical studies and to contemporary Western knowledge overall. As a result, I also began to conceive of the project as a means of encouraging those unacquainted with China to discover some of the things that might be important and interesting to their own work. The book, therefore, also aims at presenting a self-contained, though by no means comprehensive, introduction to the social, political, and intellectual history of China that will, hopefully, be useful for this purpose.

One approach I take to conceptualizing the revolution and its relationship to the past is to make a self-conscious effort to bring the story of the nineteenth and twentieth centuries into accord with what might be called the traditional version of earlier Chinese history as portrayed by American specialists on that era and to draw the necessary consequences for the story of the revolution. This approach is useful because the historiography of pre-revolutionary China has, as opposed to the study of recent times, been comparatively uninfluenced by Western theories. As a result, there has been something of an inconsistency between the specialist's image of the earlier era, as presented, for example, in Charles Hucker's text, *China's Imperial Past*,[1] and the baseline for the revolution implied by many studies of modern times. Simply noting this situation and working to overcome it by giving full respect to scholarship on the earlier era help to understand the character of the revolution and its relationship to the past.

The other strategy that I have adopted is to narrate and analyze the story in terms of traditional Chinese historiographical concepts, generally from the Confucian tradition. I continue this strategy even when the West comes on the scene, as it does, of course, in an important way. As a result, not only do I follow the recent trend in scholarship that stresses internal causation rather than the foreign impact, but, even more fundamentally, I analyze the role of the Occident and its influence in terms of the Chinese story and the Chinese categories rather than the other way around.

My approach, I believe, obviates a major difficulty that is inherent in interpretations that derive from Western outlooks: the tendency toward an excessively simplistic understanding of the society that gave rise to the revolution, seeing it as static and homogeneous, perhaps, or without an opposition tradition, or conceiving of it as sociopolitically ''backward,'' as similar to the ancien régime in the West, ''traditional'' in the technical sense of the social sciences or ''feudal'' for Marxists. Clarifying such misconceptions leads, in turn, to a fundamental reinterpretation of the relationship between modern China and the past, of the West's impact on the revolution, and, to some extent, perhaps, of our understanding of the modern West itself.

Two concepts from traditional Chinese social theory are of particular importance to the analysis: *fengjian* and *junxian*.[2] These were what we would today call ''ideal types'' or theoretical models for alternative forms of sociopolitical organization and were commonly used to understand the history of China before the dominance of Western theories. There are two basic elements that define and distinguish fengjian and junxian. Under the fengjian system society is not run directly by the king. Rather it is governed in a decentralized fashion, by hereditary local lords whose families have been granted a piece of territory to administer. Junxian society is run from the center with the country divided up into local units administered through bureaucrats appointed by the monarch. The other distinction between the two systems is closely related. Fengjian society has an elite of hereditary aristocrats and sharp and clearly defined class lines, whereas junxian has an elite based on wealth, talent, or education and a relatively open social system.

In addition to these basic meanings there are at least three other characteristics that traditional social theorists commonly associated with the two systems. First

of all, in fengjian there are powerful sociopolitical restrictions on the sale of land, labor, and goods. In junxian there is comparatively free sale of these commodities. Second, a fengjian society has a military mentality; junxian, a civilian or mercantile outlook. Finally, the fengjian order is deeply religious and spiritual in ideology, while the junxian tends toward the humanistic or secular.

Fengjian, then, implies decentralized authority, sharp class lines, the absence of a free market, and military and religious values. It is commonly translated as "feudalism." There is no accepted translation for junxian, though it is sometimes called the "prefectural" or the "bureaucratic" system. Perhaps "capitalism" in its most general sense of postfeudal society or "modern times" and thus of centralized bureaucratic government, a market economy, and civilian and secular values gives something of the feel, though, as we shall see, the fact that we have no obvious word for the system may be the more interesting point.

Roughly speaking, China was fengjian for the first one thousand years of its history, from about 1700 to 500 B.C. Then the initial development of junxian began, reaching a peak with the brief Qin Dynasty (221–206 B.C.). The next millennium saw something of a revival of fengjian and then, toward the end, the final reemergence of junxian. China entered its full junxian era in the Song Dynasty, which began in A.D. 960, and the system reached maturity in the Ming (1368–1644) and the Qing, which began in 1644. Thus a junxian system, with at least a thousand years of history behind it, was on the scene when the revolution began in 1800.

It should be noted that using traditional Chinese terminology to structure the story of the era prior to 1800 is, not coincidentally, fully compatible with the standard view of American specialists on that period, for while fengjian and junxian have not been systematically employed, the terms have been sufficiently analyzed and used to understand and apply them effectively. More interestingly, however, these categories were so central to traditional Chinese historiography that they lie behind almost all work influenced by those views rather than by the West. They are, therefore, almost taken for granted by scholars on the earlier era, however much they may disagree about other points. As a result, the terms not only provide a good way of summarizing the standard image but in a few places, I hope, help to tie things together and clarify some points, as one might expect when an important, but implicit and even unconscious, key to understanding is systematically revived.

Thus, for example, the Chinese concepts help to clarify the so-called Naito Hypothesis, which is widely accepted in the historiography of traditional China, though its implications for the nineteenth and twentieth centuries are often ignored.[3] The most influential feature of Naito's analysis, which centers on a transition from aristocratic to commoner society in about the tenth century A.D., is not only fully compatible with an analysis in terms of fengjian and junxian but was, indeed, developed under the influence of Chinese historians thinking along such traditional lines.

On the other hand, while the approach in this book does not basically alter

our understanding of China before 1800, as I have noted, it suggests an entirely new perspective on the history since then and one that, I think, helps to conceptualize the revolution and relate it to the past in a clear and parsimonious way. I analyze the revolution as a movement within and against a junxian society and, from the point of a long-standing and vigorous opposition tradition of the time, an overripe and decaying junxian system.

In addition, this aspect of the analysis suggests the reevaluation of the interrelationship between China and the West. To understand this further, it is necessary to describe another term from the Chinese tradition, the concept of *datong*. Datong, which literally means the "Great Unity" and in sociopolitical terms has been translated as the "Great Community," was an image of the good society that played an important part in the thought of the opposition during the junxian age.[4]

The datong ideal called for a number of things that are discussed at length in the book. What is most essential for understanding the role of the West, however, was the notion that the proper social organization should be a blend of the best in the past and, in particular, of fengjian and junxian. As a result, by the seventeenth century, one of the major goals of revolutionaries and social critics was to supplement what they considered to be the excessively junxian character of their society with the strengths of fengjian. For example, they said that centralized, bureaucratic rule had become dictatorial and that the free market in land was causing extremes of inequality and argued that such problems could be resolved by reestablishing what they considered to be the liberal political style of the fengjian age or its constraints on private ownership.

This perspective on the opposition leads to the new analysis of the critical role that the West played in the revolution. First of all, I should note that I do not disagree with the existing interpretations when they say that the impact of the Occident took the form of modern science and technology and the notion of transcendent progress. However, I do argue that a major influence of the Occident also came from the fact that as China's junxian society decayed, the West was in a transition from fengjian to junxian.

As a result, the West proved a fountainhead of fengjian ideas and practices for Chinese radicals seeking to correct the junxian excesses of their own society. This analysis differs from and, indeed, reverses the prevailing view, which tends to see China as "backward" in comparison to the West not only in terms of science and technology but also in relation to the sociopolitical categories described by fengjian and junxian, and which tends to assume, almost unconsciously, that the West was more junxian than China, and that Chinese revolutionaries wanted China to become more junxian and sought to learn the system from the West.

I am not unaware that what is unusual here is not simply that I revise the impact of the Occident in this way but also that I use Chinese categories to understand the West. Indeed, it is, perhaps, the most novel aspect of the book. However, though unorthodox, it is central to the goals of the work and, I believe, historically reasonable. As it turns out, it also opens the way to "translating"

Chinese history for the use of specialists on the West and to some fresh views about what can be learned from the study of China.

First of all, the Occident cannot be related to the story of modern China (nor, indeed, can any two cultures be connected in a single narrative) without a common vocabulary or categories of analysis. Since the purpose of this study is to see how the Chinese revolution relates to Chinese tradition and how it is a part of Chinese history rather than a subcase of Western experience, using Chinese concepts to compare the two societies and to analyze their interaction is necessary and appropriate.

Second, while the categories fengjian and junxian are Chinese, employing them to generalize about recent Western history does not involve any serious deviation from our usual approaches, and, indeed, I focus on them to some extent because of their utility as one way of relating China and the West in the nineteenth and twentieth centuries. Thus, the transition in the West from the ancien régime to the "new," from feudalism to capitalism, or from traditional society to modern is fairly described in sociopolitical terms as a shift from aristocratic and decentralized government to centralized bureaucracy, from a controlled and limited market to laissez-faire practices, and from warlike and religious values to more civilian and secular ones. These changes did not all occur simultaneously, of course, and the pace was different in different countries; overall, though, it seems reasonable to use fengjian and junxian to describe a process of change that has been occurring in Western society over the past several hundred years.

Third, these categories were actually used to describe the West by the last generation in China that saw the revolutionary process primarily in indigenous terms, the group that came to prominence in the 1890s and is generally known as the Reform Movement of 1898. I have, indeed, been particularly influenced by this group, which I have studied for many years and which felt that China had become excessively junxian and saw the West as a source for long lost fengjian traditions.[5]

Finally, as I have noted, using a Chinese frame of reference as the basis of one's analysis may help to make Chinese history and theory more interesting and useful to colleagues in other fields. Most of us who study China would, I think, still be forced to agree with E. G. Pulleyblank when he wrote that China remains peripheral to Western historiography and learning, not because of the lack of specialized knowledge about China but, rather, because of "the lack of the means of fitting the vast mass of detail of Chinese history into familiar patterns of Western history" and that

> to be rendered intelligible to Western readers Chinese history must undergo a process of translation, and not of words alone, but of whole concepts and systems of concepts. Further, if it is to be made congruent with Western history, our concepts of dealing with Western history must also come under criticism and new concepts must be devised which will be adequate to render each culture intelligible in terms of the other.[6]

Simply introducing the nonspecialist to Chinese history and tradition by using Chinese concepts and theories to analyze important and interesting material, the story of China and of her interaction with the West represents, I believe, one approach to such problems, for it displays the strengths and relevance of Chinese information in a respectful and, hopefully, effective manner. The approach also directly highlights the utility of Chinese history and thought since, as we shall see, Chinese social theory originally began in a fengjian-junxian transition and was then further developed as junxian society matured. Therefore, it would, along with the history involved, be invaluable in understanding many aspects of the modern West.

For example, the information from China suggests that the combined weight of science and technology and a belief in transcendent change have often obscured the fact that the modern West has been in a transition from fengjian to junxian and that we are in a relatively early phase of the latter system. This understanding, in turn, leads in many possible directions ranging from support for Schumpeter's analysis of imperialism as a "feudal atavism" to an appreciation of Montesquieu's belief in the importance of a vigorous aristocratic heritage to the development and success of liberalism. More broadly, it is an understanding that brings out the fact that the dominant historiographical problematique for the past 150 years has tended to define the issues of the modern West in terms of the relationship or conflict between junxian and postjunxian society and that an analysis in terms of junxian society and the past might be more realistic and accurate.

The validity of such assertions can, of course, be evaluated only when the book has been read. However, one example may, at least, help to show the suggestive character of the approach and also explain one reason why "translating" Chinese history has proven difficult; for it turns out that the understanding of junxian and the terminology needed to analyze it, indeed, the very concept itself, developed in China only when the system was well along and several hundred years after political theory in general came into existence. It is suggestive of the historical situation of the modern West, then, to discover that, as opposed to fengjian, our vocabulary has no generally agreed upon set of terms for junxian society. Thus, for example, we have a reasonable translation for fengjian, "feudalism," but none for junxian itself. Similarly, we have a precise word for the elite of a fengjian society, "aristocracy," but none for that of junxian, and a word for the average person in the former system, "commoner," but none for the latter.

In conclusion, I should say that though readers may, by this point, feel that this book approaches things in an excessively theoretical fashion, they will, I hope, be pleasantly surprised to find that the body of the work, while embodying my particular perspectives, is written as a straightforward narrative. Specialists will also note that even in the discussion of the modern period, the book avoids introducing novel or controversial facts. There are, naturally, places where I have differed from the usual approach in terminology or emphasis, and I have discussed these fully in the notes.

I have adopted this format partly because of my hope that the book may provide a self-contained and stimulating translation of Chinese history for the nonspecialist. Equally important, though, I believe that a new interpretation is best demonstrated and judged by its success in integrating existing information into a coherent story and in my case, most importantly, by its ability to relate Chinese tradition to the revolution in a smooth and convincing manner.

Part I of the book tells the story of China from its beginnings in the second millennium B.C. to about A.D. 1800. It is important in its own right and also for understanding the Chinese social thought that forms the basis of the analysis and the character of the society in which the revolution took place. For this reason it pays particular attention to the opposition tradition. The section concludes with a chapter on foreigners that, among other things, sets the West into a Chinese frame of reference.

Part II picks up in 1800 and deals with the revolution proper. It describes the problems which began to accumulate, the developing movement against the junxian system and the reigning Qing Dynasty, and the overthrow of the latter in 1911. It also details the story and character of the Western impact from the Opium War through the May 4th Movement and the victory of the Communists in 1949.

The final chapter discusses the People's Republic. This is, of course, the most tentative part of the work, not only because it deals with the contemporary scene but also because Chinese communism has, thus far, repudiated the traditional framework of analysis that I employ in favor, generally, of Marxism. I suggest that the People's Republic has brought some needed improvements to society but has by no means been successful in attaining the goals of those who opposed the junxian system. In addition, I argue that a major and ironic cause for the problems of the past forty years, most starkly exemplified by dictatorship, economic problems, and ever mounting dissatisfaction, is the fact that China remains out of touch with the dynamic side of her own traditions. As a result, the nation has had difficulty both in learning from its own national heritage and in assimilating the strengths that earlier generations saw in the West.

Yang Lien-sheng read the chapters on the traditional era with great care and made extensive and extremely useful comments that have done much to save me from error in dealing with the vast amount of territory on which he is so expert. Paul Cohen also made particularly thorough and important suggestions.

I have also profited from the comments and assistance of many people, including: Rudolph Binion, Cyril Black, Joseph Coggins, Albert Craig, Irene Eber, Robert Entenmann, John Fairbank, Joshua Fogel, Lars Freden, B. Michael Frolic, Bradley Geisert, Kathleen Hartford, Hsu Cho-yun, Akira Iriye, Marius Jansen, Gary Jefferson, Sungha Kim, James T. C. Liu, John McLellan, Roderick MacFarquhar, Min Tu-ki, Jean Oi, Mary Rankin, Edwin Reischauer, Benjamin

Schwartz, Florence Trefethen, Michael Walzer, David Wiesen, Robert Wolfe, and Ernest Young.

The book received its original stimulation from my participation in the Graduate Program in Comparative History at Brandeis and I owe a great debt to it and to my colleagues in the History department as a whole. I have been trying out the various ideas and approaches in the book on undergraduates at Brandeis for longer than I would care to remember and I would especially like to thank them for the myriad ways in which they helped to focus and shape the final product. My membership in the Fairbank Center for East Asian Research at Harvard and access to the marvelous collection of the Harvard-Yenching Library have been of immeasurable importance to my work and I am very grateful. While working on the book I spent a year at the Institute for Advanced Study in Princeton and am immensely thankful for the financial support and intellectual climate that that uniquely pleasant place provided.

I would like to thank John Harney for doing so much to see the manuscript to press, Ina Malaguti and Judith Brown for their secretarial help, and Carol Lucas and Alicia Merritt for their editorial and production work.

It is impossible to thank all the personal friends who have been supportive and helpful in what has sometimes been a difficult project. Some of these include Robert Brandfon, Sidney Coleman, Milton Hindus, Stanley Kelley, Jr., Richard and Nadine Lindzen, Jocelyn Nash, Alan Scribner, Thomas Tuttle, and Thompson Williams.

My sons, Michael and Daniel Schrecker, have been wonderful throughout the project.

Needless to say, with so much help, all errors and weaknesses which remain in the book are solely my responsibility.

THE CHINESE REVOLUTION IN HISTORICAL PERSPECTIVE

Part I

CHINA THROUGH 1800

1

Ancient China and the Development of Chinese Thought

HISTORICAL SETTING AND BASIC CONCEPTS

One of the most remarkable features of Chinese history is its great age and continuity. This is not to say that China has been changeless or static but simply that she has had over three thousand years of an unbroken cultural and political tradition and is the oldest country in the world. In many ways, China today and the revolution that brought her into being are but the latest stage in this long history. It should not, therefore, be surprising that a book that deals primarily with the nineteenth and twentieth centuries should begin with the ancient era.

There have been humans or protohumans in what later became China at least since Peking Man, about four hundred thousand years ago. About seven thousand years ago the area entered the Neolithic or New Stone Age, an era marked by settled communities subsisting on agriculture. We know about the three thousand years of the Neolithic era almost entirely from archaeological deduction since, except for a few primitive symbols, it was preliterate.

Neolithic society was spread all over China and was organized into tribes. The group of greatest interest to historians and the one about which we know the most lived in North China and became the main source of later Chinese civilization. Like many tribal societies in other parts of the world, this group did not have a hereditary ruler or king, an institution often associated with later developments in the evolution of politics and society. Rather, it seems to have selected a chieftain on the basis of his ability and charisma. For example, we have semihistorical legends from this group that speak of the sage ruler Yao, who selected his successor, Shun, on the basis of merit, as did Shun when choosing his successor, Yu.

About 2000 B.C. this Neolithic tribal society began to give way to a larger and more coherent political system. This first Chinese state took shape in the middle reaches of the Yellow River and is associated with the earliest of the so-called *San Dai*, the Three Dynasties of ancient China. The first dynasty was the semilegendary Xia (ca. 2000 B.C. to 1700 B.C.). The second of the Three Dynasties was the Shang or Yin (ca. 1700 B.C. to 1100 B.C.), which is fully historical, as is the following Zhou Dynasty (ca. 1100 B.C. to 256 B.C.).

A dynasty in China means a ruling family and also denotes an era when a given family is in control. When the ruling family changes, the dynasty changes. The legend says that the Xia, the first of the San Dai, was ruled by the family of Yu. He had wanted to select the most virtuous person to succeed him in the tribal tradition of Yao and Shun but was prevailed upon by the people to choose his son as the next ruler. Thereafter the hereditary principle prevailed. The Three Dynasties are roughly coterminous with the Bronze Age of China, though in the second half of the Zhou, iron made its appearance. From the Shang onward, the civilization was literate and used a writing system based on ideographs that is the direct ancestor of contemporary Chinese script.

The Three Dynasties, at least the thousand or so years up to the late Zhou, had a sociopolitical system that in traditional Chinese terms was called *fengjian*. In traditional terminology a fengjian system was generally contrasted with an alternative form of organization known as *junxian*. It was in the late Zhou that China, for the first time, began to move from a fengjian to a junxian society, and the history of the era did much to establish the fundamental understanding of the two systems. The concepts fengjian and junxian eventually developed into what we would, today, call ideal types or theoretical models, useful for understanding not only ancient China but the entire subsequent course of Chinese history.

There are two basic elements that define and distinguish fengjian and junxian. Under the fengjian system, society is not run directly by the king. Rather, it is ruled in a decentralized fashion by hereditary local lords whose families have been granted a piece of territory to administer. Junxian society is run from the center with the country divided up into local units administered through bureaucrats appointed by the king. The other distinction between the two systems is closely related. Fengjian society has sharp class lines and an elite of hereditary aristocrats, whereas junxian has a relatively open social system and an elite based on wealth, talent, or education.

In addition to the basic meanings of fengjian and junxian, there are at least three other characteristics that traditional social theorists commonly associated with the two systems. First of all, in a fengjian system there are powerful sociopolitical restrictions on the sale of land, labor, and goods. In a junxian society there is comparatively free sale of these commodities. Second, a fengjian society has a military mentality; a junxian society, a civilian or mercantile outlook. Finally, the fengjian order is deeply religious and spiritual in ideology, while the junxian tends toward the humanistic, secular, or atheist.[1]

In the Xia (if it existed) and the early Shang, the fengjian system still had something of a tribal flavor, and its highest development came in the early years of the Zhou. The Zhou had been a semi-independent group on the edges of the Shang state. Several generations before they conquered the Shang, they had become part of the system. When they overthrew the government, they claimed that they were doing so because the Shang rulers had become evil and profligate in personal behavior and in governing society. In particular, they claimed that the last ruler, a vicious debauchee named Zhou Xin (no relation to the Zhou), had lost the "Mandate of Heaven" to rule. The notion that rulers remained legitimate only so long as they continued to behave virtuously and that a given political order was worthy of support only so long as it was just remained basic to Chinese social theory from then on.

The ruler of the Zhou was the king. He claimed to be the ruler of "all under heaven," and the Zhou extended the sway of the Chinese state to most of the territory north of the Yangtze River. There had now been three ruling dynasties, and the tradition was well established that there should be one government for the Chinese culture area, and that it should not be divided up into competing political units. This tradition was also an ideal that was handed down to succeeding generations, and disunity and interstate conflict within China remained a deviation from the ideal ever after.

The Zhou king stood at the apex of a decentralized fengjian hierarchy. From top to bottom this hierarchy was an aristocratic one, based on hereditary position. Below the king were about one hundred hereditary domains run by great lords, many directly related to the Zhou family. The lords had various titles depending on their rank and relation to the Zhou central line. The territories they controlled were received as fiefs from the king and could not be privately enlarged, bought, or sold. Each lord, in turn, subdivided his area among sublords with lesser titles who also served as ministers to him. At the bottom of the hierarchy were the lowest aristocrats, the *shi*, who managed estates for the higher lords. They were a sort of gentry class, not terribly powerful politically but important to the day-to-day management of society.

The aristocrats were military men, and one of their highest obligations to the Zhou king was military service. Warfare was limited to aristocrats, who generally used bronze weapons to fight each other from chariots. Military loyalty helped to keep the Zhou state united. The system also held together because of the familial connections between the aristocrats and the Zhou line and because of elaborate ritual behavior that clearly specified the appropriate relationship among the various aristocrats and among different levels of the hierarchy.

The Zhou aristocracy was very religious. Its outlook combined three elements that were to remain essential features of Chinese religion ever afterward, though the overall importance of religion declined as humanistic values came to the fore. One part of the Zhou faith was a simple animism, a worship of spirits associated with different places, crops, natural forces, the ghosts of dead people, and so on. A second element was the worship of ancestors in one's family line.

Finally, there was a belief in a supreme deity, *Ti*, or *Tian*, generally translated as "heaven." The Zhou kings associated their ancestral line with heaven and also, of course, claimed the Mandate of Heaven to rule. In Chinese, the Mandate of Heaven is *tianming*. When the Western word *revolution* came to China in the late nineteenth century, it was translated as *geming*, "to change the Mandate." Religious practices in the Shang and early Zhou could be extremely cruel and, among other things, included human sacrifice.

We do not know much about the common people of the Zhou. They lived in villages spread over the countryside. There were merchants and artisans, tied, for the most part, to various lords; however, the great mass of people worked the land. They were bound to the soil of the lords as serfs and could not, of course, buy or sell the land they were allotted. It is not clear exactly how agriculture was organized, though it seems to have included some communal labor for the lord. Commoners were not involved in the military activities that were so important to the aristocracy. In addition, within the rigid hereditary system, they had no chance to rise into the ruling class, nor did they share in the elaborate ritual life of their masters. The religion of the people, as far as we know, involved animism and shamanism, the possession of holy people by spirits.

The Zhou brought effective and comparatively stable government to China for almost four hundred years. There was internal peace, for the most part, and reasonable prosperity. Among other accomplishments, the first real books in China were compiled in these years, works that were to remain the classics of the nation thereafter. One of these classics was the *Shujing* or *Book of History*, which tells the story of China from the beginning through the Zhou. The early parts on Yao, Shun, and Yu are more or less legends, since no records remained from the tribal age. However, from the Xia onward, the book has the flavor of history. The parts on the late Shang and on the Zhou itself provide a rich source of material on the history of society and its values.

Another of the classics is the beautiful *Shijing* or *Book of Poetry*, which was to exert great literary and philosophical influence. Finally, there was the famous *Book of Changes*, the *Yijing*. In the *Yijing* is to be found the conception that remained basic to Chinese epistemology, that reality can be seen as the product of the two complementary principles, often referred to later as *yin* and *yang*, the active and the receptive, the masculine and the feminine. These are envisioned as endlessly interacting with one another, rising and then falling in mutual influence and power.

The Zhou system began to come apart in the eighth century B.C. We know more about the details of what happened than about why because the philosophers and historians who were shortly to write about the collapse had never experienced such a change before, and the less experience a society has with a historical phenomenon, the harder it is to understand. More particularly, the breakdown of the Zhou involved not simply the end of a dynasty but also the decline of the fengjian system and the first development of junxian society, something unprecedented in Chinese history.

One approach to understanding the fall of the Zhou and the decay of the fengjian order is suggested by a principle of the *Book of Changes*, a principle that was to become basic to Chinese social theory. This says that any institution or phenomenon that reaches completion or full development is doomed to decline. One might expect a transformation since the fengjian system had reached perfection as the Zhou, too, came to its zenith. Another approach to analyzing the decline of the Zhou order is suggested by the work of the greatest philosopher of China, Confucius, who emphasized the role of the family to a stable social order. As the aristocratic population increased and families grew larger, their interconnections weakened. By the seventh century B.C. the great lords had begun to take different surnames from the Zhou king. At the same time their military loyalty and ritual propriety to him had seriously declined. A third approach, in harmony with the modern Western emphasis on economic development, is that the coming of iron, which entered China at about this time, created broad changes that undermined both the Zhou and the fengjian system.

The event that traditionally marks the beginning of the end for the Zhou occurred in 771 B.C., when an incompetent king was on the throne. One of the vassals made a direct attack on the Zhou capital and murdered the ruler. The dynasty moved its capital to the east, but its power was gone. The period after 771 is known as the Eastern Zhou. It is generally divided into two eras, which do not exactly overlap. The first runs from the beginning of the Eastern Zhou to about 500 B.C. and is called the Spring and Autumn Period. The second is called the Warring States Period and runs from the fifth century B.C. to 221 B.C. The Warring States era includes the official extinction of the Zhou Dynasty in 256 B.C.

The late Spring and Autumn Period and the era of the Warring States are when China made the initial transition from fengjian to junxian. This transition was by no means thorough or complete. Many people and areas were not affected. However, the direction and nature of the change are crucial, for the transition set the background for the great philosophers of the age, philosophers who were to establish the broad problematique of Chinese thought ever after. As a result, Chinese philosophy was permanently to bear the imprint of a transition from fengjian to junxian.

In political organization the changes began with the breakdown of Zhou authority. The various lords began to fight among themselves and no longer looked up to the Zhou king as ruler. In the Warring States Period, the decline of the Zhou king was complete. He was virtually a forgotten figure, and various powerful lords began to call themselves kings rather than use lesser titles, such as duke or marquess, which implied subordination to the Zhou.

On the other hand, as the chaos of the Warring States era reached its peak, centralized authority began to reemerge. The more powerful lords began to gobble up the weaker ones and to establish large kingdoms. These then fought it out with one another for complete control of China, a situation that gave the Warring States Period its name. By the third century B.C. there were only seven great kingdoms left, fighting and intriguing against one another. At the same time, the new countries were increasingly junxian in character. In 221 B.C. one of them, Qin, laid low its last rival and once again united China. Qin was the most thoroughly junxian of the new states, and as it conquered its foes, it spread the system to areas where it had not yet taken hold and, eventually, to the whole nation.

The kings of these new states did not divide their lands into hereditary fiefs. Rather, they appointed officials directly responsible to the crown. One reason they did this was because they did not trust the aristocrats; for not only was there constant warfare between the various kingdoms but also there was chaos within them. We hear repeatedly of fights between aristocratic factions, of murders and intrigues, and even of aristocrats who deposed kings. Raising men of lower status to power, people without independent authority and military traditions, seemed a far safer and more secure course for a ruler than using aristocrats to govern.

As a result, as governments became more centralized, the power of the aristocracy began to decline in favor of a junxian elite based on talent, luck, or money. The aristocracy also declined because it could not remain intact in an era of combat and retribution. When two aristocratic factions fought within a state, one side or the other lost and was often exterminated, requiring new men to fill their place and leaving positions available in the government. Similarly, when one country conquered another, the aristocracy of the defeated side was no longer trustworthy. The new bureaucrats often came from the old shi class of gentry, though their power now rested primarily on their rank in the government rather than on their status at birth. Commoners, too, entered the new elite. As a result, social mobility became one of the most striking features of the society to the men of the time, however few people may actually have risen.

In the Warring States era, there was also movement toward a junxian economic system, as land and other goods began to be bought and sold more freely. This process was intimately related to the sociopolitical shifts of the time and, in turn, further enhanced these changes. The junxian economy resulted partly from the decline of the aristocracy. Landholding came to involve landlords who rented to tenants rather than lords who owned serfs. At the same time, there was a general rise in productive capacity, which increased the exchange of land and goods and encouraged the development of a mercantile spirit.

The rise in production rested in the first instance on the peace of the early Zhou and on the introduction of iron. Iron tools were far more efficient than ones made of bronze or wood. With more to exchange, money came into large-scale use for the first time. Since a free market stimulated production, the various governments often encouraged the new developments for the sake of national wealth and strength; they also built public works, irrigation systems, and roads, all of which further increased production and the exchange of goods.

The economic changes, in turn, reinforced the changes in class relations. Commoners (peasants, merchants, and artisans) could accumulate land and wealth. Indeed, as actual producers, they were often better fitted to benefit from new opportunities than were aristocrats. This situation provided such people with an additional entrée into the elite. At the same time, rulers often found such men more talented and certainly safer to employ than aristocrats. Public works and economic development also required the kings to use specialists with technical expertise.

While the junxian system broadened the elite, it should be stressed that the commercialization of the economy did not necessarily help the mass of people. For now, cut off from the security of the fengjian order, peasants were left open to the play of the market, and many were ill-prepared for the change. Some could become wealthy and powerful, but many others were left without land or sustenance. Those who rented were at the mercy of landlords, who felt few constraints other than those of the marketplace, and everyone was open to the rapacity of governments. The warfare of the time could also bring heavy taxes, as well as the constant danger of pillage and death.

Partly because of the incessant warfare, there was a revulsion against military values during the Warring States era, an attitude that was to contribute to the civilian character of junxian society. Almost all the great philosophers had a powerful civilian thrust. At the same time, the elite was no longer made up simply of aristocratic warriors. It now included a wide range of people, from specialists in administration and diplomacy to businessmen, who were not militarily minded. In some ways, though, the fighting of the time helped the rise of the junxian system. Battles were no longer fought between handfuls of aristocrats; instead, governments now employed large armies with masses of infantry armed with iron. This change threw off the social hierarchy, which had rested partly on the aristocratic monopoly over military life. Commoners were now involved, opening an additional path to social mobility through the army and military expertise.

Secular values were also in the ascendancy in this era, and men became skeptical about the religious system handed down from the Shang and Zhou. Human sacrifice came to an end during the Spring and Autumn Period, and other aspects of Zhou ritual observance declined. In junxian fashion, the new states lacked and often did not claim the religious aura that had surrounded the Three Dynasties. The most striking sign of the shift, however, was the work of the great thinkers, which was, for the most part, deeply humanistic.

CONFUCIANISM

The philosophical era of the Warring States is so varied and rich that it is generally called the time of the "Hundred Schools of Thought." The various philosophies ranged from systematizations of animistic beliefs to others concerned with pure logic. All of them, however, shared certain characteristics that mark them as products of the great transition from fengjian to junxian, for they all sought to reestablish peace and order in a time of political confusion and change and to reestablish effective values in a time of intellectual disillusionment and fluidity.

The most significant of the philosophical schools was Confucianism, not because it was the most popular during the Warring States era but because it was to emerge as the most important and dominant philosophy later on and to become the greatest intellectual influence on the subsequent course of Chinese history. At the same time, to the extent that other schools of the time survived, it was generally through accretion onto Confucianism rather than the other way around. Ultimately, the reason for the power of Confucianism is that it was the most profound and comprehensive of the Hundred Schools. Indeed, it is one of the very greatest systems of thought ever propounded at any time or place in history.

Confucius (551–479 B.C.), the founder of the school, lived at the juncture of the Spring and Autumn Period and the Warring States era. We do not know much about his life. However, he seems to have come from a poor family of the lower aristocracy, the gentry class. His personal goal was government service; however, he did not find a ruler sympathetic to his approach and so, except for a few brief stints in service, did not work in administration. He spent his life in teaching and scholarship. Confucius's words are preserved in terse statements passed along by his students and soon compiled into the work known as the *Lun Yu* or *Analects*. A history of his native state of Lu, called the *Spring and Autumn Annals*, is also attributed to Confucius, and he may also have worked on editing the classics.

Confucius's greatest followers in the Warring States era were Mencius (372–289 B.C.) and Xunzi (300–237 B.C.). These two worked out different possibilities within Confucius's thought and expanded and developed his ideas. The most famous distinction between the two is that Mencius believed that man's nature in an undisciplined state tends toward good, while Xunzi believed it tends toward evil. Both, however, stressed that a good Confucian society was possible.

Essentially, Confucianism is a sociohistorical analysis combined with an ethical system, all tied to methods for spreading the philosophy and its attendant benefits. In more technical language, one might say that it is a normative sociology that includes an educational theory. It is a very subtle outlook and in its analysis deals with all aspects of human life, from personal psychology to the political system, from religion to the family. Its integrative thrust and power stem, in part, from Confucius's desire to renovate society, to restore a sense of value to it in a manner appropriate to the fengjian-junxian transition.

This is evident in the ideological underpinnings of the theory. For Confucianism, in a junxian fashion, rests on an analysis of human life and experience rather than on religious speculation or on the gods. It is deeply humanistic. "Zilu [a student] asked how one should serve ghosts and spirits. The master said, 'Till you have learnt to serve men, how can you serve ghosts?' Zilu then ventured upon a question about the dead. The master said, 'Till you know about the living, how are you to know about the dead?' "[2] And, as the *Analects* record, "The master never talked of prodigies, feats of strength, portents or spirits."[3] "Respect the ghosts and spirits but keep them at a distance"[4] was his general view.

On the other hand, Confucius linked religious sentiment to his system by arguing that the good order he propounded was possible, though by no means certain, because the natural order, heaven, was on its side. "He who does not understand the will of Heaven cannot be regarded as a virtuous person"[5] and "Heaven beget the power that is in me. What have I to fear from such a one as Huan Tui [a powerful official]."[6]

The goal of Confucianism is to develop an effective, peaceful, and ethical society, with a decent life for the people. Mencius describes such a society for a ruler whom he is urging to improve:

If the mulberry is planted in every homestead . . . then those who are fifty can wear silk; if chickens, pigs and dogs do not miss their breeding season, then those who are seventy can eat meat; if each plot of land . . . is not deprived of labor during the busy seasons, then families with several mouths to feed will not go hungry. Exercise due care over the education provided by the village schools and discipline the people by teaching them the duties proper to sons and younger brothers, and those whose heads have turned grey will not be carrying loads on the roads. When those who are seventy wear silk and eat meat and the masses are neither cold nor hungry, it is impossible for their prince not to be a true king.[7]

The Confucians often spoke as if such a good society had existed in earlier times, and they idealized the sage rulers of the tribal era, Yao Shun and Yu, and the great kings of the Three Dynasties. However, the Confucians were very critical of the political and moral breakdown that they perceived around them. For example, after Mencius described the good society, he criticized the king to whom he was speaking:

Now when food meant for human beings is so plentiful as to be thrown to dogs and pigs, you fail to realize that it is time for garnering, and when men drop dead from starvation by the wayside, you fail to realize that it is time for distribution. When people die, you simply say, "It is none of my doing. It is the fault of the harvest." In what way is that different from killing a man by running him through, while saying all the time, "It is none of my doing. It is the fault of the weapon". . . . There is fat meat in your kitchen and there are well-fed horses in your stables, yet the people look hungry and in the outskirts of cities men drop dead from starvation. This is to show animals the way to devour men. Even the devouring of animals by animals is repugnant to men. If, then, one who is father and mother to the people cannot, in ruling over them, avoid showing animals the way to devour men, wherein is he father and mother to the people?

Using the past to criticize the present established a powerful tradition in Confucian thought. Confucianism at its best, in the hands of its serious thinkers down through history, has been a critical philosophy, one that saw a great gap between the possibilities of humanity and the reality of any given era. In this sense it is very radical and progressive. It returns to roots to make a basic critique of the present. At the same time, it lays a heavy responsibility on those in power, for by proper example and wise policies, they are to initiate and further a process that, ideally, will raise everyone to their level. Education has been defined as a relationship of inequality whose purpose is to destroy itself,[8] an excellent expression of the Confucian sensibility.

On the other hand, Confucianism has a conservative side. Because of the era in which it developed it has a thirst for order and stability, and its emphasis on rulers and their responsibilities can have a patriarchal and elitist flavor. More importantly, it does not admit that any sort of change is possible at any given time. It is too steeped in history, too aware of the limitations of social and psychological reality for that claim. This is not to say that it cannot support broad and even comparatively rapid reform. Confucius said, "If only someone were to make use of me, even for a single year, I could do a great deal; and in three years I could finish off the whole work."[9]

However, it is too skeptical, too respectful of order, to accommodate the belief in a transcendent break with the history. "Those who in private life behave well towards their parents and elder brothers, in public life seldom show a disposition to resist the authority of their superiors. And as for such men creating chaos no instance of it has ever occurred." And even, "I have never seen anyone whose desire to build up his moral power was as strong as sexual desire."[10] As a result of Confucianism's conservative side, when people down through history felt strongly pressed and ready for revolution, they might do so within a broadly Confucian outlook. However, they have often turned to other more religious and metaphysical belief systems for sustenance in their hopes for victory.

In general, then, the goals of Confucianism are highly radical and idealistic, but its methods and analysis are conservative and realistic. A basic way in which Confucianism reconciles its radical and conservative sides is through the crucial concept of *zheng ming*, the "rectification of names." This is the idea that all people and social institutions have specific ethical and practical obligations in life, which are summarized by the names used for them. If they fail to fulfill the names they assume, they lose the claim to the names and to the respect and loyalty that they may imply. Thus, a king, for example, who governs badly no longer behaves truly like a king and has lost the claim to the throne. Even rebellion is permissible then, though it is technically no longer rebellion because the ruler is technically no longer ruler.

It was with this theory, for example, that Mencius justified the overthrow of the Xia and the Shang and their evil kings, Jie and Zhou Xin:

> King Xuan of Qi asked, "Is it true that Tang [the founder of the Shang] banished Jie and King Wu [founder of the Zhou] marched against Zhou Xin?" "It is so recorded," answered Mencius. "Is regicide permissible?" "A man who mutilates benevolence is a mutilator, while one who cripples righteousness is a crippler. He who is both a mutilator and a crippler is an *outcast*. I have indeed heard of the punishment of the *outcast Zhou Xin*, but I have not heard of any regicide!"[11]

The fundamental way in which Confucianism seeks to achieve the good society is through a hierarchical system permeated with a sense of responsibility by those above and obligation from those below. This hierarchical system was envisioned in various ways, and the perspectives on the issue provide a further example of the general relationship of Confucianism to the transition from fengjian to junxian. One way of describing the hierarchy was in terms of the fengjian class structure of the Zhou: at the top are the rulers, then come peasants, then artisans, and finally merchants. Another way, used by Mencius later in the Warring States Period, when the system of hereditary classes had decayed, was based on the distinction between those who worked with their minds and those who worked with their hands. The former were assumed to be on top.

However, the most important and lasting way that the Confucians envisioned the hierarchy was in ethical terms, with the most virtuous and perfected people on the top and the least virtuous, the worst, on the bottom. "When the Way prevails in the empire men of small virtue serve men of great virtue and men of small ability serve men of great ability. But when the Way is in disuse, the small serve the big, the weak serve the strong." In the ethical hierarchy the highest obligation of those on top is to develop and perfect those below, to eliminate gaps, to initiate the grand educational process that will develop and enhance the moral tone of the whole society. "Heaven, in producing the people, has given those who first attain understanding the duty of awakening those who are slow to understand; and to those who are first to awaken the duty of awakening those who are slow to awaken."[12]

This ethical hierarchy represents a junxian approach to society. It takes the fengjian values of loyalty and obligation based on hereditary class and universalizes them into an ethical system appropriate to an age that had increasing doubts about whether goodness and virtue were to be equated with noble birth. From the point of view of the "rectification of names," one might say, it expressed the idea that the Zhou aristocracy no longer lived up to its claims as the best people, the true noblemen.

This sense of transition is clearly evident in the words used for perfected and unperfected people, for the word for a good person is the old Zhou word for aristocrat (*junzi*), and the word for a bad person is the old word for commoner (*xiaoren*). Confucius still harbored some hopes that the Zhou junzi could become the ethical junzi, that name and reality could be again reconciled. However, both in his work and in the work of Mencius and Xunzi, who had lost this hope, the words are used almost exclusively in their ethical sense.[13] The notion that society should take the form of an ethical hierarchy and that the obligation of those on top is to elevate those below provided one of the most dynamic concepts in Chinese history.

What does it mean to be a good person, to be a junzi? Essentially, it is someone who manifests a set of virtues that are at the core of Confucian ethics. There are many virtues discussed. For example, "Zizhang asked Confucius about humanity. Confucius said: 'To be able to practice five virtues everywhere in the world constitutes humanity.' Zizhang begged to know what these were. Confucius said: 'Courtesy, magnanimity, good faith, diligence, and kindness.' "[14]

What is striking about these and the other Confucian virtues is that they are all social values. They are required for people to live well together, to relate effectively to one another; they alter and improve both the giver and the receiver, and so help to spread virtue and improve society. "Zigong asked: 'Is there any one word that can serve as a principle for the conduct of life?' Confucius said: 'Perhaps the word *reciprocity*: Do not do to others what you would not want others to do to you.' "[15]

Much of Confucian theory is devoted to the environment and methods through which a person becomes perfected and develops the requisite virtues. In this part of the analysis the remarkable integrative power of the philosophy becomes clear, for the methods involve and unite all aspects of life and belief into an organic and interdependent whole. Overall, the individual must see the proper examples and live in the proper environment. He must learn to learn and to practice what he has learned. Ultimately, he must replicate his experience for others, to serve society by improving it.

The first and most crucial part of a person's upbringing is to live in a family where the virtues are practiced. "The empire has its basis in the state, the state in the family, and the family in one's own self,"[16] says Mencius. The family is the basic sphere of activity of the individual and the basic unit of society, where the person must learn the basic relationships and forms of propriety that are at the core of virtuous behavior. It is here, too, that he is most often called upon to act correctly.

Just as there are many virtues in Confucianism, there are also many important relationships, and a majority of the most crucial ones are in the family. Thus, the most important were often said to be the so-called *san gang* or Three Bonds: husband-wife, father-son, and ruler-minister. There were also the famous "Five Relationships," which include the san gang and add elder brother-younger brother and friend-friend. For society to be well ordered, families must be well ordered. Once when Confucius was asked how to bring a good society, his famous answer was: "Let the prince be a prince and the minister a minister; the father a father and the son a son."[17]

Another prerequisite for goodness is that a person have a decent standard of living and economic security. One of the deepest beliefs in Confucianism is that people whose level of welfare is too low, who are hungry and unsure of their livelihood cannot easily achieve goodness. Security and welfare do not mean great wealth, but they do mean a common level of decency. One of the highest obligations of good government is to assure this. If average people, writes Mencius:

have no certain means of livelihood they surely cannot maintain a steadfast heart . . . and as the people's livelihood is ordered at present, they do not have enough to serve their parents on the one hand or to support their wives and children on the other. Even in good years life is one long struggle and in bad years death becomes all but inevitable. Such being the case, they are only anxiously trying to stay alive. What leisure have they for cultivating decorum and righteousness?[18]

One particular reason for the economic emphasis in Confucianism was the insecurity and difficulty that faced many peasants in the market economy that accompanied the arrival of the junxian system of the Warring States era. Mencius, therefore, emphasizes the need for every peasant to be assured land. He does this by idealizing the fengjian system of land tenure of the Zhou and developing his famous image of the "well-field system." The image is based on the Chinese ideograph for "well," which looks like a tic-tac-toe board. According to Mencius, in the early Zhou, the land was divided into well-field units. Each peasant family received one of the outside fields for its personal use, and they all cultivated the central field together for their lord. Mencius held that the system was far more amenable to social welfare and good government than the open, competitive atmosphere of his time:

At the bottom of all humane government, we might say, lies the system of land division and demarcation. When the land system is not in proper operation, then the well-field farms are not equally distributed among the farmers or the grain for salaries equitably apportioned among the ministers. So a wicked lord or a corrupt magistrate usually lets the land system fall into disuse. When the land system is in proper operation, on the other hand, the distribution of land and the apportioning of salaries can be settled.[19]

In addition to having a virtuous family and economic welfare, a person, to become good, must receive an education in a formal sense. When Confucius "was going to Wei, Ran Qiu drove him. The Master said, 'What a dense population!' Ran Qiu said, 'When the people have multiplied, what next should be done for them?' The Master said 'Enrich them.' Ran Qiu said, 'When one has enriched them, what next should be done for them?' The Master said, "Instruct them.' "[20]

In line with the junxian sensibility of their time, the Confucians not only emphasized that education rather than heredity was the basis of virtue but felt that nearly everyone was capable and worthy of receiving an education and so of becoming good. "By nature men are pretty much alike; it is learning and practice that sets them apart," Confucius said (an eloquent statement about the inherent equality of all people that was selected, twenty-five centuries later, as the essential truth about human nature in a United Nations (UN) "Statement on Race").[21]

Down through history, Confucius has been known in China as the great "Teacher," and he proudly said, "From the very poorest upwards—beginning even with the man who could bring no better present than a bundle of dried meat—none has ever come to me without receiving instruction."[22] Mencius carries these implications to their utmost by suggesting that everyone could even become a sage, a person who initiates or qualitatively enhances the very process of improving society at a fundamental level. "Cao Jiao asked, 'Is it true that all men are capable of becoming a Yao or a Shun?' 'Yes,' said Mencius."[23]

Education for the Confucians meant a broad study of human life and achievement. Above all, it meant learning about the past, the study of the classics and history. Confucius said, "I for my part am not one of those who have innate knowledge. I am simply one who loves the past and who is diligent in investigating it."[24] The study of the past was particularly important because, from the humanist stance of the theory, experience, for a person or a society, was the prime source of wisdom. "The master said, 'Zhou could survey the two preceding dynasties. How great a wealth of culture! And we follow upon Zhou!' "

The classics and history can also orient a person in time and put him in touch with the deep flow of human reality. This orientation is another aspect of being a sage in Confucian terms. "Zi-zhang asked whether the state of things ten generations hence could be foretold. Confucius said, 'We know in what ways the Shang modified ritual when they followed upon the Xia. We know in what ways the Zhou modified ritual when they followed upon the Shang. And hence we can foretell what the successors of Zhou will be like, even supposing they do not appear till a hundred generations from now.' "

In addition to the study of the past, a Confucian education also meant a good grounding in the rules of propriety and ethics and in ritual, music, literature, and the arts. "These were the subjects on which Confucius often discoursed: poetry, history, and the performance of ceremonies." "Confucius said: 'Personal cultivation begins with poetry, is made firm by rules of decorum, and is perfected by music.' " "Confucius took four subjects for his teaching—literature, conduct, loyalty, and truthfulness."[25] For later generations, of course, education also included training in the Confucian theory itself.

Besides environment and education, attaining virtue also requires an intense effort on the part of the individual, self-cultivation, as it is sometimes called. Self-cultivation means learning to learn and also acting correctly: observation, study, self-reflection, and proper behavior. There is a powerful emphasis in Confucian theory on the unity of thought and action. "Zigong asked about the good person. The master said, 'He does not preach what he practices till he has practiced what he preaches.' "[26] In a particularly famous passage, Confucius makes the unity of thought, of action, and of virtue the highest attainment of human life: "Confucius said, 'At fifteen, I set my heart on learning. At thirty, I was firmly established. At forty, I had no more doubts. At fifty, I knew the will of Heaven. At sixty, I was ready to listen to it. At seventy, I could follow my heart's desire without transgressing what was right.' "[27]

Ultimately, then, in Confucian theory, everyone is responsible for the goodness of society in some way. However, the junzi, the virtuous person, has the greatest responsibility. In this way the theory makes the crucial link between personal and political morality. For the highest goal of the perfected individual is to serve in the government. This is his obligation toward society and is the capstone of his own development and practice. "Zilu asked about the qualities of a virtuous person. The master said, 'He cultivates in himself the capacity to be diligent in his tasks.' Zilu said, 'Can he not go further than that?' The master said, 'He cultivates in himself the capacity to ease the lot of the whole populace. If he can do that, could even Yao or Shun find cause to criticize him?' " With regard to his own inability to achieve a post of authority Confucius bemoaned, "As far as taking trouble goes, I do not think I compare badly with other people. But as regards carrying out the duties of a virtuous person in actual life, I have never yet had a chance to show what I could do."[28]

In Confucian theory not only does the good person have the obligation to enter public service, but the government should be made up of the virtuous. In fengjian times the junzi, in the sense of aristocracy, ruled. Now, in the transition to junxian, the Confucians began to envision the junzi as a ruling meritocracy. In this period, and even later in the full junxian era, China had a hereditary ruler at the top. This situation was, in some ways, a compromise with the Confucian ideal; and Confucians often had a soft spot in their hearts for tribal times, when rule passed to the most worthy, rather than in a monarchical fashion.

Within this compromise, however, the obligations of the ruler were met if he himself was a good person and if he selected and relied on virtuous people to govern. As Mencius said to one ruler, "If you honor the good and wise and employ the able so that outstanding men are in high position, then virtuous men throughout the Empire will be only too pleased to serve at your court."[29] It was for this reason that Confucianism considered the relationship between ruler and minister to be one of the crucial Three Bonds.

As a result, the expectations of a ruler and the burden on government were immense in Confucian theory, for those in power were particularly, and even ultimately, responsible for the goodness and success of society. "Mencius said, 'When the prince is benevolent, everyone else is benevolent; when the prince is dutiful, everyone else is dutiful.' "[30] Good government, indeed, was crucial to bringing about the good Confucian society, a society with good families, good education, stable public welfare, and a high moral tone. The very practicality and general optimism of Confucian theory made the burden on those in power all the greater. Success was possible. "If there is indeed anyone whom I have praised," said Confucius, "there is a means by which he may be tested. For the common people here round us are just such stuff as the Three Dynasties worked upon in the days when they followed the Straight Way."[31]

Though the Confucians placed great emphasis on the importance of correct rule, they felt that the good government should have a laissez-faire attitude toward people and society. This position was by no means dogmatic, especially in the light of the many responsibilities laid upon the state. However, ideally speaking, the good ruler was someone who shared his power with others, did not weigh heavily on the people or needlessly interfere with them, and, in a sense, ruled basically by example. "Govern the people by regulations, keep order among them by chastisements, and they will flee from you, and lose all self-respect. Govern them by moral force, keep order among them by ritual and they will keep their self-respect and come to you of their own accord."[32]

In fact, if society is truly in good order and the ruler truly virtuous, he need do nothing. "The master said, 'Among those who ruled through laissez-faire, surely Shun may be counted. For what action did he take? He merely placed himself gravely and reverently with his face due south; that was all.' "[33] In its emphasis on light government one again sees the blend of fengjian and junxian values that is typical of Confucianism. The sense that the ruler should share his authority with others comes from the former and is an aristocratic ideal opposed to the centralizing, bureaucratic tendencies of the latter. On the other hand, the notion that people should be allowed to follow their own destiny without excessive constraints is a product of the new freedoms and opportunities associated with the junxian system.

From a Confucian point of view one particular danger to society was a government that wasted money and extracted too much wealth from society. As Mencius wrote, "A good ruler is always respectful and thrifty, courteous and humble, and takes from the people no more than is prescribed. . . . Yang Hu [an upright official] said, 'If one's aim is wealth one cannot be benevolent; if one's aim is benevolence one cannot be wealthy.' " And in another admonition on economic matters:

> In the market-place, if goods are exempted when premises are taxed, and premises exempted when the ground is taxed, then the traders throughout the empire will be only too pleased to store their goods in your market-place. If there is inspection but no duty at the border stations, then the travelers throughout the empire will be only too pleased to go by way of your roads. If tillers help in the public fields but pay no tax on the land, then farmers throughout the empire will be only too pleased to till the land in your realm. If you abolish the levy in lieu of corvee and the levy in lieu of the planting of mulberry, then all the people of the empire will be only too pleased to come and settle in your state.[34]

Another particular danger to the welfare of society, in Confucian eyes, was needless warfare. The Confucians were not pacifists. However, they deeply opposed the military spirit that still pervaded their time and the constant fighting it provoked. Mencius said:

> It can be seen that Confucius rejected those who enriched rulers not given to the practice of benevolent government. How much more would he reject those who do their best to wage war on their behalf. In wars to gain land, the dead fill the plains; in wars to gain cities, the dead fill the cities. This is known as showing the land the way to devour human flesh. Death is too light a punishment for such men. Hence those skilled in war should suffer the most severe punishments.[35]

War, if it was to be waged at all, was to be a last resort. Confucius said, "Only when men of the right sort have instructed a people for seven years ought there to be any talk of engaging them in warfare. . . . To lead into battle a people that has not first been instructed is to betray them." The name for Confucianism in Chinese is *ru xue*, literally, the "philosophic school of scholars," of those who wield the writing brush rather than the sword. "Duke Ling of Wei asked Confucius about the marshalling of troops. Confucius replied saying, 'About the ordering of ritual vessels I have some knowledge; but warfare is a thing I have never studied.' Next day he resumed his travels."[36] In the long run, one of the great contributions of Confucianism was to further the development of the civilian values that were part of the junxian outlook and, of course, a major advance for human life in general.

The image of the bad society in Confucianism is the reverse of the good one. It has evils ranging from poor ministers to a bad educational system; it has a poor moral tone. As Xunzi wrote:

> These are the signs of a disordered age: men wear bright colored clothing, their manner is feminine, their customs are lascivious, their minds are set on profit, their conduct is erratic, their music is depraved, and their decorative arts are vile and garish. In satisfying the desires of the living they observe no limits, but in burying the dead they are mean and stingy. They despise ritual principles and value daring and shows of strength. If they are poor, they steal, if they are rich they commit outrages.[37]

When this sort of society develops, the rulers and the elite are, in the first instance, at fault, and, if things become bad enough, they can lose the Mandate of Heaven. Mencius wrote much about this issue, and he is often credited with developing the so-called right of revolution in China. The notion is based partly on the concept of the rectification of names: if a dynasty or political system no longer lives up to proper expectations, it can, indeed it must, be overthrown. This outcome had happened to the Xia and the Shang and was now happening to the Zhou. Unlike Confucius, Mencius and Xunzi, living later in the Warring States era, no longer had any hopes for the Zhou.

The right of revolution is also based on the belief that the people are the ultimate basis of the state, that a government with the Mandate is recognized by the fact that the people support it:

> Wan Zhang said, "Is it true that Yao gave the Empire to Shun?" "No," said Mencius. "The emperor cannot give the empire to another." "In that case, who gave the empire to Shun?" "Heaven gave it to him." "You say Heaven gave it to him. Does this mean that Heaven gave him detailed and minute instructions?" "No. Heaven does not speak, but reveals itself through its acts and deeds. . . . In antiquity, Yao recommended Shun to Heaven and Heaven accepted him; he presented him to the people and the people accepted him. Hence I said, 'Heaven does not speak but reveals itself by its acts and deeds'. . . . [The *Book of History*] says, 'Heaven sees with the eyes of its people. Heaven hears with the ears of its people.' "[38]

Elsewhere, Mencius said, "It was through losing the people that Jie and Zhou Xin lost the Empire, and through losing the people's hearts that they lost the people. There is a way to win the empire; win the people. There is a way to win their hearts; amass what they want for them; do not impose what they dislike on them. That is all.'' And, in another place: ''The people are of supreme importance; the altars to the gods of earth and grain come next; last comes the ruler. That is why he who gains the confidence of the multitudinous people will be emperor.''[39]

OTHER PHILOSOPHIES; THE CONCEPT OF DATONG

In addition to Confucianism, many other philosophies developed at the time of the Hundred Schools. Each in its own way contributed to later developments in China, though generally as accretions onto Confucianism. The most important of these were Mohism, Taoism (pronounced Daoism), and Legalism. Another idea, of comparatively minor significance during the Warring States but of great importance later on (particularly from the viewpoint of revolution), was the notion of datong or the Great Community.

Mohism, named after its founder, Mozi, was an extremely popular school in the Warring States era, though it died out almost completely thereafter as an independent philosophy. It emphasized universal love, an intense belief in God, and a deep interest in pure logic. It was deeply and profoundly meritocratic and clearly rejected hereditary claims on authority. Its antiaristocratic thrust contributed to the junxian spirit of the Warring States Period and helped to bring out this aspect of Confucianism.

Taoism, of all the Hundred Schools, was able to maintain its independent identity most strongly later on, though it, too, deeply influenced Confucianism. Taoism's basic text is the great *Dao De Jing, The Book of the Way and Its Power*, authored by the semimythical ''Old Master,'' Laozi. Taoism developed during the Warring States era, but it emphasized simplicity and idealized a society of communities living virtually in tribal isolation from one another. Its most famous concept was *wuwei*, effectiveness through inaction. Politically, wuwei suggested a laissez-faire spirit in human relations and in government policy. As a result, Taoism encouraged the laissez-faire tendencies within Confucianism, the sense that a government should not lean heavily on the people and that one of the greatest dangers for a society was an overactive state.

Legalism was particularly important because the thinkers in this school, Shang Yang, Shen Buhai, and, above all, Han Fei Zi, led the way in conceptualizing the idea of a junxian society.[40] In addition, the state of Qin, which united China along the lines of the new system, was officially Legalist in outlook. Like Mohism, Legalism was sharply opposed to aristocracy. The Legalists said that there should be no formal class distinctions in society, but rather that society should be organized around clear laws of reward and punishment applicable to all. In addition, Legalists emphasized that the proper form of government was a powerful and highly centralized bureaucracy whose members were selected on the basis of merit rather than a decentralized structure based on hereditary position.

The Legalists were also actively concerned with creating a rich economy. In the short run this was for strength in war, which was considered necessary for uniting the nation. In the long run economic development was to be for the sake of prosperity, required for good order and control. The Legalists advocated public projects and government monopolies where these were needed to increase national wealth. In line with their junxian values, however, they were basically for a competitive market economy. To accomplish their chief goal of agricultural growth, they urged the abolition of all fengjian restrictions on the private ownership and sale of land. They argued that such limitations discouraged initiative and bred inefficiency, and they attacked the Mencian dream of a well-field system on the same grounds.

Despite their emphasis on the need for a strong army, the Legalists also stressed that bureaucratic, junxian-style government, with its corps of civilian officials, was ultimately more peaceful than a fengjian order, with its elite of independent and militarily minded aristocrats. Finally, though Legalist rulers were sometimes superstitious, Legalist theory was extremely antireligious and stressed that a ruthless and pragmatic atheism was the only rational outlook.

The datong approach was not so much a separate school of thought as an ideal that developed out of an eclectic background during the Warring States era and shortly thereafter.[41] Datong means, literally, the "Great Unity" and, in sociopolitical terms, can be translated as the Great Community. There were three basic elements to the concept. The first was that all of society should relate as if it were one great family; the second was that it should be as egalitarian as possible; and the third was that the proper social organization was a blend of the best in the past and, in particular, of tribalism, fengjian, and junxian.

The classic statement of the familial ideal in the datong outlook, considered to be the basic image of the good society among those who followed the tradition thereafter, is to be found in the *Book of Rites* (the *Li Ji*), a Confucian work with strong Taoist influences and perhaps some Mohist ones:

> When the great Dao [the correct way] was in practice, the world was common to all; men of talents, virtue, and ability were selected; sincerity was emphasized and friendship was cultivated. Therefore men did not love only their parents, nor did they treat as children only their sons. A competent provision was secured for the aged till their death, employment for the able-bodied and a means of upbringing for the young. Kindness and compassion were shown to widows, orphans, childless men, and those disabled by disease. In this way, they all had the wherewithal for support. Men had their proper work and women had their homes. They hated to see the wealth of natural resources undeveloped, but also did not hoard wealth for their own use. They hated not to exert themselves, but also did not exert themselves for their own benefit. Thus selfish scheming was repressed and found no development. Robbers, filchers, and rebellious traitors did not show themselves, and hence the outer doors were left open. This was the period of the Great Community.[42]

The *Book of Rites* also suggests the notion that the datong will be a blend of the best in history; for the book associates the ideal with the distant past, tribal times, which later declined into the era of individual families, ritual propriety, and war, a period that was represented, for all of its greatness, by the fengjian system of the Three Dynasties.

Now that the great Way has fallen into obscurity, the world has been divided into families. Each loves but his own parent and treats as children only his own children. People accumulate material things and exert their strength for their own advantage. Great men take it as proper behavior that their states should descend in their own families. Propriety and standards of justice they regard as bounds whereby to keep in its correctness their relation between ruler and subject; in its generous regard, that between father and son; in its harmony, that between elder and younger brother; in a community of sentiment, that between husband and wife. They use them to formulate institutions, lay out lands and hamlets, adjudge courageous and wise men as superior, and regulate accomplishments for their own advantage. Hence scheming practices come thereby and militarism arises. It was in this way that Yu [founder of the Xia], Tang [founder of the Shang], Kings Wen, Wu, Cheng, and the Duke of Zhou [founders of the Zhou] obtained their distinction. Of these six great men, each paid great attention to propriety. They displayed their justice, tested their sincerity, exposed errors, exemplified virtue and discoursed about courtesy, thus showing the people the invariable constants. All rulers who did not follow their course lost power and position, and all regarded them as pests. This was the period of Small Tranquility.

Confucian writers were also a powerful source of the concept that the Great Community would combine the best in the past, for overall, Confucianism sought a good society uniting the strengths of fengjian and junxian, a society that joined the security and spirituality of the former with the justice and humanism of the latter. An excellent example of this blend in economic matters is provided by the policies of Mencius. Thus, in a fengjian fashion he calls for the public ownership and allocation of land through the well-field system. At the same time, however, in accord with junxian ideals, he advocates a laissez-faire spirit toward trade and commerce, emphasizing the need for low taxes and the free movement of goods.[43]

A similar approach is found in the influential work known as the *Zhou Li*, the *Rites of Zhou*. Like the *Book of Rites*, to which it is related, it is a book purporting to be a product of the early Zhou, but was actually written much later. It, too, became part of the Confucian corpus and an important text for the datong tradition. The *Rites of Zhou* uses Legalist language and thought to redefine the fengjian norms of the Zhou in a manner appropriate for recreating them in a junxian age. The book describes a society that is hierarchical and lays great stress on ritual behavior. At the same time, however, it is an extremely centralized system, and its emphasis on rites seems to rest more on a desire for social order than on transcendent concerns. The work even has a powerful military sensibility, though it aims at peace and a civilian society.

The third aspect of the datong ideal was egalitarianism and democracy, economic leveling, access for all to education and culture, and responsibility to all for the governance and welfare of society. One source of this element of the datong was, again, Confucianism, for the Confucian political process places responsibility on a good government and a virtuous elite to make everyone else into a good person, cultured and responsible for society. In this sense the philosophy calls for expanding the polity and the benefits of society to all and so supports the notion of democracy as an ideal. In addition, Mencius stresses that government ultimately rests on the will of the people, and his well-field system aims at establishing equity in land-holding; so does the call for *tu jun*, "the equal distribution of land," in the *Rites of Zhou*.[44]

Nevertheless, the Confucians of the Warring States era were quite elitist and rather skeptical about the possibilities for equality in their own time. "The common people can be made to follow the Way;" said Confucius, "they cannot be made to understand it."[45] The most important representative of egalitarian thought in the Warring States era was the school known as the Agriculturalists. The most famous advocate of this school was Xu Xing, who, we are told, traveled about with his followers, "numbering several score, all wore hemp, and lived by making sandals and mats."[46] Xu Xing's own words have been lost; however, their intent is preserved by Mencius, who attacks and perhaps parodies them.

Basically, Xu Xing advocated a society with no distinction between those who worked with their minds and those who worked with their hands, between the rulers and the ruled.

> The prince of Teng [he is quoted as saying] is a truly good and wise ruler. However, he has never been taught the Way. To earn his keep a good and wise ruler shares the work of tilling the land with his people. He rules while cooking his own meals. Now Teng has granaries and treasuries. This is for the prince to inflict hardship on the people in order to keep himself. How can he be a good and wise prince?

Mencius's response to this argument is to say that efficiency and the division of labor require the present system. He asks: "Does Xu Xing use an iron pot and an earthenware steamer for cooking rice and iron implements for ploughing the fields?" "Yes," answers a follower of Xu. "Does he make them himself?" "No. He trades grain for them." So, says Mencius,

> To trade grain for implements is not to inflict hardship on the potter and the blacksmith. The potter and the blacksmith for their part also trade their wares for grain. In doing this, surely they are not inflicting hardship on the farmer either. . . . Now, is ruling the empire such an exception that it can be combined with the work of tilling the land? There are affairs of great men and affairs of small men. Moreover, it is necessary for each man to use the products of all the hundred crafts. If everyone must make everything he uses, the empire will be led along the path of incessant toil. Hence it is said, "There are those who use their minds and there are those who use their muscles. The former rule; the

latter are ruled. Those who rule are supported by those who are ruled." This is a principle accepted by the whole Empire.

As may be evident, the three elements that make up the concept of the datong have a contradictory quality. Families are inherently hierarchical by virtue of age and, in the Chinese case, because of patriarchy. Similarly, combining ideals that are often opposites from different social systems cannot be defined abstractly but requires specific and concrete determinations on every issue. Nonetheless, the notion of community does, in fact, include just such logical contradictions, and the result was to make the datong an important and durable sociopolitical goal. Indeed, a thousand years later, when society had garnered much experience, when junxian values were well established and the country was much richer and better educated, even the immediate pessimism of Confucianism about egalitarianism and its long-term optimism began slowly to be reconciled, and a vigorous datong tradition came into being within the philosophy.

QIN: THE FIRST JUNXIAN STATE

In 221 B.C. Qin, having destroyed Zhou thirty years earlier, conquered its last rival, Chu, and established the first junxian state in China. At the top was the king of Qin, who now proclaimed himself the emperor of China. He had to invent a new word to distinguish himself from the fengjian kings of the Three Dynasties and their petty successors. The term he coined, *huangdi*, remained, until the twentieth century, the name for the supreme ruler of the land, though the junxian system was not permanently entrenched until many centuries later. The new emperor hoped his dynasty would last forever, but, in fact, it was very short-lived. Our name for China, however, is said to derive from the name Qin (pronounced Chin).

The policy of the new government was to spread the junxian system of Qin to the whole country. In line with its Legalist philosophy and the immensity of the task, it did so with great harshness and a brutal eye to conformity. In a manner reminiscent of the French Revolution, the nation was placed under a uniform code of law and divided up into prefectures run by bureaucrats appointed by the central government. There were harsh measures against the remaining aristocrats, and it is recorded that thousands of noble families were killed or moved.

There was ideological uniformity as well. All philosophies except Legalism and some of the more superstitious schools of the late Zhou were banned. The prime minister, Li Si (a student of Xunzi, who went in the direction of Legalism rather than Confucianism), hated people who "praised the past in order to disparage the present."[47] The result was the infamous "burning of the books," in which many classical texts were lost. This was done on a nationwide basis, no mean task, and indicates the high degree of control and efficiency achieved by Qin. In addition, we are told, Li Si organized the "burying of the scholars," in which four hundred noted intellectuals were murdered.

The Qin continued to encourage the commercialization of the economy and also undertook massive public works. The most famous project was the completion of the Great Wall. It is said that one million people died toiling on the construction, ex-aristocrats and commoners alike. There was military action in all directions, which gave the lie to the Legalists' claim that they represented peace. Overall, Qin proved extremely unpopular, and, indeed, forever after the name has remained a byword in China for tyranny and excessive uniformity.

When the emperor died in 210 B.C. the dynasty had too many enemies to survive, both among the common people of the former countries and among the ex-aristocrats. Rebellion broke out, led by a peasant, Chen She. In starting what, in fact, was probably the first large-scale revolution in human history, he proclaimed:

> It has been several decades since the Qin began to oppress the world with its unprincipled government and ruthless laws. In the north there was the building of the Great Wall and in the south there have been the military outposts at Wu-ling. These have created a great turmoil both within and without, driving the people to exhaustion. Grains for military expenses have been collected according to the number of persons in a family. The sources of both wealth and physical energy have been exhausted, and the people are left without any resources. On top of this, the imposition of despotic laws and ruthless punishment has so disturbed the empire that not even fathers and sons can live peaceably together.[48]

The ensuing struggles destroyed the Qin and in 206 B.C. brought a common laborer, Liu Bang, to the throne as the founder of the Han Dynasty. As it turned out, the fifteen years of Qin rule were to mark the high point of the junxian system for many centuries to come.

2

Junxian China

THE HAN, DISUNITY, AND THE REVIVAL OF FENGJIAN

The development of a junxian system did not follow a simple linear path in China. Indeed, one of the most striking features of the thousand years that followed the fall of Qin is the degree to which fengjian characteristics made a comeback, reversing the trends of the late Zhou and the Warring States era. It was only in the seventh and eighth centuries A.D. that these characteristics began permanently to recede in favor of a junxian order. By about A.D. 1000 or so the latter system was again dominant, however, and the next nine hundred years were the great junxian age of China, with the system eventually taking hold far more broadly and completely than had ever been the case in the waning years of the Zhou.

Generally speaking, the fengjian revival took place because the transition to junxian had not been thorough in the Warring States era, nor had society had sufficient experience with the system to develop social groups committed to it or institutions capable of maintaining it. In other words, the reversal occurred through force of habit. Fengjian values were still deeply held in society. When problems developed, men tended to gravitate back to older ways of doing things. They felt comfortable with hereditary and localized power, and they did not really feel comfortable with a free market. Few people were deeply committed to civilian or humanistic outlooks. In the later junxian period the system proved more durable because it was based on a long accumulation of historical experience and rested on social groups committed to its values.

The Han Dynasty (206 B.C.–A.D. 220) was, on the whole, a glorious and prosperous era and one with a magnificent cultural flowering. Forever after, the Chinese have referred to themselves as *Han Ren*, the Han People. One striking reason for the popularity of the dynasty was that it tried to bring itself into accord with the actual situation in society. This goal meant compromising with the powerful fengjian tendencies that still existed and that the Qin had tried to break off too abruptly. The Han softened the extremes of Qin while maintaining a stable political community that, indeed, gave the dynasty something of a datong quality. It was this approach that began the fengjian revival.

In political organization, the Han blended centralized bureaucracy with aristocratic power, and the latter ultimately won out. At the beginning of the dynasty, its founder, Liu Bang, enfeoffed relatives and others who had helped him to win. For the first forty years of the Han, the emperors had to work to regain power from the new aristocrats who had been created. This task was more or less completed by the reign of the most powerful Han ruler, the famous Wudi. He put the finishing touches on a bureaucratic system similar to Qin's, though not quite as harsh overall or with as much central domination.

Thereafter, however, the new officialdom and the relatives of empresses gradually began to amass wealth and land and to form great families that increasingly dominated government power, locally and centrally. They used public influence for long-term private ends and began to look very much like an aristocracy. Indeed, one name that was applied to these families was *su feng*, which means something like "those who have been informally enfeoffed," an unofficial aristocracy.[1]

Economic life was officially open; however, a fengjian land system developed in practice. The great families accumulated more and more land in their home areas, and the local peasants increasingly turned into their retainers. One mechanism for this process was the ability of the unofficial aristocracy to use its political power to evade taxes. As a result, the burden on the average person became all the heavier. The peasants were thus encouraged to yield their land to a powerful family who could protect them and cushion them against economic disaster.

The Han government tried repeatedly to limit land-holding. The means included outright bans on land accumulation and efforts to prohibit primogeniture, the fengjian practice of leaving all one's property to a single son, rather than dividing it equally among all. All such measures failed, and the Han fell in A.D. 8, partly because of the divisiveness caused by the power of the great families. In A.D. 23 the dynasty was restored, and it lasted another two hundred years. However, the Latter Han, as it is called, never really obtained control of the nascent aristocracy, which grew ever more powerful.

The aristocratic spirit permeated all aspects of life. In the early years of the dynasty historians still celebrated the fact that the common people had been crucial to the overthrow of Qin and the founding of the Han. They wrote plainly that Chen She, who had launched the rebellion, was "born in a humble hut with tiny windows and wattle door, a day laborer in the fields" and that Liu Bang was from a mean background and "rose from the lanes and alleys." By the

Latter Han an elaborate lineage had been developed for Liu Bang, a lineage which traced his family back to the sage ruler Yao.[2]

The Han, as befitted a society with a powerful, aristocratic spirit, was successful militarily. The dynasty filled out the basic boundaries of the Chinese nation. It also went on the offensive against the tribal nomads beyond the Great Wall and expanded its territory into the steppes of the north and the deserts and mountains of the west. In some periods the empire extended outward over a thousand miles, almost to the borders of India. The Han also established military garrisons in Korea and took over the northern part of Vietnam, where an independent Viet state had been developing.

Humanism went into decline. Confucianism became the official philosophy of the government, partly because it was well suited to the blend of fengjian and junxian that the Han sought. At the same time, it adapted itself to the role of legitimizing the state by developing what has come to be called "Imperial Confucianism," an ideology that was to make a lasting imprint on Chinese political life. However, in at least one crucial respect, Han Confucianism became a very different outlook from that of the classical period, for Han Confucians were heavily influenced by animism and became deeply religious in spirit. Heaven was no longer the fundamental but subtle guarantor of goodness; it became active and humanized, more like God. In addition, the Han Confucians were often simply superstitious, with a deep interest in spirits, divination, and portents.

The image of Confucius himself changed. No longer was he simply a wise teacher or a sage. In line with the aristocratic tendencies of the time he began to be viewed as a great lord or king and then as a semidivine being:

> Confucius' mother, Zhengzai, once while taking a walk happened upon the mound of a large tomb, where she fell asleep and dreamed that she received an invitation from a Black Emperor. She went to him and in her dream had intercourse with him. He spoke to her saying: "Your confinement will take place within a hollow mulberry tree." When she awoke she seemed to feel pregnant and later gave birth to Confucius within a hollow mulberry tree.[3]

Similar stories, which not only claim a noble descent for Liu Bang but even a divine origin, appear in histories of the Latter Han.

The Han Dynasty fell in A.D. 220, a victim of the great families, popular rebellion, and invasion by northern tribes. One notable feature of its fall was a wave of opposition against the government by intellectuals and students, the first example of a phenomenon that was, thereafter, to become a common feature of Chinese political life.

The end of the Han ushered in four hundred years of political disunity and foreign domination. This Era of Disunity continued the fengjian tendencies of the time and, indeed, brought them to their peak. South China remained under the political control of native Chinese. However, it had a succession of short-lived dynasties, which were generally a cloak for coups and forced abdications. In the face of such weak government, to which they themselves contributed, the great aristocratic families became all the more dominant.

North China fell to nomadic invasions. The various groups gradually became assimilated to Chinese ways and tried to rule in a monarchical fashion, establishing various kingdoms and dynasties. The conquerors, however, placed themselves over the native Chinese (whom we can henceforth conveniently call the Han peoples, or simply the Han, in Chinese fashion). The result was the creation of a new elite, which paralleled the great families in the south, though with an even greater hereditary and aristocratic character.

The position of the average peasant again resembled that of a serf. In the south, many became "guest families" of the mighty, who could offer them political security and economic protection. In the north, the Han often became servile labor for their tribal conquerors. Commerce declined, and even the use of money waned. Overall, though, it must be stressed that this period was no Dark Age. Even the north retained a relatively advanced culture, and in the south Han civilization lived on, and there were many great intellectuals and artists. Technological progress also moved forward; the most significant development of the time was chemistry, which led, among other things, to the invention of gunpowder.

The march from humanism also continued with the rise of Buddhism. Buddhism is an Indian religion that believes that the world is an illusion. A person is doomed to live in the world of illusion in an endless cycle of rebirths until he has attained enlightenment, which is achieved through following the Buddhist way, recognizing that the world is a world of pain and that pain comes from desire. Renouncing desire allows one to see through the illusion of reality and so attain liberation. By the time Buddhism reached China it had, in addition to its rich metaphysics, acquired a panoply of spiritual beings whose propitiation was an aid to salvation. In the course of time the religion was to make a great, even incalculable contribution to Chinese life and culture. Eventually, too, Chinese Buddhism became comparatively this-worldly and practical. However, from the point of view of intellectual trends in the Era of Disunity, it represented the ultimate triumph of religious thought over the humanism of the late Zhou.

Buddhism first entered China from Central Asia in the middle of the Han, and the way was prepared for it by the religious atmosphere of the time. In the Era of Disunity it achieved incredible success, for in a time of chaos and suffering it gave people solace and support. It also proved particularly popular and influential among the tribal groups in the north because these peoples had a powerful religiosity that easily gave way to the sophistication and artistic splendor of Buddhism. In addition, it may have appealed to the nomads because it was foreign and because by adopting it, a great universal religion before which all people are equal, they could achieve a feeling of equality and cultural parity with the Chinese whom they conquered. Ultimately, however, Buddhism spread to virtually everyone, north and south. Among other things, Buddhist monasteries developed and began to amass land and serfs, and this phenomenon further contributed to the fengjian flavor of the time.

Chinese philosophies could not resist the march of Buddhism. Its only serious rival was Taoism. Originally, Taoism had been a school that used Zhou naturalism as a basis for a subtle philosophy of human conduct and political action. In the Han it had begun to change to a more religious style, and this changeover was complete during the Era of Disunity. This later form of Taoism is generally called ''religious Taoism'' to distinguish it from the Zhou version, which is called ''philosophic Taoism.'' Indeed, Taoism came under powerful Buddhist influence and could rival the new faith only by copying and blending with it.

Buddhism and Taoism dominated culture and gained a firm grip on society for the next seven hundred years or so. Confucianism went into deep decline. The philosophy had triumphed in the Han only in a markedly religious form, and now it simply had no way of resisting the new beliefs. People might retain a Confucian style in their families, and it had some influence on political life; however, it lost all vibrancy and had few serious adherents. No Confucian thinker of note was to appear again until the ninth century.

THE SUI AND TANG AND THE REEMERGENCE OF JUNXIAN

In 589 one of the aristocratic families of the north, the Yangs, succeeded in conquering all rivals and once again united China, ushering in the era of the Sui and Tang dynasties. This period of 350 years was in many ways a high point of Chinese civilization, with great achievements in all areas from the arts and sciences to literature and government. Paper had been invented in the Han, and now printed books came on the scene. From our point of view what is most significant is that in this era the fengjian revival reversed itself and China entered its fully mature junxian age.

The Sui (589–618) was a brief dynasty, somewhat reminiscent of the Qin in its harshness of rule, massive public works, and foreign adventures. It sought to recapture too much power from the aristocrats who had run the country for so long and fell to a coalition of great families. Its successors were the Li family, also a clan from the north with a mixed Chinese and tribal background, who established the Tang Dynasty (618–907). The Tang government was a compromise with the powerful aristocratic groups, and for the first half of the dynasty China retained a rather fengjian atmosphere. Overall, the Tang was often considered a particularly glorious and just time, again perhaps, as with the Han Dynasty, because the mixture of fengjian and junxian that it represented gave it something of a datong quality.

One reason that the Tang and the Sui before it were able to reunite the country was the famous system of land distribution that they organized: the so-called *jun tian* or equal-field system. Under it, every adult upon reaching maturity received land from the government. The person had use of the land for his lifetime, though he could not sell it. When the person became old or died, the land reverted to the government for redistribution. In return for the land, the person or his family owed the government grain, cloth, or other products and service on public works and in the army.

The equal-field system first developed among some of the nomadic kingdoms of the north. It was made possible by the fact that the population had declined in the face of conquest, leaving free land. It was also encouraged as a concept by tribal traditions of public rather than private land tenure and supported ideologically by arguments that equated it with the well-fields of Mencius and the policies of land equalization in the *Zhou Li*. In practice, during the early Tang the government did not disturb the holdings of friendly aristocrats or of the monasteries. There was still free land available to distribute. Through the system, however, the central government was assured of more financial and military power than any aristocratic group and so could maintain authority.

To run the equal-field system and its attendant levies, the Tang established a government modeled on the Qin and Han, though far more developed and rationalized in terms of bureaucratic organization and techniques; it was, thus, in political organization that the junxian system began to make a comeback. There were specialized government ministries in the capital and local officials who were part of a centralized hierarchy. There were regular evaluation of bureaucrats and rules of avoidance and rotation, which meant that no official could serve in his home area and none could hold an office for too long. This policy guarded against the tendency in the Han for officials to make government positions into private fiefs. Perhaps the most important innovation of the Sui-Tang era was an examination system to aid in selecting officials, something that had existed only in a rudimentary form in the Han and was later to contribute to the end of an aristocratic elite in China.

Nonetheless, like the equal-field system, in the early Tang the central government existed alongside of considerable and independent aristocratic power. Furthermore, the bureaucracy itself was dominated by aristocrats who achieved their positions through connections or by monopolizing the examination system. There were important fengjian elements in other areas of life as well. Buddhism and Taoism continued to flourish and received patronage and support from the government. In addition, China once again went on the military offensive and, as in the Han, conquered deep into central Asia.

There are many ways of marking the end of the fengjian resurgence and the full resumption of a junxian tide. No single event or date can ever be of great significance in a grand historical process of this sort that stretches out over centuries. Nevertheless, if a symbol of the reversal is worth picking, none is better than the year A.D. 751 and the battle of Talas River. Here, in central Asia, a Chinese army moving westward met defeat at the hands of an Arab army moving eastward. This defeat was the turning point for the military power of the Tang and, indeed, for the Han people. Never again would a native dynasty have the power to create an international empire, and the Han would generally be on the military defensive. In earlier times an aristocratic military spirit had remained strong. Now, for the first time, a truly civilian culture was to emerge in China.

The full resurgence of junxian that began in the eighth century was, in many ways, a replay of the late Zhou, though now with far more historical experience behind it and at a much higher technological plane. In the short run, the immediate cause of the changeover was the success of early Tang society. China was stable and prosperous, population grew, and commerce burgeoned. One result of this success was that the equal-field system collapsed and a free market in land developed, for the rising population made redistribution difficult and the commercial atmosphere created people eager for private property. As the system declined, the government could no longer collect grain and products from the people or requisition the necessary labor and military service. It responded by creating new bureaus and levels of government to manage and tax the society, and it turned from a militia to a professional army.

Because of the changes both in the economy and in the government, the elite began to open up. No longer was it primarily made up of aristocrats ruling over peasants. Now it came to include many intermediate groups, such as landowners, merchants, professional military men, and specialists of different sorts. These new middle classes, both the products and the agents of the rise of the junxian system, were used by the government in the new administrative organs, further encouraging their emergence and giving them additional opportunities for influence.

As these changes were taking place, humanism began to revive with a renewal of interest in Confucianism. An early sign of this vigor was the work of Han Yu (768–824), who not only turned on Buddhism and Taoism but also sought to go back to the original Confucianism of the Zhou rather than the religious style of the Han. As he wrote:

> After the decline of the Zhou and the death of Confucius, in the time of Qin's book burnings, the Taoism of the Han, the Buddhism of Wei, the Jin, the Liang [dynasties of the Era of Disunity] and the Sui, when men spoke of the Way and power, of humanity and righteousness, they were approaching them either as followers of Yang Zhu [a Taoist] or of Mozi, of Laozi or of Buddha. Being followers of these doctrines they naturally rejected Confucianism. Acknowledging these men as their master, they made Confucius an outcast, adhering to new teachings and vilifying the old. Alas, though men of later ages long to know of humanity and righteousness, the Way and inner power, from whom may they hear them?[4]

In the ninth century the government broke up the great Buddhist monasteries and confiscated their estates, partly for economic reasons and partly because of the developing reaction against Buddhism.

SONG THROUGH QING: OVERVIEW OF THE JUNXIAN ERA

The Tang fell in 907. In the short run the dynasty was the victim of popular rebellion and disloyal military men, and in the long run, of the social dynamism and resultant dislocations that its own success had helped to engender. After the collapse of the government, China again fell into disunity, the era of the so-called Five Dynasties and Ten Kingdoms. This chaos was, however, short-lived and lasted less than sixty years. It came to an end partly through warfare and partly through negotiation among the powerful generals. One of these generals, Zhao Kuangyin, became emperor and established the Song Dynasty (964–1279). The new tendencies of the late Tang picked up great momentum in the Song, and by the middle of the dynasty the society was essentially junxian.

The Song was followed by the Yuan Dynasty (1279–1368), the Ming Dynasty (1368–1644), and the Qing Dynasty (1644–1911). The Song and the Yuan may be considered the early junxian age. The Ming and the first half of the Qing brought the system to maturity, and it reached completion, one might say, in the early eighteenth century. Then it began to decline. Overall, in the junxian era, China had a centralized government with no competing political units. The elite was of wealth or talent and not of birth. Families moved up and down the social hierarchy, and class lines grew vague. Education and political sophistication spread, and the population at large played an important role in politics. The economy rested on private enterprise, and values were comparatively civilian and humanistic. Confucianism became the dominant ideology.

The changeover to the junxian era is immediately evident in the names of the dynasties it includes. Hitherto, dynastic names had been based on the aristocratic titles claimed by the founders prior to their accession to power. The Li family, for example, had been Lords of Tang, and even the peasant Liu Bang used a title he had picked up as Lord of Han when he named his dynasty. Now, except for the Song, which was named in the era of transition, dynastic names became sobriquets like New and Fair Deal, selected for their political effectiveness and auspicious meanings. The name of the Yuan Dynasty means "basic" or "fundamental." Ming means "bright," and Qing means "pure."

The junxian age is also striking, at first approximation, because of the military weakness it brought to China. In fengjian times the nation had often gone on the offensive and had never been completely conquered. Now China was under partial or complete foreign domination for over half the time, and when independent, it was generally on the defensive.

When the Song came to power in 964, it never succeeded in recapturing parts of the northeast, which had fallen to tribal peoples during the Five Dynasties. The nomads continued to nibble at the borders and conquered the whole northern half of the country in 1126. The rest of the Song fell to the Mongols in 1279, and they ran the Yuan Dynasty. The Ming was again a native dynasty, but it was constantly under pressure from the north. In 1644 China fell to the Manchu tribes who ruled the Qing. In the nineteenth and twentieth centuries, one might add, the nation came under great imperialist pressure from the West. In general, the northern conquerors, and especially the Qing, assimilated themselves quickly to Chinese ruling styles and to Chinese society. Nevertheless, the importance of foreigners increased greatly in this era, and we will devote the next chapter to the topic.

Another striking feature of the junxian age was its wealth and prosperity. China had already been a large country. In the Han and the Tang the population reached 60,000,000. Now it soared. In the Song it reached 100,000,000, and by the Ming it stood at 150,000,000 to 200,000,000. By the middle of the eighteenth century there were 300,000,000 people.[5] Along with the population rise there was a sharp increase in economic productivity. Urbanization increased, and there were many great cities and innumerable lesser towns and hamlets. Most people lived on the land; however, the population density was so great and the general social integration so high that the distinction between urban and rural was unimportant in terms of values.[6] The majority of people lived in great regional megalopoli, and, as Hucker notes, by 1800 there was no one in the country "not well enough acquainted with city ways to be something of a suburbanite in outlook." In fact, to one knowledgeable European in the late sixteenth century, China looked like "but one body and but one city."[7]

Finally, the junxian period is clearly set off from the past by the increased importance of the average person in political life. This importance was true in everyday affairs and is most immediately evident in the way dynasties changed. Popular rebellion had been an important feature of the Chinese political scene at least since the revolution that overthrew the Qin. In the fengjian revival from the Han through the Tang, however, all rebellions failed, and when dynastic change occurred, it was through struggles within the elite, regicides, and military coups. In the junxian age all dynasties except the Song, which fell to foreign invasion, came to an end because of broad-based political movements that culminated in a successful revolution. Mencius's dictum that government ultimately rested on the will of the people had, in other words, become a practical reality.

Overall, there were sharp ups and downs in the junxian era, and, particularly because of the high population density, poverty, destitution, and famine were always possible and all too often occurred. Nonetheless, for the most part, the age was one of remarkable public welfare, security, and justice. As Fairbank notes, the Ming was "one of the great eras of orderly government and social stability in human history" when a huge population "was maintained during 276 years in comparative peace."[8] The same can certainly be said for much of the rest of the age.

The great exception to the generally successful, generally integrated character of junxian China was the status of women. The history of Chinese women has yet to be written in detail. However, the general fact that women suffered a decline in status with the arrival of the new system, particularly in contrast to the leveling that took place among men, is clear. In fengjian times women had been subordinated as a matter of course. However, in a society with sharp class lines based on birth, their position was roughly commensurable with that of their men. In the Tang, for example, women received land in the equal-field system, and among the aristocrats they had considerable independence of action. It is probably no coincidence that the only female emperor of China, Wu Zhao, reigned at this time. By contrast, in junxian times, a self-conscious emphasis in thought and action developed concerning the subordination of women.

The most striking manifestation of the change was the introduction of foot binding. Girls had their feet bound when they were young, and the limbs remained undersized and deformed throughout their lives. The custom was considered attractive and erotic, but it was painful and cruel. It also had repercussions far beyond sexual matters, for it was both a symbol of the subordination of women and a powerful factor that contributed to their continuing loss of independence and to blocking their possibilities for equality. Foot binding began in the Song among the elite and by the Ming had spread in varying degrees to the whole population, baleful testimony to the general integration of society.

The reasons for the decline in the status of women must, at present, remain a matter of speculation. However, it would seem in some ways to be intimately tied to the very arrival of the junxian system itself. Thus, in the new age, status at birth was no longer accepted either in theory or in practice as the basis of social stratification. Since gender is the ultimate genetic difference, the new emphasis on the subordination of women may have been an effort to guarantee male supremacy when the social and ideological justifications for inequality between the sexes had disappeared. In addition, in the junxian era, China not only lost its martial vigor, but the male ideal came to emphasize intellectual refinement and the polite arts and to denigrate physical prowess and strenuous activity. As a result, the heightened repression of women may also have been a psychological response to the need to keep sharp distinctions between men and women in this new situation.

While women do not appear often in the historical record of the junxian age, they do become visible in times of unrest and rebellion. One suspects, indeed, that fundamental female dissatisfaction with society and culture in this era probably had a far greater and more constant influence than we yet know or appreciate. Certainly, when the system declined and the revolution against it developed, women were to play a vital role.

SOCIETY, GOVERNMENT, AND ECONOMY

Though, apart from women, the social structure in junxian China was open, it can, for any specific segment of time, be analyzed as a hierarchy of levels. At the top were still an emperor and a hereditary dynasty. The imperial family was not supposed to wield political influence, but, as we shall see in our discussion of government, the power of the ruler actually increased in comparison to the situation in earlier times. Below the dynasty came society as a whole.

In the Song, near the beginning of the new era, its character can still be described in terms of the old fengjian classes of elite, peasants, artisans, and merchants, though one's position was no longer formally determined by birth and the elite formed a continuation of the new middle classes of the late Tang rather than an aristocracy.[9] By Ming and Qing, however, the general blending and growing complexity of society brought a more fundamental distinction to the fore: between an elite that worked with its mind, and average people who worked with their hands. Mencius had emphasized this social differentiation late in the first junxian era, and by this period it provides the most satisfactory description of the realities of Chinese society. As this simple distinction became paramount and the lines between the two levels remained open, the whole notion of class grew weak, though the concept of an elite remained powerful and, in general, the prestige of those who worked with their minds was considerably higher.

The vast majority of those who worked with their hands were farmers or farm laborers. The rest included a diverse mixture ranging from canal boatmen to the army rank and file, from miners and artisans to workers in factories. The elite included an overlapping group of landowners, government employees, merchants, army officers, and a range of other nonmanual occupations. The division between the elite and the nonelite was, to some degree, visually evident, for those who worked with their hands, both rural and urban, tended to wear short jackets and trousers, while those who claimed elite status wore long gowns, a division roughly analogous to our differences between blue and white collar.[10]

The most important distinction within the elite was between those who passed the imperial examinations, the so-called degree-holders, and the rest. The examination system was the central institution in junxian China guaranteeing the maintenance of nonaristocratic society. The purpose of the exams was, theoretically, to produce important government officials, though in practice only a small percentage of those who passed worked for the state. The rest lived at home and provided the leaders for society in general.

The degree-holders were expected to be experts in human relations and public administration. In order to insure this result the exams tested candidates in philosophy, history, literature, and Confucian theory rather than in specialized knowledge. The degree-holders, representing the highest echelons of the elite and certified by society, were, in a sense, like the professionals in contemporary America, men who claimed the greatest status and were especially privileged.[11]

Except for degree-holders we do not have figures on the number of people in each category of society, for there were no formal distinctions among the various groups and the government kept no tabs, except on the men who passed its exams. We know that at any given time in the Ming there were about a half million degree-holders and in the early eighteenth century, about one million. These figures would mean that, including immediate families, about 2 percent of the population was at the degree-holding level.

For every person who passed the exams we know that there were many more who pursued elite occupations and who tried but failed to obtain certification or did not try at all. A very rough approximation of the long-gowned group as a whole might be 10 percent of society, or 15 million in the Ming and 25 million in the early eighteenth century. The remaining 90 percent were short-jacketed workers, and of these, farmers constituted perhaps 80 percent or 130 million in the Ming and 200 million in the Qing.

A number of factors combined to keep status lines vague and society open in the junxian era. One was that there were few if any legal or customary bars to social interaction or social mobility. Indeed, except for an insignificant number of people in supposedly disreputable occupations, all males could sit for the exams. Even these groups were enfranchised by the eighteenth century. The values and ideals of meritocracy were now long-standing and deeply embedded. People really believed that ability rather than hereditary ascription should determine one's place in society and that everyone should have a chance to prove himself. At the same time there was, at least among the population at large, if not always among those at the top, a healthy sense that the actual distinctions in society were not necessarily based on talent, but that luck, money, and connections could play a vital role.[12]

In addition to its meritocratic and egalitarian spirit, society was also comparatively integrated because there were a large number of people on the boundary between elite and worker. Such people could serve as intermediaries for the two groups. For example, clerks in the government and in private enterprise were in this position, as well as many smaller landlords who engaged in long-gowned activities but also tilled the fields. Another factor that tended to mix the population was that in many parts of China, there were powerful clan organizations. A given clan could include people from all walks of life who, nonetheless, had varying degrees of familial connections.

A result of these elements and in itself the capstone that maintained social integration was the fact that people moved from one level to another, families rose and fell, and, therefore, the different parts of society were not differentiated in the course of time by permanent sets of people. Again we do not have specific figures except for degree-holders. However, what has been deduced from this and other information indicates a steady rise and fall in society.

Thus, a family might retain degree-holding status for three generations or so and then lose it, and the cliché of the time and other evidence indicate that if a family did not maintain such a position, it would soon drop in status; for administrative opportunities associated with degree-holding, rather than land or investments, were often its major source of wealth. Furthermore, in the junxian age primogeniture was a thing of the past. Now a father divided his property equally among his sons, thus discouraging permanent accumulation in a few hands. Finally, in a family of wealth and leisure the children might easily lose the necessary drive and discipline to get ahead, and the system was such that no family could rest on its laurels for too long without a sharp decline.

Aside from luck and talent, what a person needed to rise in the system was leisure time and education. In other words, a family required sufficient wealth to spare a son from labor and to provide him with the necessary schooling for elite status. As a result, in the more prosperous eras of the junxian age and, in that sense, the era as a whole, there was a real possibility of advancement. There was also an educational boom in this period that furthered the process and is an indication of the demand for schooling. Beginning in the Song and picking up momentum in the Ming, a network of private elementary schools spread across China. These schools were inexpensive, and, if a child could be spared from work, it was not difficult for him to attend. In any case, if a child proved particularly talented, a rich relative or the community as a whole might support him.

One result of the easy access to education was that literacy reached unprecedented levels. One foreign resident wrote that "with few exceptions, every Chinese knows how to read and write, at least sufficient for the ordinary occasions of life."[13] This statement was certainly an exaggeration, particularly if one keeps women in mind, but it gives the general feeling. According to a recent estimate, at least 50 percent of the males were literate as well as a substantial, though far smaller, number of women. Along with literacy, popular literature boomed, and the average man seems to have enjoyed relaxing over a good book.[14]

The general openness of status lines and the possibility of advancement did not mean, of course, that any large number of workers became degree-holders. The possibility was there, and the "log cabin myth" of the humble farmer's son who became a great official was a popular tale with good overtones, but such a reality was not likely. Nonetheless, as Hucker notes, despite the rarity of such happenings, the average person had "every reason to expect that one of his sons, with hard work and luck, could improve the family fortunes and status substantially by rising into the lower level of the managerial elite, so that the family could escape from the drudgery of hard manual labor at least for a generation or two."[15] Of course, once someone was in the elite for a while, degree-holding status became possible for a few in the endless rise and fall that characterized the age.

The open social situation was not without its costs. The system could breed a competitiveness and insecurity that accompanied people no matter who they were. Would they rise? If they did, were they truly worthy? Would family problems or a depressed economic situation cast them down? Among other things, such problems could sometimes lead to an intensely elitist behavior among those on top, attitudes exemplified at the highest levels of society by the old Western word "Mandarins" for the degree-holders. Such behavior was at odds with the general nature of society. As a result, particularly when times were bad, sharp social cleavages could rapidly develop, marked by an intense competition for what was available and coupled with insensitive arrogance on top and angry resentment below.

The government in junxian China took the form of a well-organized and highly centralized bureaucracy. Nonetheless, it normally did not weigh heavily on society. It was, in a sense, the supreme arbiter and mediator of the system. It was ultimately responsible for peace and order, for the defense of private property, and for a basic level of welfare. It also took care of national defense and major public works. It collected the necessary taxes to do these things. However, it was not a particularly large or interventionist state and was generally committed to a laissez-faire attitude toward society.

At the top of the government stood the emperor, whose power as the chief executive of the system actually rose in comparison to the situation in fengjian times. This process began in the Song, picked up momentum in the Yuan, and culminated in the Ming and Qing. To some extent, the increased power of the ruler was a result of the influence of foreign conquest on political life. However, the more basic reason was that in the earlier era, the elite was composed of great families and aristocrats with independent influence and prestige. Indeed, such families might have as much prestige as the dynasty itself. Now, with such groups gone in favor of a government and society made up of an open and shifting citizenry, the uniqueness of the emperor increased.

There were many signs of the new status of the ruler. One striking symbol was in protocol. In the Tang, officials in his presence could sit in an informal manner. In the Song, they had to stand at attention, and by the Ming, they customarily knelt or lay prostrate. Through the Yuan, the government included a powerful prime minister who often functioned as the actual chief executive. The Ming emperors abolished the post and gathered its power into their own hands. Overall, the ability of government officials to disagree with the ruler or safely to criticize him declined. In former times, the censorate, a watchdog agency in the government, had the dual task of overseeing the bureaucracy and remonstrating with the ruler. Now, all too often, its function became simply to keep an eye on other officials for the emperor.

In practice, there were checks on what the emperor could do. Confucian ethics, the obligation of a ruler to behave in a virtuous and effective fashion, were important. So was his obligation to pick the best subordinates and, at least in theory, to listen to their criticisms. If the bureaucracy disagreed with a policy, it could also drag its heels, and, in any case, the emperor was expected to follow a host of bureaucratic procedures that he could overlook only at great peril to his effectiveness and the loyalty owed to him.[16] Finally, the generally low level of government activity also served to limit the ruler's authority.

Nevertheless, there was no real legal limit on the emperor's power within the government or toward society. The Ming rulers earned a reputation for being particularly harsh and insensitive to their subordinates. Censors and others who criticized the emperor or his favorites were sometimes publicly beaten at court. Later in the dynasty the nation was often at the mercy of the imperial family and court eunuchs working under the protection of an evil emperor or the neglect of a poor one. It is no wonder, then, that a hallmark of Confucian radicalism in the junxian age became opposition to the new authority of the emperorship, for not only had the power of the position risen, but its legitimacy had weakened at the very same time. In fengjian times, the hereditary emperorship sat atop a society committed to aristocratic values. Now, the position was the last important hereditary one left, and it ruled a nation that no longer believed in such claims to authority. This situation constituted one of the greatest contradictions in junxian China.

Peking was the capital for most of the time from the Yuan onward. Here the emperor resided, and here, too, were located the highest echelons of the bureaucracy. There were many bureaus with specialized functions and responsibilities; among the most important were the so-called Six Ministries: Personnel, Revenue, Rites (which, among other things, ran the examination system), War, Justice, and Public Works. Subordinate to the Peking bureaucracy were provincial governments and various sublevels below these down to the local district, the *xian* (as in junxian). Various central government agencies also had offices in different parts of the country, and there were censors and others moving around the system to keep an eye on things.

The government included people from all levels of society. Senior degree-holders filled almost all the executive positions, and, in theory, the purpose of the exams was to create such personnel. Lower positions, depending on the job, could be held by younger degree-holders, other members of the elite, or workers. Their employment ranged from staff positions to secretaries, from policemen to tax collectors. In general, only degree-holders could rise in the system. For them, promotion was basically by seniority, though talent and connections also helped. Family background before one entered the service, however, was not, as such, of particular importance.[17]

The government was not as large, in proportion to the population, as it had been in fengjian times. This fact was a reflection of the laissez-faire spirit of the age and was particularly evident on the local scene, where the government interacted with the people. At any one time in the early eighteenth century, only 10 percent of the degree-holders, or about forty thousand men, were in service. In addition, there may have been two or three million other government employees, excluding the military. In other words, government personnel, at all levels combined, totaled about 1 percent of the population at most. In the Ming and Qing, despite the rise in population, the number of local districts was no greater than it had been in the early Tang. In the Qing, for example, there were about thirteen hundred districts and about fifteen hundred subprovincial units in all. To have kept pace with population growth since the Tang would have required eight thousand districts and ten thousand subprovincial units.[18]

In Ming and Qing times the district magistrate was considered to be the crucial link between the society and the government. He represented the legal and administrative authority of the state and was responsible for peace and order and for collecting taxes. He was expected to be au courant about his area and the people in it. Among other things, everyone in the district was registered at his office, through the so-called *baojia* registration system. Nonetheless, he was supposed to work in close cooperation with the local citizenry and not to be needlessly interventionist. Indeed, the job was structured in a manner that insured this result.

The magistrate was an outsider where he served, for by the rule of avoidance he could not hold office in his home province. He was never at his post for too long, because rotation after two or three years was the rule. When he arrived at his district, which often had two or three hundred thousand people, he came only with a few trusted advisers. The vast bulk of his staff of clerks at the district office (the local *yamen*) were local people, numbering two or three thousand. As a result, if he was to be a successful official he had to depend on the cooperation and initiative of local society, and this dependence encouraged him to act more as a general supervisor and transmission belt than as an active administrator.

The people selected their own local leaders, who would often be well-known members of the elite but could also be average persons. These leaders were selected, ideally, on the basis of talent and effectiveness, either by consensus or election. Age was particularly prized, and the "local elder" was an honored figure. As far as possible, the locality was supposed to handle its own affairs and deal with its own problems. If there was a problem or dispute that could not be resolved without recourse to the magistrate, people could then turn to him. For example, legal disputes that could not be adjudicated locally ended in the magistrate's court. There were also some particularly serious matters, such as murder, that the magistrate was obliged to investigate. But, in general, he was meant to rule with a light rein.

If the magistrate could not handle a problem himself or if the local people raised issues of broader provincial or national policy, the magistrate was supposed to pass the matter upward in the bureaucracy. Each district also had degree-holders who could circumvent the magistrate if necessary and make their voices heard higher up. At the provincial level officials had the right to write memorials directly to the throne. Since the flow of documents upward was essential to an effective and just functioning of the system, there was great emphasis in political theory on the notion that the *yan lu*, the paths of communication up the hierarchy and ultimately to the throne, remain open.

In normal times the system worked rather well. If the local elite was oppressive, the people had recourse to the magistrate. If he was corrupt, the locality could resort to noncooperation or an appeal to higher-ups. Similarly, if an official was dissatisfied with his superior, he could remonstrate with him or, if necessary, complain to those above, directly or indirectly. If complaints against an official proved founded, the result would be a blackmark on the man's record and a blow to his career. However, when times were bad, problems could mushroom all along the line.

If the local elite and the magistrate were both unprincipled, the average person might be left with no solution to his problems. Or, if the highest officials were corrupt, there was no recourse for those lower down but the emperor. If he, too, was hopeless, then the only appeal for upright people throughout the system was heaven, that is to say, rebellion. There were frequent cases of local noncooperation, tax riots, and minor unrest throughout the junxian age. Often these were simply to bring a bad situation to the attention of higher officials or of the ruler. However, in the late Yuan and Ming and, as we shall see, at the end of the Qing, all the negative factors combined to bring down the dynasty.

From the Song onward, the army and military service did not have much prestige as compared to private life or work in the civilian bureaucracy. The general feeling in the junxian era was expressed in the famous couplet "*hao tie bu zuo ding, hao ren bu zuo bing*," "good iron is not made into nails, good people do not become soldiers." This attitude, of course, contributed to the decline of Chinese military power in this period. In general, armies were conscripted, and service was not popular. Dynasties also used various means to maintain a strong army and a good military spirit. In the Yuan and Qing the core of the army comprised hereditary units made up of Mongol and Manchu troops. The Ming also experimented with enfeoffment and hereditary military establishments in strategic places. This approach, which was unusual in junxian China, was defended on the reasonable grounds that a fengjian organization was better for the military spirit.[19] Whatever policies were used, however, all armies, conquerors or natives, rapidly deteriorated in the face of the powerful civilian bias of society.

When there was need for military power, one solution was the formation of militia units. These local corps, as they are called, were organized in time of trouble to maintain order in an area and to keep out intruders. The corps often supported the government. However, if things were going badly, they could turn on the officials. The inherent military strength that remained on the local scene was another check on government abuse and a prop for rebellion when this came on the agenda. Since those who worked with their hands were most likely to find themselves in the rank and file of the army and of the militia, military skills, if not a liking for the military life, were greater among those lower down in society than among the elite.

The economic system in junxian China rested on a free market and a cash nexus. Landowners could buy and sell their land. Farmers owned their land, rented it, or worked as laborers. Almost all other economic activity was also private. In the Song there were still several government monopolies; however, by the Ming and Qing, salt was the only important one left.[20] Government connections and support might be necessary for major economic activity, but there were few, if any, restrictions on trade except with foreigners. There were taxes on land, produce, and trade, though these were supposed to be kept light, and when they rose, the increase was taken as a sign of government misrule.

The junxian system encouraged initiative and efficiency, and when the population did not press too heavily on resources and the government was effective, it contributed to the creation of a vigorous economy. There was an agricultural revolution in the Song in crops and techniques, and progress continued afterward. When contact with the New World began in the sixteenth century, potatoes, corn, and peanuts further increased yields, often on what had been marginal land with older crops. Throughout the period, the best seeds, new crops, and various technical improvements spread with amazing speed from wherever they were introduced, testimony to the pressures of the market and the sophistication of Chinese farmers. There was efficient use of manpower and animals. Natural fertilizer was employed with great care, and night soil and sewage were not only saved on the farm but collected from the cities for use on the land. Prior to the development of chemical fertilizers in the twentieth-century West, China almost certainly had the highest yields per acre of any country in the world.

Along with agricultural growth, industry and commerce also boomed. The chief products of industry were consumer goods: textiles, food products, porcelain, and items for home consumption. There was a well-developed trade and banking system resting on the market town and smaller cities and spreading upward to encompass the great regional zones and, in some cases, the nation as a whole. There was an active overseas trade, particularly to Southeast Asia. By the late Ming, this involved thousands of ships, mostly in Chinese hands, the largest up to one thousand tons (about the size of a clipper ship), with crews of over two hundred.

The free market that contributed to the great economic progress of the age was not without its problems, of course. In the Song landlordism was widespread, and excessive accumulation of property in the hands of the wealthy continued to be a recurring problem later on. Indeed, inequality, competition, and insecurity were, in a sense, endemic to the system. However, those who rented land or worked for others could, to some extent, rely on leases, community traditions, and their own power to protect themselves from abuse. In addition, the government, though basically committed to the privileges of private property, intervened when necessary to alleviate extreme hardship or to avoid sharp social cleavages. It could do anything from controlling rent to providing work to supplying food.[21]

As a result, when the economy took a downturn, those affected would quickly turn to political and social activism. This might help to redress the problems and so keep society on an even keel. On the other hand, if things did not improve, the possibility of broader unrest and rebellion was always present. In these ways, the character of the open marketplace provided a further impetus to the development of mass politics in junxian China.

NEO-CONFUCIANISM

In the junxian era humanism and, in particular, Confucianism became the dominant outlook of society. The reinvigoration of the philosophy began in the late Tang, and in the Song it became the vehicle of thought for the new meritocratic elite that was coming to characterize China. The Confucianism that developed in the Song is generally called Neo-Confucianism, and its creation is associated with a succession of famous thinkers and political figures, including

Zhang Zai, Zhou Dunyi, Shao Yong, Wang Anshi, the Cheng brothers, Hao and Yi, and, above all, the great synthesizer of the system, Zhu Xi.

In the Song the goal of these men was to revive Confucianism and to bring the government and society around to its views and values, to *xin min*, "renovate the people," as they put it. As a result, by the Ming, Confucian learning had become the basic curriculum for the proliferating network of schools and had permeated all levels of society. At the same time, the Song interpretations of Confucian theory had become official in the sense that they provided the ideological basis for the government and were the required viewpoint on the examinations for degree-holding status.

It should be emphasized that religion by no means died out in junxian times but rather served to complement the basic Confucian outlook. A syncretic faith, often referred to as "Chinese popular religion," grew out of Buddhism, Taoism, and various other traditions, including Confucianism itself. There were those who considered themselves Buddhists and Taoists primarily, and almost everyone sought the consolations of religion from time to time. In general, however, serious religious devotion was associated more with outsiders, the young, the poor, and women than with the elite. As we shall see, therefore, religion often played an important role in rebellions and other movements for radical change.

Neo-Confucianism was a good representation of the thought of Confucius and Mencius. However, it had at least one major feature that the classical thinkers had lacked, a well-developed cosmological underpinning. This cosmology represented a subtle and profound mixture of many elements from the past, including the *Yijing*, Taoism, Han Dynasty naturalism, and, above all, Buddhism; indeed, the Song thinkers developed their cosmology partly because the long centuries of Buddhist predominance had made people sensitive to the need for such things and, partly, because of the desire to combat Buddhism's own rich metaphysics.

Generally, Neo-Confucian cosmology centered on the idea of the *taiji* or great ultimate, a grand integration of everything quite beyond human comprehension and similar to the Tao of the Taoists or, perhaps, to an ultramodern view of God or the cosmos. Humans can perceive reality only through the yin-yang complementarity, which, generated by the taiji and rising and falling in influence, governs and generates all that we can know. At the same time, all reality is made up of *li* (principle) and *qi* (material force). All things, the Neo-Confucians said, had a principle (li) which provided their basic nature and form. At the same time, they are composed of material force, which gives them their actuality and physical reality. All things of the same sort share the same li. However, they are not necessarily the same because the qi of which they are composed can be relatively clear or relatively turbid, revealing the li or obscuring it.

The Neo-Confucians used this cosmology to understand all reality; however, their main effort was to use it to support Confucian sociomoral theory. For example, the so-called Four Books that Zhu Xi selected as representing the essence of Confucian thinking (*The Analects, The Mencius, The Doctrine of the Mean*, and *The Great Learning*) are all primarily concerned with ethics, society, and politics. Essentially, what the Neo-Confucians argued was that the principles (li) of goodness and virtue were inherent in all people and the way to bring them out was through the basic Confucian means of good environment, good education, and good behavior.

Furthermore, they stressed that the principles of good environment (including government), good education and behavior, and, indeed, of all socioethical matters could be discovered through Confucian theory and practice. Thus, Neo-Confucian cosmology supported the Confucian view at all points and aimed at developing good people and a good society in a Confucian sense. It is worth pointing out that Neo-Confucian cosmology is a comparatively rare phenomenon in history, for it was created to enrich a well-developed social theory rather than to rationalize a religion; as a result, it may be of considerable contemporary interest.

The Song Neo-Confucians were extremely optimistic men. They rejected Xunzi and supported Mencius's view that the nature of man tends toward the good. Their optimism was based essentially on their deep belief in the power of Confucianism to effect a good society.[22] At the same time, one may surmise, it rested on the fact that the junxian system was bringing commoners, the group they represented, to power.

In the Song, the Neo-Confucians worked at all levels of government and society to carry out their goal of "renovating the people," of inculcating a Confucian spirit of goodness and moral behavior appropriate to the new era. Thus, they were deeply committed to the idea that environment, education, and attitude, rather than status at birth, were critical for developing virtue; indeed, they even went beyond Confucius himself in stressing this point. As Cheng Yi put it:

> *Question*: Since man's nature is originally enlightened why is it sometimes obscured? *Answer*: This must be investigated and understood. . . . Man's nature is universally good. In cases where there is evil it is because of one's capacity. The nature is the same as principle, and principle is the same whether in the sage emperors Yao and Shun or in the common man in the street. Material-force is the source of capacity. It may be either clear (and reveal the basic nature) or turbid (and obscure it). Men endowed with clear material-force are wise, while those with turbid material-force are stupid.
>
> *Further question*: Can stupidity be changed? *Answer*: Yes. Confucius said: "The most intelligent and the most stupid cannot be changed." But in principle they can. Only those who ruin themselves and cast themselves away cannot be changed. *Question*: Is it due to their capacity that the most stupid ruin and throw themselves away? *Answer*: Certainly. But it cannot be said that capacity cannot be changed. Since all have the same basic nature who cannot be changed? Because they ruin and cast themselves away and are not willing to learn, people are unable to change. In principle, if they were willing to learn, they could change.[23]

In addition to their commitment to meritocracy, the Neo-Confucians were also in general agreement with the other aspects of the junxian system. They were for centralized, bureaucratic government but often worked to keep the role of that government light. Many were famous for encouraging and developing means for local cooperation and social management in fields ranging from education to economic development. Most were deeply civilian in background, and, of course, they led the way in the revival of humanism.

Despite their optimism and basic commitment to the new system, however, the founders of Neo-Confucianism, like all great Confucians, were far from being simply upholders of the emerging status quo. They often found themselves in political opposition and suffered severe damage to their careers because of their outspoken views. Some, indeed, in grappling with basic problems they saw developing in the junxian system, made a major contribution to the formation of the opposition tradition of the coming era.

For example, a number of them were particularly distressed by the inequalities associated with the free market system and hostile to the growing power and undemocratic character of the junxian emperorship, both themes of great importance to social critics in later times. As Zhang Zai wrote:

> If the government of the empire is not based on the well-field system, there will never be peace. The way of the Zhou was simply this: to equalize. . . . The well-field system could be put into effect with greatest ease. The government needs only to issue an edict and the whole thing can be settled without having to beat a single person. No one would dare to occupy and hold land as his own. Moreover, it should be done in such a manner as to obtain the people's ready compliance, nor cause those with much land to lose all their means.
>
> This is the basis of the people's subsistence. In recent times no provision has been made for the people's means of subsistence, but only for the commandeering of their labor. Contrary to expectation, the exalted position of the Son of Heaven [the emperor] has been used for monopolizing everything productive of profit. With the government thinking only of the government and the people thinking only of themselves, they have not taken each other into consideration.[24]

Nonetheless, while the Song Neo-Confucians were, in general, liberal-minded people and even radical at times, their thought bore the seeds of the official ideology that it later became, a way of bolstering the authority of those on top. The most serious problem was the possibility that their views could be understood not as indicating a dynamic ideal toward which society should proceed but as an actual description of society as it existed. For example, one of the most famous pieces of writing was the "Western Inscription" of Zhang Zai. It began: "Heaven is my father and earth is my mother, and even such a small creature as I finds an intimate place in their midst. . . . All people are my brothers and all things are my companions. The emperor is the eldest son of my parents (Heaven and Earth) and the great ministers are his stewards."[25] Zhang surely meant the latter statement as an ideal; however, it was just the sort of sentiment that could easily be misconstrued into an orthodoxy.

The other serious ambiguity in the outlook of the Neo-Confucians concerned two other mutually related issues: how much to emphasize formal education and learning as a prerequisite for virtue and how much practice was necessary to supplement knowledge and thought in its pursuit. The important Neo-Confucians, working to renovate Chinese society, were all deeply interested in scholarship. On the other hand, they emphasized the importance of good behavior and did not shrink from political activism. Nevertheless, their writings could be interpreted as a denigration of action as opposed to theory and as setting a very high standard of learning as a prerequisite for virtue and, hence, for political power.

For example, Zhu Xi wrote:

> Even Confucius, magnificent as his talents were, was nevertheless diligent in his efforts. For anyone of lesser endowments, to let things develop of themselves, willy-nilly, is unheard of. . . . So let us now set our minds on honoring our virtuous natures and pursuing our studies. Let us every day seek to find in ourselves whether or not we have been remiss about anything in our studies and whether or not we have been lax about anything in our virtuous natures. This spirit also makes us broadened by literature and disciplined by propriety, able to penetrate higher things by studying lower things. If we urge ourselves on in this way for a year, how can we not develop? Every day we must seek some amount of improvement, learning what we do not yet know and changing for the better whatever is not good; thus, we shall improve our virtuous natures. In reading books we must seek for righteous principles, and in making compilations, we must assemble in order things that are relevant, not merely copying along, always becoming more widely acquainted with former precepts and past examples; thus, we shall improve our studies. We must never relax for a moment. If we pass our days in this fashion, then in three years we might have made a bit of progress.[26]

As in the case of Zhang Zai, this statement should be taken in the context of the times. In a sense, it may even reflect the frustrations of Zhu's career and his subsequent pessimism about the possibility of effective action; he may have felt it was better to cultivate oneself and work for posterity. However, it was the sort of thing that could be misconstrued to suggest that the average citizen had neither the leisure nor the education to become truly virtuous and to discourage political action by any but a handful.

As a result, though the Song Neo-Confucians contributed to the rise and success of junxian China, when their views became the official outlook, those in power could use them to argue that the status quo was necessarily the good Confucian society; for the orthodox philosophy suggested that there was a sage ruler on top who selected his subordinates through examinations in Neo-Confucianism and so assured that they were the best people.

In this way, the official outlook might be used to reverse the Confucian principle that the best should be on top and to associate it with the ultimately un-Confucian idea that being on top meant that one was the best. Given the open, skeptical, and practically minded society of the time, how successful those who supported this idea were in convincing anyone but themselves that it was true is open to question. However, it could be a very elitist and objectionable outlook that could lead to poor human relations and bad government. When times were difficult, it could even tarnish Confucianism itself and in the twentieth century contributed to giving the philosophy a bad name in China.

THE OPPOSITION TRADITION

In the junxian era, in addition to the official Neo-Confucianism espoused by the government, a vigorous opposition tradition also existed. Like the orthodoxy, this tradition had deep roots in the Chinese past, overlapped considerably with the original Neo-Confucians, and came into full development with the Ming. By then, it appeared basically in two forms. The first was associated with those lower down in the social scale, popular rebellion, and religion. The other was more tied to the upper echelons of society, formal social criticism, and Confucianism.

As might be expected in the light of the open and comparatively homogeneous society of junxian China, the two strands interacted with one another, had much in common, and could frequently blend. Indeed, given the character of Neo-Confucianism, even the line between the opposition and the orthodoxy was often not so much in theory as in political attitudes and self-interest. Like the official viewpoint, the opposition contributed greatly to the welfare and justice of the junxian era.

The tradition of popular opposition and revolution can be traced as far back as the rebellion that overthrew the Qin Dynasty, a movement that included both commoners and ex-aristocrats.[27] The broad ideology that informed the rebels was the general notion of the Mandate of Heaven. This was the idea that went back to the early Zhou and that said that governments or persons in authority remained legitimate only as long as they maintained a good society. Once they had lost virtue, "to oppress the world with . . . unprincipled government and ruthless laws," they were no longer worthy of support.[28]

This idea had become common coin in the thought of the Warring States era and is particularly associated with Mencius's argument for the right of revolution in terms of the rectification of names. The concept of the Mandate of Heaven was to remain the basic outlook behind all great rebellions and revolutions thereafter. It was, of course, bolstered as an ideal by the revival of the junxian system in the late Tang and the apotheosis of Mencius by the Song Neo-Confucians.

The rebellion against Qin placed the commoner Liu Bang on the throne. After that, until junxian times, though popular rebellions succeeded only in weakening governments but not in overthrowing them, the tradition continued to develop. In the Han two other elements were added. One of these was the ideal of datong, the Great Community, and the other was religion.

As we have noted, the concept of datong envisioned a society that would relate like a great family, provide human equality, and integrate the best in past social systems. The concept first gained prominence early in the Han in the Confucian book known as the *Li Ji*. It appealed both to intellectuals and rebels and yielded a number of works that seem to have served as tracts for revolutionaries active in the latter years of the dynasty. With the opportunities and insecurities inherent in the reemergence of junxian from the late Tang onward, of course, datong ideals became particularly relevant.

Familial forms of organization within disaffected groups and as a goal for society became common. Similarly, egalitarianism, sometimes including women, developed into a recurring element within the opposition. Finally, of course, the notion of redressing the problems of the new era with the strengths of fengjian came sharply into focus. This latter idea could take many forms. One was religion. Another might be an emphasis on chivalric and military ideals within a rebel band rather than civilian or bureaucratic ones. An especially significant and practical manifestation was the demand that the government again play the active role in the economy that it had in the earlier system and, in particular, that it do so in the direction of equalizing land-holding.

In the short run, this aspect of rebel ideology was a response to the breakdown of the equal-field system of the Tang and the fact that the average person was now left open to the play of the marketplace and to destitution in time of trouble. A similar situation in the earlier transition to junxian had impelled Mencius to idealize the justice of fengjian land relations in his concept of the well-field system, and his arguments had, in fact, influenced the development of Tang land policy. The first rebellion that had equalization of land as a major goal was the massive unrest that shook, but did not destroy, the Tang. Its leader marched under a banner that proclaimed him to be the "Heaven-Commissioned Great General to Equalize Inequality."[29] Thereafter, redistributing and equalizing land became a prominent theme in virtually every important popular rebellion.

Religion also entered rebel ideology in the Han. It had a strong appeal to outsiders, was egalitarian in outlook, and could provide a deep faith that an evil order should and would be destroyed. It could also supply an organizational basis for action in the form of congregations of believers. For example, the rebellions that shook the late Han had roots in religious Taoism. They used "magical arts" for healing and in confessionals, preached that a millennium was at hand, and showed an interest in equality for women.[30]

In junxian times religion continued to play a crucial role in rebellion. By then it was, in a sense, part of the datong outlook, for a religious sensibility harks back to fengjian rather than junxian values. Sometimes the basis of opposition was the general "popular religion" of the age. At other times it was various specific faiths, ranging from Manichaeism to Vegetarianism, with the most important being the belief in the Maitreya Buddha. The Maitreya was the Buddha of the paradise to come, the divine being who was to appear after one hundred million years and establish a new order on earth. This ideology was perfect for rebellion, and down through the centuries rebels claiming to be the Maitreya or his herald repeatedly appeared.

In the Song, a final element was added to the tradition of rebellion, nationalism, which we shall treat at greater length in the next chapter. All these elements could combine in different ways in different rebellions, and some uprisings did not have them all. However, the general pattern of popular opposition included the notion of the Mandate of Heaven, datong ideas, religion, and nationalism. All were joined, for example, in the great revolution that overthrew the Mongol Yuan Dynasty.

This was the first successful revolution since the one that had destroyed the Qin and established Zhu Yuanzhang, a farm worker turned Buddhist priest, on the throne as the founder of the Ming. At first, Zhu was quite tough on the existing elite. He made some efforts to redistribute land and also sought a religious foundation for his authority. However, he soon abandoned such efforts and did not claim the Mandate on the basis of either datong ideas or religion but rather in terms of Confucianism and a stable junxian order. Ultimately, his reign marked the decisive step in the establishment of Neo-Confucianism as the state orthodoxy and the creation of the powerfully authoritarian emperorship of the later dynasties.[31]

As should be evident, the original neo-Confucians were, in some ways, part of the tradition of popular opposition. This fact is not surprising since, at the start, they represented the interests of middle-class commoners opposed to the declining aristocratic order. In a sense, these Neo-Confucians were arguing that the Mandate had passed from fengjian to junxian. They were often sympathetic to datong ideals and, though not basically religious, worked to infuse Confucianism with the power and commitment of religion.

Perhaps the revival of rebellion (by now with powerful egalitarian goals) as an effective means of changing the government provided a direct stimulus to the separation of the elite from the popular opposition. Things could become too dangerous. Another factor, of course, was the rise of Confucianism to dominance and the fact that religion had, therefore, become an inappropriate vehicle for elite politics. In any case, in the Ming, which was the product of a revolution and the dynasty that firmly established Neo-Confucianism as the official outlook, the elite tradition of opposition came into full development.

The most important figure in this process was a man particularly tied to the datong tradition. He was Wang Yangming (1427–1529), the most dynamic and influential thinker in China after the Song. In the latter part of the Ming his views rivaled the orthodoxy in popularity, though they were never officially recognized. In later centuries Wang's thought spread to all parts of East Asia and continued to have an important influence in China.[32]

Wang Yangming came from a family with a long tradition of culture, one with a love of literature, philosophy, and music. For the most part, however, the family had not been wealthy and lived basically as farmers or teachers. Wang Yangming was said to resemble his grandfather, a man who wept one day when he realized that his only property was a few trunks full of old books. Wang's father, however, came in first in the imperial exams and made an excellent career. Wang's approach to the datong, always a bit theoretical (he did not emphasize land reform, for example) but with a deep sense of community and a profound faith in the average man, is understandable in this light.

As a young man, Wang was very taken with Buddhism and Taoism and in this sense was close to the popular tradition of opposition. However, he returned to Confucianism and worked to bring out its egalitarian and communitarian side. He was also much taken with the military arts, a rather unusual taste for someone with his background but also something that brought him closer to the average person, and later in his career he became famous not only as a civil official but also as a general.

Wang passed the exams with flying colors and had a long career in public service. He combined his official life with his theoretical writings, which took the form of a branch of Neo-Confucianism alternative to that of the orthodoxy. His thought was geared to the possibilities and problems of the junxian era, and this focus accounts for his great influence. He was not, however, a revolutionary and, indeed, helped to suppress a number of rebellions. Times were generally good, and he did not challenge the Ming's claim to the Mandate. Nonetheless, Wang preferred to dwell not on society's successes but on its problems and never believed that the existing hierarchy paralleled the moral one, the crucial issue on which the opposition differed from the official view. He suffered difficulties because of his personal integrity and his unorthodox views and once was publicly beaten in court and exiled.

One of Wang Yangming's main points was that everyone could become a good person, even a sage. This point did not differ, in theory, from the official position or, indeed, from the view of Confucius and Mencius themselves. However, unlike the orthodoxy, Wang stressed that goodness did not require excessive book learning or scholarly attainment. He was not against education in due proportion, of course, but felt that the necessary amount was within reach of all citizens. He also recognized that the orthodox concept of education had become overrefined and was being used primarily as a way of dividing people into a hierarchy, thus undercutting the basic Confucian thrust toward perfecting everyone and negating the pedagogic process and egalitarian imperatives that he saw as the heart of the philosophy.

This situation was particularly bad, he felt, because education in his time was too competitive and directed toward social advancement rather than wisdom and virtue. In this sense, it defeated the basic purpose of learning and undercut the merit that those who succeeded presumed to represent. In Wang's view, everyone should work to create community and to develop virtue and human potentiality, not to compete or to repress the possibilities of individuals or of society. In his vision the sage became a man committed to attaining the datong. As he wrote in a famous passage of his *Instructions for Practical Living*:

> The mind of a sage regards Heaven, Earth and all things as one body. He looks upon all people of the world, whether inside or outside his family, or whether far or near, but

all with blood and breath as his brothers and children. He wants to secure, preserve, educate, and nourish all of them, so as to fulfill his desire of forming one body with all things. . . . He therefore extends his humanity which makes him form one body with Heaven, Earth, and all things, to teach the world, so as to enable people to overcome their selfishness, remove their obstructions, and recover that which is common to the substance of the minds of all men. The essentials of this teaching are what was successively transmitted by Yao, Shun, Yu and what is summed up in the saying, "The human mind is precarious and liable to mistakes, the moral mind is subtle and follows the moral law."

At the time of Yao, Shun, and the Three Dynasties, teachers taught and students studied only this. At that time people did not have different opinions, nor did families have different practices. Those who practiced the teaching naturally and easily were called sages and those who practiced it with difficulty were called good people, but those who violated it were considered degenerate even though they were as intelligent as Dan Zhu [the son of Yao, a man both intelligent and well connected]. People of low station—those in villages and rural districts, farmers, artisans, and merchants—all received this teaching, which was devoted only to the perfection of virtue and conduct. How could this have been the case? Because there was no pursuit after knowledge of seeing and hearing to confuse them, no memorization and recitation to hinder them, no writing of flowery compositions to indulge in, and no chasing after success and profit. They were taught only to be filially pious to their parents, brotherly to their elders, and faithful to their friends, so as to recover that which is common to the substance of the minds of all men. All this is inherent in our natures and does not depend on the outside. This being the case, who cannot do it?[33]

The second thing that Wang emphasized as essential to the development of virtue was the unity of thought and action, of knowledge and practice. Once again, this idea was not fundamentally different from what had come before. However, for Wang, it meant that for people and society to be worthy of the name of Confucianism, they had to live up to the philosophy's claims in everyday behavior, in political life, and in a belief in the possibilities of the Great Community.

Once a student said he did not understand Wang's concept of the unity of thought and action. "For example," the young man said, "there are people who know that parents should be served with filial piety and elder brothers with respect, but cannot put these things into practice. This shows that knowledge and action are clearly two different things." Wang responded:

The knowledge and action you refer to are already separated by selfish desires and are no longer knowledge and action in their original substance. There have never been people who know but do not act. Those who are supposed to know but do not act simply do not yet know. When sages and worthies taught people about knowledge and action, it was precisely because they wanted them to restore the original substance, and not simply to do this or that and be satisfied.

Suppose we say that so-and-so knows filial piety and so-and-so knows brotherly respect. They must have actually practiced filial piety and brotherly respect before they can be said to know them. It will not do to say they know filial piety and brotherly respect simply because they show them in words. Or take one's knowledge of pain. Only after one has experienced pain can one know pain. The same is true of cold or hunger. How can knowledge and action be separated? This is the original substance of thought and action, which have not been separated by selfish desires. In teaching people, the Sages insisted only this can be called knowledge. Otherwise, this is not yet knowledge. This is serious and practical business. What is the objective of desperately insisting on knowledge and action being two different things? And what is the objective of my insisting that they are one? What is the use of insisting on their being one or two unless one knows the basic purpose of the doctrine?[34]

On the personal level Wang emphasized that proper behavior between family and friends was essential to the unity of thought and action and to attaining the good society. In politics he stressed that what was crucial was *qin min*, "loving the people," "being intimate" and "close" with them. In answer to the question "Why then, does the learning of the great man consist in being intimate with the people?" Wang answered:

To manifest a clear character is to bring about the substance of the state of forming one body with Heaven, Earth, and the myriad things, whereas intimacy with the people is to put into universal operation the function of the state of forming one body. Hence manifesting a clear character consists in being close to the people and closeness to the people is the way to manifest a clear character. . . . This is what is meant by "manifesting a clear character throughout the world." This is what is meant by "regulation of the family," "ordering the state," and "bringing peace to the world." This is what is meant by the "full development of one's nature."[35]

As far as we can tell from his reputation and public documents, Wang truly tried to practice what he believed. He was a just and effective magistrate, popular and close to the people. Once, after he had been unjustly banished from service for six years, he received reappointment to a new post and on his way there passed through the place where he had formerly been stationed. Upon his arrival,

the village elders, soldiers, and common people all came to welcome him, holding incense in their hands, and lining the streets. They filled the roads and the streets, so that it became impossible for him to move. The elders, therefore, held up his sedan chair and passed it along over the heads of the crowds until they reached his quarters in the city. Yangming invited the elders, soldiers, and the common people to come in to see him. They came in through the east gate and came out through the west gate. Some could not bear to leave him, and went in again. This went on from seven in the morning until four in the afternoon.[36]

In addition to Wang's general influence on Ming government and society he had a considerable number of direct followers. Among the most noteworthy were those in the so-called Taizhou school. One of their mottos was "The streets are full of sages," and they worked to make this a reality.[37] Often from common backgrounds themselves, they organized educational, welfare, and political activities among the people and showed a concern for the status of women. Committed to the Great Community, they tried to work out the theories of Wang Yangming in practice. On the other hand, other followers, disillusioned by the rampant corruption and competitiveness of late Ming society, turned fully to Buddhism or to an extreme individualism.

The activities of the Taizhou school paralleled and interacted with the revival of popular opposition in the declining years of the Ming. The major rebellion and the one that eventually brought down the dynasty in 1644 was led by an unemployed postal worker, Li Zicheng. His movement emphasized most of the classic themes of the opposition, including economic reorganization; to equalize the land and abolish the land tax were among its goals.[38] However, the movement did not emphasize religion, testimony perhaps to the spread of Confucianism in the Ming and to some reconciliation of popular and elite opposition. A similar phenomenon would also be a feature of the revolutionary process of the nineteenth and twentieth centuries.

Things, however, changed in the Qing. As the Ming declined and rebellion broke out, a radical opposition, often called the Donglin Movement, developed among intellectuals and students and is another and particularly famous example of this form of political activity. The Donglin was highly critical of the government, which was oppressing everyone, including the bulk of the elite. At the same time, however, the group had mixed feelings about Wang Yangming. There was considerable respect for his general ideas; however, there was also criticism for the degree to which they were contributing to social breakdown and revolution.[39] This train of thought, critical of the orthodoxy but deeply wary of the popular opposition, became the focus of elite radicalism after the Manchus overthrew Li Zicheng's brief hold on power.

In the early Qing such views were most notably represented by two great Confucian scholars who refused to serve under the new dynasty and who had powerful resonances with the datong tradition. These were Huang Zongxi (1610–1695) and Gu Yanwu (1613–1682). Both men were deeply shocked by the breakdown and disorder of the late Ming and by the fact that China had once again fallen to foreign conquest. Their approach to preventing such a disaster from recurring was an analysis of society in terms of the junxian system, which they both criticized, and a call to revitalize it with fengjian ideals and institutions.

Huang emphasized in his work that the despotic character of the junxian emperorship was the most important cause for China's problems, from economic to moral to military. He saw these evils as inherent in the establishment of the system in the Qin and brought to completion by the Mongol Yuan Dynasty, which had set the mold for the Ming and its demise in revolution and conquest. Huang wanted a return to the fengjian order, under which, in the words of Theodore de Bary, he understood China to have had a liberal "basic constitution" that insured a just and successful society.[40]

As Huang wrote:

Until the end of the Three Dynasties there was law. Since the Three Dynasties there has been no law. Why do I say so? Because the Two Emperors and Three Kings knew that mankind could not do without sustenance and therefore gave men fields to cultivate. They knew that men could not do without clothes and therefore gave them land on which to grow mulberry and hemp. They knew also that men could not go untaught, so they set up schools, established marriage ceremony to guard against promiscuity, and instituted military service to guard against disorders. This constituted law until the end of the Three Dynasties. It was never laid down for the benefit of one man alone.

Later rulers, once they had won the world, feared only that their dynasty might not last long and that their descendants would be unable to preserve their empire. To prevent what they feared from happening they resorted to laws. Consequently, what they called "law" was simply instituted for the sake of one family and not for the sake of all mankind. This was the reason that Qin abolished the fengjian system and established the junxian. They believed the junxian would serve their own personal interests. . . .

It might be argued that order and disorder in the world are unrelated to the maintenance or absence of law. Now as to this, there has been a great change from the past to the present: one complete upheaval which came with the Qin Dynasty, and another with the Yuan Dynasty. Following these upheavals nothing at all survived of the sympathetic, benevolent, and constructive government of the early kings. So, unless we take a long-range view and look deep into the heart of the matter, changing everything thoroughly in order to restore the well-field system, the fengjian system, the school and military systems of old, then even though some minor changes are made there will never be an end to the misery of the common man.[41]

Gu Yanwu was directly concerned with the possibility and, indeed, necessity of working toward the Great Community. As he wrote in a letter, "Today, saving people from misery and inaugurating the *Taiping* [Great Peace] for ten thousand generations, this is the responsibility of our generation."[42] Taiping or Great Peace was the most common synonym in the tradition for datong.[43] To achieve his goal Gu systematically attacked the existing system and presented his solution:

If we understand why the fengjian system turned into the junxian, then we will understand that as the junxian system decays there must be another change. Does this mean there will be a return to fengjian? No, this I say is impossible. But if some sage were to appear who could invest the junxian system with the essential meaning of fengjian then the world would attain order.[44]

More specifically, Gu argued for a reinstatement of small fiefs under carefully selected hereditary officials who would be controlled both by the local people and the central government. Within these fiefs the reconstruction of community and a successful polity could begin. This solution, with its call for the revival of aristocracy, is startling from our point of view but is understandable in the light of Gu's attitudes toward the long history of the junxian system in China and its present condition.

He was very clear about what would happen if a major change did not occur and in so doing provided an amazingly succinct prediction of the revolutionary process that emerged 250 years later. As he wrote, "Now, the decay of the junxian system has already become extreme, but no sage appears to change things and people go on doing everything in the same old way. Therefore, the people's livelihood grows poorer by the day, China grows steadily weaker, and we are hastening toward chaos."[45]

Nonetheless, despite the deeply critical character of their social analysis, early Qing radicals such as Huang, Gu, and others like them retreated from direct political involvement. This retreat was partly because of their reaction to the revolutionary movement of the late Ming and partly because of the power of the new Manchu rulers. Gu, in particular, though clearly concerned with fundamental problems and long-term goals, emphasized the importance of approaching issues through a careful study of narrow questions and deep scholarship. He was extremely critical of Wang Yangming and returned to the elitist notion that such scholarship and learning were necessary for attaining virtue and justifying power. Even this approach was lost or deeply submerged as the dynasty continued and proved successful.

Much of what had been the elite opposition blended with the orthodoxy into a philosophical school that stressed *kaozheng*, philology. The latter often produced extremely fine and useful scholarship, though (perhaps only on the surface) it seemed to lose a sense of the broader sociopolitical message of Confucian learning.[46] The success of the Qing continued the spread of education and sophistication within the general populace. Mass organizations flourished, both secular and religious, and some were deeply hostile to the government. Such groups, as well as the occasional rebellion that broke out in the generally stable period through 1800, indicated, however, that the opposition tradition was still alive among the people, though now rather split from the thinking of the establishment.

3

FOREIGNERS AND THE WEST

THE SETTING

Since China was on the defensive or conquered for most of the junxian age, the relationship to foreigners in that era is an important aspect of her history. It is also particularly crucial in setting the stage for the revolution of the nineteenth and twentieth centuries, when foreigners, and the Chinese attitude toward them, were to play a vital role; for the Qing Dynasty was, of course, run by Manchus and the West began to assume great significance in Chinese affairs.

Throughout her history, China was in contact with foreigners of all sorts. Among others, there were Buddhist travelers from India in the Era of Disunity, merchants from West Asia in the Tang and Song, Japanese traders and marauders in the Ming, and diplomatic missions from Korea and Southeast Asia in the Qing. However, the most persistent contacts, which did the most to structure China's approach to foreigners, were with the tribal and nomadic people on the nation's northern borders, for they threatened China militarily from the Zhou onward and ran the various dynasties of conquest during the Era of Disunity and in the junxian age.

China's northern frontier begins in the east in the forested lands of present-day Manchuria, centers on the steppes of Mongolia, and continues westward to the highlands of the Himalayas.[1] We do not know much about the origins of society in this vast stretch of inner Asia. For much of its history it remained a preliterate area. However, we do know that from early on in Chinese history, the most striking difference between the northern people and the Chinese was that the former lived basically by animal husbandry and hunting, while the latter subsisted on settled agriculture. At the same time, as Chinese society moved from its tribal origins in the third millennium B.C. into the fengjian system of the Three Dynasties and the junxian beginnings of the Warring States era, the people of the North remained tribal.

By the time of the Warring States, the gap between the two cultures was very striking, and the Chinese began to build walls to protect themselves from their northern neighbors. The Great Wall, first completed during the early junxian zenith of the Qin, became the most famous symbol of demarcation between China and the North. For most of Chinese history the two societies were to remain clearly separate, though they constantly interacted.

The basic reason why Central Asian and Chinese culture diverged and remained apart was an accident of geography and climate. Rainfall is generally sparse north of the Wall, and it is very cold much of the time. It was an area, therefore, utterly unsuited to agriculture. As a result, while Chinese culture easily moved southward, generally assimilating tribal people as it went, it could not move north. Nor could the nomads extend their style of life into China without changing their ways. Thus, the presence of the northern tribesmen provided a permanent international environment for China, which shaped and structured Chinese views of foreigners and of foreign relations. From the Chinese point of view it was a dangerous environment, for the nomads were both powerful and threatening.

The power of the northern people did not lie in their numbers, of course. The population density among them was always far lower than in China. The land area of China's inner Asian frontier is about twice the size of the traditional eighteen provinces, the heartland of China. But historically, it has supported only about one-thirtieth of the population.

The danger from the tribesmen came out of the differences between the nature of their society and that of China's. This contrast is most evident in the case of the nomads of the steppes, who were prototypical of inner Asian society and who posed the greatest threat. These tribal people were self-sufficient only for the bare necessities of life, which they obtained from their livestock, most notably the sheep for sustenance and the horse for transportation, and from hunting and gathering. The various groups had to rely on other tribes or on China for luxuries and even for many necessities. For example, to obtain metal utensils, they might have to trade or raid a tribe that had iron and that specialized in its manufacture. For agricultural products, including such important items as tea, spices, and silk, the northerners had to deal with China.

But here is where China's problems began. China was largely self-sufficient and certainly did not want as much from the nomads as they required from her. In addition, China was far richer and more productive overall. Therefore, when the nomads lacked trade goods or when an opportunity presented itself, commerce could turn to raids from the north and raiding into conquest. The probability of such activities went up dramatically in view of the high level of nomad fighting skills as compared to China.

In general, there was a much smaller gap between daily life and battle for a nomad youth than for the average Chinese farm boy. The nomad grew up in the saddle, and he was adept at hunting and at moving over long distances, often under conditions of great hardship. Through necessity and design, the nomads became particularly good warriors. They developed the stirrup to shoot better from horseback and created the compound reflex bow made of horn and wood, a compact weapon suitable for use from horseback and with a fearsome striking power. The nomads became adept at long, strategic marches and mobile striking tactics. Indeed, it has been said that the steppe warriors at their peak, under the Mongols of Chingis (Genghis) Khan, were the best light cavalry in the history of the world (the Plains Indians of the American West, who were also nomads, are said to have been the second best).

The danger to China becomes all the clearer when one adds the dynamics of the social and political organization of the nomads to their economic needs and military capabilities. Life on the steppe was difficult because of the harshness of the terrain and the rough-and-tumble competition for what resources were available. Success required tight organization and effective leadership. The tribes did not wander aimlessly. Through the year they followed complex and fixed routes in order to insure the constant food and water that their herds required. Just moving around in this way, at the mercy of sudden and unpredictable changes in the weather, required great precision and efficiency. At the same time, each tribe had constantly to defend its rights and grazing lands against other groups.

As a result of the great discipline that such a life required, the tribes were generally led by a powerful chief. The chief was selected in various ways, but the most common was by a man's charisma and abilities. Once in power and as long as he succeeded in the tasks of ruling, the chief had great authority and received great loyalty. If, however, he faltered in his responsibilities, he and his family could be ousted from command in what was often a bloody process. As a result it was urgent for the chief constantly to prove himself, and one product of this need was pressure on China, for, in addition to running the tribe and preserving and expanding its grazing privileges, the chief was, of course, responsible for obtaining the necessary goods from other tribes and China. If he could get them cheaply through raids or conquest rather than through trade, it might help his prestige all the more.

This situation existed to the north, while to the south lay China, fabulously wealthy by nomad standards and often weak. For this reason the northern frontier was a constant problem. It was not, perhaps, important for most people in China most of the time. But the success of a Chinese government was judged, in addition to the more basic questions of welfare and justice, by how well it managed relations with the North. Success in internal and external affairs was, in fact, considered interdependent. As the old adage had it, *nei luan wai huan*: "When there is internal chaos, there will be disaster from abroad."

CHINESE ATTITUDES AND POLICIES

Despite the power of the nomads, for most of the fengjian period in China, while the military spirit was strong, the nation was able to fend off the foreign threat. It was only during the three hundred years of the Era of Disunity that North China was conquered, and the nomads were never able to take over the whole country. In the Han and Tang, of course, China itself conquered far out into central Asia and controlled the tribal menace by securing considerable domination over the nomad home areas.

However, as we have noted, with the arrival of the junxian era in the late Tang and Song and the decline of a military spirit in China, the situation changed dramatically. A Mongolian people, the Khitans, kept parts of North China out of the hands of the Song and established the Liao Dynasty, which lasted from 947 to 1125. Tibetans of the Tangut tribes also held parts of the Northwest and established the Xi Xia Dynasty (1038–1227). A fresh wave of northerners, Juchen tribesmen from Manchuria, destroyed the Liao and drove the Song to the south of China, establishing the Jin Dynasty in the North. In the thirteenth century the Mongols destroyed the Xi Xia and the Jin and then took all of China by destroying the Song in 1279. They ruled until 1368, when a native dynasty, the Ming, once again established control, though often under pressure from the North. In 1644 Manchu tribes, descendants of the Juchen, recaptured China and established the Qing Dynasty, which lasted until 1911.

In the first flowering of the junxian system, the Chinese had begun to build walls to defend themselves against the nomads, who seemed ever more backward and dangerous. Now, as the system took firm hold, the gap was wider than ever. Not only was China threatened, but she often succumbed. At the same time, the foreigners seemed all the more primitive, avaricious, and vulgar barbarians without real history or culture. In response to this situation, two sets of attitudes toward the northern tribesmen developed among the Han peoples. One of these can be called a culturalist approach; the other, nationalistic. (I should note that in designating the latter position as nationalism rather than using a term like xenophobia or patriotism, I have departed from common usage. Chinese nationalism has been one of my own areas of expertise, and after considerable thought, I have decided that the term is appropriate because it is relatively value-free, is historically reasonable, and helps to relate the history of the nineteenth and twentieth centuries to the past. For a fuller discussion of the issue see the note.)[2]

The culturalist point of view stressed that what was important about a person was the degree to which he accepted and practiced Chinese culture. It was not particularly important where that person was born or what his ethnic background was; if he learned the ways of civilization, he became Chinese. The purpose of foreign relations was to control and manage foreigners by any means possible, while working to educate and assimilate them. If they conquered China, they should be judged in terms of their behavior, and the goal of the Han people should be to make them as Chinese as possible as rapidly as possible.

The nationalist approach stressed that what was important about a person was whether or not he was born within China and was a Han Chinese. In foreign policy it asserted that a unified and effective Chinese nation and the aroused and cohesive actions of the Chinese people could and should resist all foreign threats. What barbarians really understood was power; they should be kept out when they were beyond the Wall and driven out when they were within. Dynasties of conquest, nationalists said, were never proper.

The culturalist and nationalist positions were by no means incompatible. Both believed in the superiority of Chinese civilization, both saw the northerners as dangerous, and both, in a sense, saw the highest goal as universal peace and order, while admitting the need for force. Neo-Confucianism, in fact, provided a neat formula for reconciling the two views. Essentially, the Neo-Confucians argued that the tribesmen were inherently as good as the Han, for they, like everyone else, had the same nature and were born with the same innate principles (li) of goodness. This aspect of their analysis was a powerful basis for culturalist attitudes. On the other hand, the Neo-Confucians conceded and, indeed, often emphasized that the material force (qi) of the northerners was so turbid that, in practice, the good could not show through. This proposition was a way of saying that the nomads were so bereft of the proper upbringing, formal educational possibilities, and economic level (all of which China presumably provided) that they were deeply and hopelessly barbaric and there was little chance of improving them. Such ideas supported nationalism.

Overall, there seems to have been more nationalism after the arrival of the junxian era than there was in the late fengjian period. One short-term reason was that North China had been under tribal domination during the Era of Disunity and had grown used to foreign rule. Furthermore, the Sui and Tang were governed by elites with powerful infusions of northern blood; it was both natural and in their interest to emphasize culturalist perspectives. More generally important, however, is the fact that the culturalist view rested on success in relations with the North. It was the more optimistic view. The failure and consequent pessimism that developed in junxian times, when China found herself at the mercy of the northern peoples, supported nationalism.

The likelihood that an individual in China would adopt a culturalist or nationalist position at any given moment was dependent on a number of factors. One of these was the nature of the foreign group involved and how civilized it seemed. The Neo-Confucian formula allowed different foreigners to be seen in different ways. Some were considered more cultured than others, depending on their style of life and their relations to China. For example, Korea and the nations of Southeast Asia, comparatively old countries that generally did not present a threat to China, were not considered barbaric at all; they were more likely to elicit a culturalist attitude. A dangerous northern tribe, the very quintessence of barbarism in Chinese eyes, was more likely to elicit a nationalist response.

Another factor determining a person's attitudes was whether he was from the north or south of China. Northerners developed a reputation for being more culturalist; southerners, more nationalistic. This difference may have been because northerners had more experience with foreigners and foreign control than did southerners. More politically significant was that a person's outlook was influenced by his position in Chinese society. In general, the official and orthodox position was culturalism, while the opposition was associated with nationalism.[3]

The most general reason why those in power tended to be culturalist was probably that they were used to control and influence, to success and optimism. This sort of mentality encouraged culturalism in an individual as it had for the nation in fengjian times. Another reason for the distinction was that those in authority were directly responsible for Chinese security, and moderation often seemed the only reasonable course in view of the nation's military weakness. Finally, of course, when China was conquered, the foreign rulers emphasized the culturalist approach to justify their own legitimacy, for it placed emphasis on the degree of sinification of the alien dynasty and on how well it ruled rather than on its place of origin or ethnic background.

As a result, in the junxian age, Chinese foreign policy was generally structured along culturalist lines, though, in practice, it could have powerful nationalistic features. The pillar of this foreign policy was the famous tribute system. It assumed, at least formally, that everyone was part of the civilized Chinese order and used this assumption to deal with foreigners in a variety of ways. In the short run, the purpose of the tribute system was to manage and stabilize relations with foreigners, to avoid tension and military confrontation with them, and to cushion and protect Chinese society. In the long run, the purpose was to civilize those who seemed to need it and to bring them to the point where they were not a threat to China. Success in dealing with foreigners, it should be reiterated, was crucial to the government internally. Dangers on the borders or foreigners out of control in China were both taken as serious evidence of misrule and the need for political change and, if things became bad enough, as evidence that the Mandate was in jeopardy.

The tribute system was a procedure by which surrounding rulers recognized the suzerainty of the Chinese emperor. He, in turn, invested them with authority to govern. Their domains, thus, were not part of the Chinese junxian state, rather, they were integrated indirectly, in a fengjian fashion. The way the system worked was that at prescribed intervals the different groups sent missions bearing tribute for the Chinese emperor. The high point of the mission was when the emissaries performed obeisance before the ruler (the famous *kowtow*), presented what they had brought, and, in return, received patents of authority and gifts.

The ideology behind the system fitted the needs of the emperor and the government very nicely. It enhanced their status both at home and abroad and, thus, their claims to authority, for, with culturalism the official ideal, the sense that the emperor was governing the world was an important part of his image. The missions often came after New Year's, when Chinese officials also arrived in the capital to pay their respects to the ruler. Both groups could then see that a world polity existed, the emperor ruled, and all was well.

In addition, the actual practice of the system established an effective and flexible framework for foreign relations, whether China was strong or weak. First of all, it was an opportunity to impress foreigners with the might of China.

The nation as a whole and the capital, in particular, were well equipped to awe and amaze the average visitor from the northern steppe. If need be, the government also made certain that the emissaries saw masses of troops as well as groups of loyal officials. In addition, the mission was a good time for the Chinese government to involve itself in the internal politics of the North. One tribe might be favored over another in granting patents, and the system could provide the basis, if China had the strength, for justifying military intervention. Finally, the missions were an effective way of controlling and overseeing foreigners while they were in China.

Not only did the tribute system assist China and her rulers, but it also held out concrete inducements to the foreigners involved. Tribute missions were the only way to trade within China, rather than on the borders and, in particular, to do so in the capital. All tribute missions carried trade goods, and the journey was very lucrative and useful to those whom it represented. This result was particularly important for the northern chiefs, who needed Chinese products as a mark of their good rule and for whom a mission could represent a substantial increase in income.

Indeed, the benefits for those who joined the system went beyond simple trade. The gifts that the emperor bestowed on a mission were generally far more valuable than the tribute that he received. This custom was based on the formal assumption that the emperor was generous and bestowed more benefits than he needed to receive. In practice it also meant that the tribute system could be used as a face-saving way for the Chinese government to give bribes to a foreign tribe or group that was too dangerous to handle in other ways. Overall, in fact, it was so appealing to participate in the tribute system that many foreign groups that did so had no belief whatsoever that they were subordinate to China. In other words, from the Chinese point of view, in addition to its ideological overtones, the tribute system was a deeply practical way of managing foreign relations.

The pragmatism of Chinese foreign policy could, in fact, reach a point where the government was willing to abandon the tribute system if good relations or efficiency required such action. Memoranda within the Chinese bureaucracy might continue to couch relations in tribute language, but the practice bore no relation to the theory. For example, in the Song, China faced northerners who were much stronger than she and who would not recognize Song suzerainty over themselves or, indeed, over China. The Liao Dynasty of the Khitan and the Jin Dynasty of the Juchen claimed to be the legitimate governments of China. The Song, to keep the peace, acknowledged the suzerainty of the two groups and gave them large, regular payments.

Another instance of international relations not within the tribute framework was the trade to Southeast Asia in late Ming and early Qing times. The ports the foreigners could use were limited, the government licensed Chinese firms to deal with them, and the whole operation was closely monitored. However, no serious effort was made to fit the trade into the tribute framework.

Of course, Chinese foreign policy, of whatever sort, could fail, and the whole country could fall to northern invaders, as when the Mongols established the Yuan Dynasty and the Manchus established the Qing. Both dynasties naturally used culturalist rhetoric to justify the legitimacy of their rule. In practice, however, there was comparatively little justification to the claim on the part of the Mongols and a great deal on the part of the Manchus. The two dynasties were very different. The difference lay in the background of the two groups and in the experience that China had garnered in handling foreigners.

The Mongols were from comparatively far out in the steppe, so that they were relatively uninfluenced by Chinese ways. At the same time, during their rise to power, they were separated from the Song by other tribesmen of the Tungusic Jin. In the twelfth century Chingis Khan (Genghis Khan) welded the separate Mongol tribes into a powerful coalition. He was clearly a political and military genius but was still a rough chieftain of the steppes. "Man's highest joy," he reportedly said, "is in victory: to conquer one's enemies, to pursue them, to deprive them of their possessions, to make their beloved weep, to ride on their horses and to embrace their wives and daughters."[4]

Under Chingis, the Mongols began to construct what was shortly to become the greatest land empire that the world has ever known. At its height in the thirteenth century, it stretched from the shores of the Pacific to Southwest Asia and Eastern Europe. China was only a part, though the Mongols considered it to be their most important conquest. On the whole, however, they did not penetrate deeply into Chinese society, nor did they particularly assimilate Chinese ways. Overall, China remained a military satrap of the conquerors. For example, they often used men from other parts of Eurasia to run the country. Marco Polo is the most famous example of such a person. As the Yuan matured, the Mongols lost their military edge, increasingly adopted Chinese ruling styles, and worked through Chinese officials. Nevertheless, the dynasty lasted only a brief hundred years.

The Manchus who conquered China four hundred years later were quite different and created a very different sort of dynasty. In a sense, their rule could be seen as a triumph of the culturalist approach and of the civilizing possibilities of Chinese culture. One reason that Chinese influence was able to work on them was that they were not from the distant steppe. Indeed, they were not from the steppe at all but rather from the forests of Manchuria, a group related to the Juchen, who had established the Jin Dynasty earlier.

The Manchus were tribesmen who lived basically by hunting and gathering. However, in southern Manchuria, where they bordered on the Ming and where the group that conquered China originated, they had adopted to agriculture and lived a more settled life. They also came under the influence of Chinese social organization and in the late Ming moved from tribalism to a fengjian political system. After they entered China they adapted quickly to the junxian order. As a result, as the noted Japanese scholar Miyazaki Ichisada has written, "In an extremely short time the Manchu peoples recapitulated the 3000-year history of

China."[5] The Qing lasted a healthy 250 years, roughly the same as the Song and the Ming.

Needless to say, the Manchus were deeply committed to upholding and encouraging the culturalist view of foreigners. They established a government based on Ming models and even made some badly needed reforms in the system. For example, they ended the abusive behavior of the court, which had so marred the preceding dynasty.

To win over the elite, the Manchus did not undertake any serious program of land reform like the one at the start of the Ming. At the same time, they became great patrons of Chinese culture and learning and sponsored many activities that gave employment and status to degree-holders and intellectuals: schools, encyclopedias, and scholarly projects of all sorts. They also adopted policies meant to have broad appeal to the average citizen. The chaos of the seventeenth century seems to have done much by itself to equalize land-holding as compared to the late Ming, and the Manchus supported the situation by setting low taxes and promising not to raise them. They encouraged activities that would ease the lot of the poor, and it was the third Qing emperor, Yongzheng, who enfranchised the last groups that had been kept from participating in the examination system.

In foreign affairs the Qing was a triumph, essentially solving the problem of inner Asia for China. The Manchus combined a knowledge of central Asia ways with military skill and an understanding of Chinese techniques in foreign policy. They used the tribute framework to create a Sino-nomadic system that, more than at any time in Chinese history, united the societies north and south of the Wall into a single unit. The parts outside were still ruled essentially through fengjian techniques but were no longer a threat. The borders of China today, which include Manchuria and large portions of central Asia, are a product of the diplomacy and conquests of the Qing in the seventeenth and eighteenth centuries.

The Manchus gradually assimilated to Chinese life. After conquering China, they developed policies aimed at maintaining their separate identity as a group, since this was essential to keeping their military potential. Such policies did not, however, prove particularly effective and, in fact, were somewhat at odds with the overall strategy of behaving like a Chinese dynasty. By the late eighteenth century, Manchus were not very distinguishable from Han Chinese. A person knew if he was Manchu or not, and Manchus had certain perquisites, including reserved places in the government. But, in general, they were giving up their particular cultural traits, forgetting their language, and losing their martial vigor.

THE OPPOSITION AND NATIONALISM

As we have noted, while culturalism was, in general, the official position, nationalism was associated with the opposition, basically because weakness and problems in foreign affairs provided an added basis and incentive for criticizing those in power. Furthermore, nationalism suggested that internal unity was China's greatest strength, and culturalist compromises could easily appear as policies designed to avoid mobilizing the nation internally and thus facing the needs and political demands of the average person. When times were bad, it might even appear that barbarians were being appeased at the expense of the people or even, indeed, in order to allow the government to put down internal unrest. If the dynasty in power was a foreign one, of course, nationalism provided a direct basis for political opposition.

The relationship between opposition and nationalism begins to be evident in the late Tang, at the beginning of the junxian era. Han Yu, the most influential figure in the revival of Confucian humanism and, in his time, a political critic, opposed Buddhism not only because it was religious but also because it was foreign. In a famous memorial to the emperor, he wrote:

> Now Buddha was a man of the barbarians who did not speak the language of China and wore clothes of a different fashion. His sayings did not concern the ways of our ancient kings, nor did his manner of dress conform to their laws. He understood neither the duties that bind sovereign and subject, nor the affections of father and son. If he were still alive today and came to our court by order of his ruler, Your Majesty might condescend to receive him, but it would amount to no more than one audience in the Xuanzheng Hall, a banquet by the Office for Receiving Guests, the presentation of a suit of clothes, and he would then be escorted to the borders of the nation, dismissed, and not allowed to delude the masses.[6]

Han Yu was a great prose stylist, often considered the greatest in Chinese history. His writing is extremely compact and subtle. In his memorial he may not have been trying to allude to the Tang rulers, who were both Buddhist and from a Central Asian background. However, the emperor for whom it was written was deeply angered. Han Yu barely escaped execution and was exiled to the southernmost regions of the country, an area reputed to have an unhealthy climate and filled with various groups not particularly assimilated to Chinese ways.

The link between opposition and nationalism continued in the Song. The Neo-Confucians developed the position that could harmonize the culturalist and nationalist positions and that, on balance, turned into the culturalist orthodoxy. However, as we have noted, in their own time the founders of Neo-Confucianism were often in opposition and, as a result, could be sharply critical of the pusillanimous and compromising policies of the Song government toward the northern invaders. On the popular level such attitudes were even more evident. For example, the most famous uprising of the time had powerful nationalist sentiments and clearly showed how the average citizen could link personal injustice with a weak foreign policy. Fang La, a petty manufacturer and the leader of the rebellion, reviewed the hardship of the people in one speech and then went on:

> Whatever remains undissipated is presented to the enemy, so that thanks to what we provide they grow more and more prosperous. Even so, they encroach upon the border and you are sent to resist them. If you fail to expel them there are no limits to your punishment. And despite their aggression, annual tribute to the enemy is never discon-

tinued. Do you like this?... Silver and silk running into the millions go to the two barbarian states to the north and west. All this is drained from our life blood, we of the southeast. When they receive these gifts the barbarians become ever more contemptuous of China, and harass it incessantly. The court presents tribute, not daring to stop, and the ministers of state regard this as a long-term plan for preventing border strife. It is only we who labor from one year's end to the next; it is our wives and children who freeze and starve, their hunger never sated for a day. How do you gentlemen feel about it?[7]

The greater nationalism of South China was, to some extent, the product of the withdrawal of the Song to that area. The retreat brought the most zealous patriots along, leaving the North under a foreign dynasty, the Jin. One of the great heroes of the Southern Song was the brave general Yue Fei. He wanted not to remain on the defensive but to recapture the North through arousing and uniting the spirit of the Chinese people. His enemy, the powerful minister Qin Gui, who had Yue imprisoned and then executed, developed a reputation for deceit and evil not unlike Quisling's.

The link between nationalism and opposition was bolstered by the experience of the Mongol conquest, as was the difference in attitudes between North and South. Overall, the Yuan Dynasty was not popular, and, as Marco Polo observed, "there were many disloyal and seditious persons, at all times disposed to break out in rebellion."[8] Mongol policy, however, created some significant gradations in the hostility.

The conquerors ranked themselves on top of society, followed by their assistants from other parts of Eurasia. Below them they placed the northern Chinese, followed at the bottom by the Han of the South. They relied more on the former because they had been under foreign domination for 150 years and were, therefore, presumably more culturalist and trustworthy. This preference further increased the relative nationalism of the South as compared to the North. At the same time the nationalism of the average person also went up because, given the comparatively small number of Mongols, the conquerors had to grant power to the Chinese upper classes and to rely on them in their rule. The higher elite, therefore, appears to have suffered less under the Yuan than was the norm and to have passed down some of the burdens and exactions of the conquerors onto the weaker elements in society.

The great rebellion under Zhu Yuanzhang, which overthrew the Mongols and established the Ming, was very nationalistic and firmly established the relationship among social unrest, resisting foreigners, and political unity. For example, in one letter seeking support, Zhu wrote, "There are two ways to get the power to rule the world: to work together in an attack upon the barbarians to give peace to China is the best way; for the Chinese to fight among themselves and make things easy for the barbarians is no way at all."[9]

In a proclamation to the people of North China he also said:

Since olden times, the condition for an emperor to rule over the empire has always been: The Chinese from within controlled the barbarians, and the barbarians from without served the Chinese. Never have I heard of barbarians ruling the empire. When the Song declined, the Yuan, who are northern barbarians, came in to rule China. . . . Later the Yuan rulers disregarded the principle of relationships between the ruler and the ministers. . . . Thus people revolted in their mind and there were uprisings everywhere. Because of this chaos, the Chinese people either died with their liver and brain mixed up in the dust or lived to see their kin scatter in all directions. . . .

It was said of old that barbarians never could have a Mandate over a hundred years. In view of the present case of the Yuan, this statement is, indeed, true. . . . Among the millions of Chinese there will be one who will drive out the barbarians and restore China. . . . I have respectfully received the Mandate from Heaven and dare not rest myself in peace. I am in the midst of planning a northward expedition to chase the barbarians out of China, in order to deliver the people from their misery and recover the dignity of the Han government. . . . For Heaven will mandate Chinese to take up the task to give peace to the Chinese; how could the government be left in the hands of barbarians?

Aside from his radical proclivities, an additional reason why Zhu was tough on the elite at the beginning of the Ming was the role they had played under the Mongol domination. In the Ming itself, however, there appears to have been some weakening of the link between opposition and nationalism, a result, perhaps, of the power of the elite opposition at the time and the influence of Wang Yangming and his datong approach. Earlier and later history indicates that there was no bar to ideals of the Great Community and nationalism going together; however, when the former was comparatively widespread and optimistic, contradictions between the two may have been evident.

Thus, Wang, while patriotic and involved with border security, was not particularly inclined to nationalism. It was incompatible with his fervent belief in the basic equality of all people, as well as with his sense that status and virtue did not necessarily go together. Indeed, he is said to have received one of his greatest insights into human equality and the unity of knowledge and action while living in exile among tribesmen in the South, the sort of area to which Han Yu had been sent. As one biographer puts it:

That this insight should have come to Yangming during his exile was not coincidence. Mencius had said that every man can be a Yao or a Shun, but Zhu Xi had specified that the road to becoming Yao and Shun lies in moral cultivation and the intellectual pursuit of moral knowledge. Yangming, however, found himself in the midst of people who had never heard of Yao and Shun. Had they and their ancestors been banned from reaching sagehood? . . .

The unity of knowledge and action was, in a sense, the only rationalization one could make in order to justify Mencius' teachings. He began to teach it, first to the few humble Chinese living there and then to the even humbler and less civilized Miaos. The response was gratifying: "When I spoke to the Chinese of the theory of knowledge and action, they were all very much pleased to hear it. After a while even the barbarians became interested and reacted in the same way. But when I came out of exile and spoke of it to scholars and officials, they raised diverse opinions, often refusing to accept what I said."[10]

Just as the comparative lack of religious ideology in the rebellion of Li Zicheng, which toppled the Ming, testified, perhaps, to the spread of Confucianism and the blending of elite and popular discontent, so did the relative absence of nationalism. Thus, Li, while certainly motivated by the problems of the government on the northern borders, did not make nationalism a prominent theme in the uprising.

In the years immediately following the victory of the Manchus, nationalism once again flourished within the opposition. Indeed, it became a hallmark of early Qing thinkers, and one of their major critiques of Wang Yangming and of the revolutionary movement of the late Ming was that they had weakened China in the face of the northern threat. One early Qing writer, whose nationalism was to become particularly famous in the nineteenth century, was Wang Fuzhi. He bitterly opposed culturalism and, in fact, argued that the fresh wave of conquest had come about precisely because China had done too much to civilize the Manchus and, as a result, had whetted both their capabilities and their desire for aggression. As he wrote:

> The strength of the barbarians lies in the paucity of their laws and institutions. As long as their shelter, food, and clothing remain crude and barbaric, as long as they continue to foster a violent and savage temper in their people and do not alter their customs, they may enjoy great advantage. And, at the same time, because of this China may escape harm. But if they once begin to change and to adopt Chinese ways, then the advantages of their situation will also change. They may thereby in time grow braver and mightier than the Chinese. . . .
>
> While the barbarians are content to roam about in pursuit of water and pasture, practicing archery and hunting, preserving no distinctions between ruler and subject, possessing only rudimentary marriage and governmental systems, ranging back and forth over their territory in accordance with seasonal demands, then China can never control or rule them. And as long as the barbarians do not realize that cities can be fortified and maintained, that markets bring profit, that fields can be cultivated and taxes exacted, as long as they do not know the glory of elaborate marriage and official systems, they will continue to look upon China as a perilous and inhospitable bed of thorns.[11]

Wang Fuzhi said that the Manchus would eventually be assimilated or expelled, though in his ardent opposition to culturalism, either outcome seemed a long way off. Other early Qing intellectuals, while deeply troubled about the fact that China had once again fallen under a foreign heel, put more emphasis on the fact that civilizing the Manchus was now the proper strategy to follow. For example, Gu Yanwu said that Han policy should henceforth be "to make use of Chinese institutions to transform the barbarians."[12] With some of Gu's students in a leading role, this idea became a chief goal of the Chinese elite in the late seventeenth century.[13] As we have seen, the Manchus responded in kind and established a successful Chinese-style regime.

Manchu policy, together with the general decline of elite opposition during the first hundred years of the Qing, combined to reduce nationalism within that group. As in political matters in general, this change tended to split the establishment from the rest of society. Important popular groups, such as the so-called secret societies, continued to have powerful nationalistic and anti-Manchu elements in their ideology, and nationalism was sufficiently popular with the reading public of the eighteenth century for the government to undertake a literary purge to remove unflattering comments on nomads and tribesmen from Chinese texts.

THE WEST

It was in the Ming and early Qing that the West, a foreign culture that was to play a crucial role on the Chinese scene, came into permanent contact with China.[14] Thereafter, many things helped to determine the relationship between the two civilizations. From the point of view of the Western impact on the Chinese revolution of the nineteenth and twentieth centuries, however, the interaction can be understood roughly in terms of three general factors.

The first of these was the scientific and technological superiority of Western culture. The second is that during the era of interaction, while the junxian system was reaching a zenith in China and then beginning to decay, the West was in a transition from fengjian to the beginnings of junxian. The third, in a sense a product of the other two, is the faith in the possibility of transcendent progress, the powerful feeling of emancipation from the bonds of history, which became such a prominent feature of Western thought in the nineteenth and twentieth centuries.

The strength of the West in science and its belief in transcendent progress are easily understood within the Western context, though we will have more to say about each as they become important to our story. Understanding the West in terms of fengjian and junxian, is, however, rather unorthodox and requires some explanation. First of all, the West cannot be related to the story of the Chinese revolution (nor, indeed, can any two cultures be connected in a single narrative) without some common vocabulary or categories of analysis. Since the purpose of this study is to see how the revolution relates to Chinese tradition and how it is a part of Chinese history rather than a subcase of Western experience, using Chinese concepts to compare the two civilizations and to analyze their interaction is necessary and appropriate.

Second, while the categories fengjian and junxian are Chinese, employing them to generalize about recent Western history does not involve any serious deviation from our usual approaches; I have, indeed, focused on them, to some extent, because of their utility at this point in our story. Thus, the transition in the West from the old regime to the new, from feudalism to capitalism, or from traditional society to modern is fairly described as a shift from aristocratic and decentralized government to centralized bureaucracy, from a controlled and limited market to laissez-faire practices, from warlike and religious values to more civilian and secular ones. These changes did not all occur simultaneously, of course, and the pace was different in different countries. England, for example, achieved centralized government four hundred years ago, while an effective military ethos and religious faith were retained virtually everywhere in the West down to the twentieth century. Overall, though, it seems reasonable to use fengjian and junxian to describe a process of change that has been occurring in Western society over the past several hundred years.

Third, understanding the relative character of China and the West in terms of these categories is essential to describing a major attraction that the West held for China in the nineteenth and twentieth centuries, an attraction that is overlooked if we simply think of Western technological power or of the notion of progress, for radicals and datong thinkers had long argued that to correct the problems of junxian China, a revival of fengjian approaches was needed. These, however, had long been lost in China. As a result, the still powerful fengjian aspect of the West, the fact that it represented a blend of the two systems, was, as we shall see, particularly to influence Chinese revolutionaries.

Though permanent and significant contact between the West and China began only in the sixteenth century, there had been intermittent communication since Han times, the era of the Roman empire. Chinese silk was much in demand in Rome, and the traffic in silk "was the most far-reaching large-scale commerce of antiquity" in which the West was involved.[15] The desire for silk in Rome outweighed desire for any products at the other end of the trade, and in the first and second centuries A.D. a serious balance of payments problem developed for the Romans, who, like the British merchants of the eighteenth century in their later dealings with China, had to export large amounts of precious metals eastward.

Most of the trade between the Han and Rome was in the hands of intermediaries, though some Chinese travelers seem to have reached as far as the fringes of Roman influence and some Romans came to the Han areas of Central Asia. With the decline of Rome and of the Han, contact fell off. In the era from the Tang through the Yuan, however, relations reopened, with travelers going in both directions. The most famous of these was, of course, Marco Polo, who reported on the wonders of Yuan China to an unbelieving Europe.

When permanent contact began in the late Ming, the Westerners who went to China were mostly merchants and missionaries. The merchants were predominantly from Portugal and Spain, though in the seventeenth century they began to be supplemented by men from northern Europe. By the eighteenth century the British were far and away the most important Western traders in Chinese waters. The missionaries were Jesuits, and the dominant influence on them was Italian and Iberian, though men from other countries went to China as part of the Catholic order. The merchants fitted themselves more or less harmoniously into the trade that went on between China and Southeast Asia, and the Jesuits worked mostly on converting members of the Chinese elite.

The Chinese image of the West in the late Ming and early Qing was quite favorable. The West was not a threat, and, above all, the Jesuits were learned men. They made few conversions in the secular atmosphere of junxian China;

however, Western practical knowledge, particularly in weaponry, mathematics, and astronomy, was well received, and some Jesuits attained prominent positions. Thus, at this early date, the strength of Western culture in terms of science and technology already began to influence China.

At the same time, Westerners were also impressed by what they saw. Indeed, through about 1800, the Chinese impact on the West was, overall, considerably greater than the Western impact on China. A crucial reason for this difference was that an early peak in the West's transition from fengjian to junxian is represented by the New Thought of the seventeenth century and by the Enlightenment of the eighteenth. It is not surprising, therefore, that many important Western thinkers of the era found the fully developed junxian system of the Ming and Qing appealing. At the same time, there were commentators who did not approve of such a society, and for them China provided a negative example.

The Jesuits and others who went to China wrote many books on their observations and experiences. These works were the source of the Chinese influence on Europe, generally presenting a sharply favorable image of the country, and also extremely popular. The best ones were translated into several languages and circulated widely, and most people who read had probably read a book about China, and, through translations, even had access to the important Confucian classics. It is probably fair to say that at no other time in Western history has there been as much of an interest in China among average intellectuals in the West or as much knowledge about her.

This interest, it should be pointed out, went well beyond its impact on social thought. For example, the gaudy taste of Qing China was a major influence on the predominant artistic style of the eighteenth century, the rococo. The *reve chinois* affected the architecture of buildings and how they were furnished.[16] Even the pigtail, so common in the eighteenth-century West, was inspired by the pigtails that all men in Qing China wore. The most significant influence, though, was to give inspiration and support to the *philosophes*, the great social and political thinkers of the eighteenth century, who were in the forefront of the battle against the power of the old regime, the fengjian system, in our terminology.

In general, the *philosophes* wanted just, united countries and also had dreams of an international order that would encompass all of Europe. The unity of China and of the whole culture under one effective and comparatively rational organization was very appealing. Indeed, many thinkers even idealized the excessive power of the Chinese emperorship and called for "enlightened despots" who would sweep away the abuses and irrationalities of Europe's past. The *philosophes* also found the other aspects of China's junxian society extremely useful in expounding their hopes for the West. After all, the Chinese did not have a hereditary aristocracy. They had an open market, peaceful values, and a humanistic philosophy.

Some selections from popular Jesuit books and from seventeenth- and eighteenth-century authors will give a sense of the relationship between the West and China. The most famous Jesuit, Matteo Ricci, wrote the following about the bureaucratic efficiency and civilian values of China:

Another remarkable fact, and quite worthy of note as marking a difference from the West, is that the entire Kingdom is administered by the order of the learned, commonly known as the philosophers. The responsibility for orderly management of the entire realm is wholly and completely committed to their charge and care. . . .

The order and harmony that prevails among magistrates, both high and low, . . . is also worthy of admiration. . . . Every third year . . . a rigorous investigation is made concerning the magistrates of every province in the entire kingdom. . . . The purpose of this investigation is to determine who shall be retained in public office, how many are to be removed, and the number to be promoted or demoted and punished, if need be. There is not respect for persons in this searching inquisition. I myself have observed that not even the king would dare to change a decision settled upon by the judges of this public investigation. . . . It is a general law that no judge may hold court in the province in which he was born. . . . This is a precaution against favoring relatives and friends. . . . No one is permitted to carry arms within city limits, not even soldiers or officers. . . . Fighting and violence among the people are practically unheard of. . . . On the contrary, one who will not fight and restrains himself from returning a blow is praised for his prudence and bravery.[17]

The openness of Chinese society and the absence of special privileges, even for churches, made a deep impression on one commentator:

Nobility is never hereditary, neither is there any distinction between the qualities of people, saving what the offices they execute make. . . . Their gods as well as men are subjected to the state and are obliged by taxes and contributions to acknowledge the emperor's supremacy. When a viceroy or governor of a province is dead, his children, as well as others, have their fortunes to make, and if they inherit not their father's virtue and ingenuity, his name which they bear, be it ever so famous, gives them no quality at all.[18]

The prosperity and self-sufficiency of China were taken for granted:

Due to the great extent of this country . . . it can be safely asserted that nowhere else in the world is found such a variety of plant and animal life. . . . Everything which the people need for their well-being and sustenance, whether it be for food or clothing or even delicacies and superfluities, is abundantly produced within the borders of the kingdom and not imported from foreign climes.[19]

The free market of junxian China, with its dense and lively trade, particularly impressed the great physiocrat and forerunner of laissez-faire economics, François Quesnay. In his book *Le Despotisme de la Chine*, he wrote:

The transportation of the various articles of merchandise is very easy in China due to the number of canals which cut through all the provinces. Traffic and marketing are very prompt; self-interest, which is the dominating passion of the Chinese people, holds them to continual activity; the highways are as crowded as the streets of our commercial cities, and the whole empire seems to be nothing less than one vast fair.[20]

The leaders in the development of rationalism and humanistic thought, of course, found Confucianism particularly appealing. For example, Leibnitz, a good Christian, marveled at Chinese social theory. In his *Novissima Sinica (News from China)*, he wrote, "Chinese missionaries should be sent to us to teach us the aim and practice of natural theology, as we send missionaries to them to instruct them in revealed theology."[21] His follower, the philosopher Christian Wolff, was once expelled from the German town of Halle, where he had been teaching, because of an address, *De Sinarum Philosophia practica* ("On the Practical Philosophy of the Chinese"), in which he praised Confucianism so highly that it seemed to imply disrespect for Christianity.

As might be expected, Voltaire, the quintessential figure of the Enlightenment, was, perhaps, the most fervent supporter of Confucian humanism and of China in general. Of Confucius, he wrote, "I have read his books with attention, I have made extracts from them; I found that they spoke only of the purest morality. . . . He appeals only to virtue, he preaches no miracles, there is nothing in them of ridiculous allegory."[22] And elsewhere:

I know a philosopher in whose room a portrait of Confucius hung by itself, with the following four verses inscribed below it:

"The solitary interpreter of reason alone
Without dazzling the world, he enlightened the spirit
He spoke only as a wise man and never as a prophet
However, he was believed, even in his own land."

Voltaire's general judgment was that "one need not be obsessed with the merits of the Chinese to recognize at least that the organization of their empire is, in truth, the best that the world has ever seen."

Attitudes toward China in the seventeenth and eighteenth centuries were not always so favorable. However, what is important to note is that those who criticized the country shared the same general image of it as those who praised it. They simply did not think that it was a good society or that it should be a model for the West. Even those who extolled China freely admitted that it was behind Europe in math and science, and others took aim at the junxian system itself.

Thus, Montesquieu criticized China for being too centralized and despotic. He understood (to use Chinese terminology) that China no longer had the powerful feng-jian traditions that he believed were necessary for sound government and liberty. His comments would have been worthy of a member of the Chinese opposition:

Our missionaries inform us that the government of the vast empire of China is admirable . . . but I cannot conceive what this honor can be among people who act only through fear of being beaten. . . . The emperor of China is not taught like our princes that if he governs ill he will be less happy in the other life, less powerful and less opulent in this. He knows that if his government be not just he will be stripped both of empire and life. . . . Such has been the origin of those regulations which have been greatly extolled. They wanted to make the laws reign in conjunction with despotic power; but whatever is joined to the latter loses all its force. In vain did this arbitrary sway, laboring under its own inconveniences, desire to be fettered; it armed itself with its chains, and has become still more terrible. . . . China is, therefore, a despotic state, whose principle is fear.[23]

Montesquieu may have had some sense that despotism had not always been the case with the Chinese emperorship: "Perhaps in the earliest dynasties, when the empire had not so large an extent, the government might have deviated a little from this spirit," he wrote, "but the case is otherwise at present."

Other people criticized the excessively mercantile spirit of junxian China, what one might call its unbridled capitalist ethos:

There is one blemish in their commerce, it is said, the lack of good faith. The Chinese are not content with selling as dearly as they can; they also falsify their merchandise. One of their maxims is that he who buys pays as little as possible, and that he would pay nothing, if he could. They infer from this that one may charge and receive the most exorbitant sum, if the buyer is so simple and so unintelligent as to pay it. "It is not the merchant who deceives," they say, "it is the buyer who deceives himself; no violence has been done, the profit taken by the vendor is the fruit of his industry."[24]

Other critics, in the still generally aristocratic and warlike atmosphere of Europe, found the civilian and middle-class values of China to be signs of weakness. "Running away is no dishonor with them; they do not know what an insult is," wrote Ricci.[25] And another commentator, generally sympathetic to China, wrote that the army there was

numerous, well looked after, duly paid and exactly disciplined . . . yet soon broke, and by the least thing in the world put into disorder. The occasion of this I apprehend to be, because in the education of their youth they never instill into them principles of honor and bravery, as we do as soon as ever they are big enough to know what weapons are. The Chinese are always talking to their children of gravity, policy, law, and government; they always set books and letters in their view, but never a sword in their hands. . . . The Chinese policy hinders hereby a great many domestic feuds and disturbances, but at the same time it does expose its subjects to the insults of foreigners, which is ten times worse.

In the eighteenth century, Rousseau used the lack of martial valor to criticize China and the reve chinois. He wrote that if the Chinese social

sciences really purified morals, if they really taught men to shed their blood for the fatherland, if they inspired courage, then the people of China would assuredly be wise, free, and invincible. . . . If neither the ability of its ministers nor the alleged wisdom of its laws nor even the numberless multitude of its inhabitants have been able to protect this realm against subjection by ignorant and rude barbarians [i.e., the Manchus], of what service have been all its wise men?

Ultimately, sympathy for Chinese humanistic philosophy came back to haunt the Jesuits. The issue was embodied in the famous "Rites Controversy," in which other Catholic orders argued that the Jesuits were compromising with idolatry in their respect for Confucius and for allowing Christian converts in China to practice the veneration of ancestors. The pope sided with the opponents of the Jesuits, whose influence was thereby retarded. In 1773, the Jesuit order was temporarily abolished, partly, perhaps, because of the role they had played in creating the Enlightenment through their propagation of things Chinese.

In the nineteenth century, a great and rather sudden change from general respect to general disrespect took place in the West's attitudes toward China. The flavor of the change is evident, for example, in the standard book on China in nineteenth-century America. In *The Middle Kingdom*, the missionary S. Wells Williams wrote, among other things, that the Chinese people were

vile and polluted in a shocking degree; their conversation is full of filthy expressions and their lives of impure acts. . . . More ineradicable than the sins of the flesh is the falsity of the Chinese, and its attendant sin of base ingratitude; their disregard of truth has perhaps done more to lower their character than any other fault. . . . Thieving is exceedingly common, and the illegal exactions of the rulers . . . are most burdensome. . . . Hospitality is not a trait of their character; on the contrary, the number and wretched condition of the beggars show that public and private charity is almost extinct. . . . The politeness which they exhibit seldom has its motive in good-will, and consequently, when the varnish is off, the rudeness, brutality, and coarseness of the material is seen. . . . Female infanticide . . . the alarming extent of the use of opium . . . the universal practice of lying and dishonest dealings; the unblushing lewdness of old and young; harsh cruelty toward prisoners—all form a full unchecked torrent of human depravity, and prove the existence of a kind and degree of moral degradation of which an excessive statement can scarcely be made, or an adequate conception hardly formed.[26]

Views on China in the nineteenth century were not uniformly hostile, and there even continued to be some influence from East to West. For example, the development of meritocracy in England was materially advanced by the introduction of the civil service examination, a concept borrowed from China. However, favorable attitudes became the exception and when the West learned something, the Chinese genesis was quickly forgotten. The momentous shift from the basic respect of the Enlightenment to the basic disrespect thereafter was deeply to affect Western policies and provided a powerful prop for the imperialist onslaught against China in the nineteenth century. Ultimately the new attitudes were also to have a significant impact on China's own self-image and to play a major role in Chinese revolutionary thought.

One reason for the shift was that China itself began to look worse in the late eighteenth century than when the Jesuits and others had collected their information, for, as we shall see, it was in this period that the Qing Dynasty and the junxian system entered upon a decline which was eventually to result in the overthrow of both. However, the crisis in China developed rather more slowly than the change in Western attitudes, and, in addition, the West did not now see China as an advanced culture that had fallen on hard times but saw her in an entirely new way, as fundamentally backward and bad. As a result, the roots of the change must also be sought in Europe and understood in terms of the general factors that have structured the relationship between China and the West in modern times: the scientific power of the Occident, the fact that it was in a transition from fengjian to junxian society, and the notion of transcendent progress, which now began fully to develop there.

The crucial manifestation of technology and science in the West of the early nineteenth century was, of course, the Industrial Revolution. The rapid economic progress that ensued brought new levels of prosperity to northern Europe and America. As a result, the respect which China had formerly achieved as a rich and developed nation now began to turn to contempt for a place that seemed ever poorer and more backward.

In addition, the new developments in the West were largely the creation of a rapidly rising urban and industrial middle class. The attitudes of this group, coupled with a long-standing urban bias in Western culture, one that closely associated cities and civilization, compounded the disrespect for China,[27] for not only was China poorer, but she remained predominantly agricultural, and in Western terms this status increasingly translated into primitive.

Two other important elements in the denigration of China grew out of the still powerful fengjian side of Western society. One of these was the revival of a doctrinaire religious spirit in the West. This often took the form of a fervent evangelical faith far less able than the worldly Jesuits of the seventeenth century or Deists of the eighteenth to tolerate differences in belief or to see value in other cultures. This faith made many in the West contemptuous of China, which was both non-Christian and comparatively secular. At the same time fengjian values and the new technology combined to make the West far more powerful than China militarily. Even in the eighteenth century the latter had been seen as weak in comparison to Europe, and now her civilian spirit was considered to be downright shameful and decadent.

Finally, in the nineteenth century the idea of transcendent progress attained prominence in the West and put the capstone on the disrespect for China. This attitude had roots deep in Western culture, most strikingly, perhaps, in a Greek heritage that played down the value of historical precedent[28] and in the powerfully transcendent character of Christianity. Now, rapid change and unprecedented wealth and strength joined with a still flourishing religious sensibility to create the new faith in progress.

Essentially, this belief asserted that the West was freeing itself from history, transcending it, and was entering an entirely new stage of human development, one that would be totally unencumbered by the problems and evils of the past. Such an outlook, of course, was bound to be very hard on China. Like other parts of the non-Western world, she was now simply part of a discredited past. Furthermore, as a culture whose age and continuity were well known, she could be considered particularly moribund and inferior.

Part II

THE REVOLUTION

4

Rebellion and Western Pressures

PROBLEMS BEGIN

In the late eighteenth and early nineteenth centuries, the Qing Dynasty and China's junxian system began to enter an era of economic, political, and moral decline. The difficulties in government and society encouraged the revival of an active opposition movement, one that, as in the past, often had a datong component. The most striking manifestation of this opposition was the renewal of popular rebellion, and the unrest culminated in the mid-nineteenth century in a number of massive uprisings, including the great revolutionary movement known as the Taiping Rebellion. However, the problems of the nation had not yet reached a point where they affected a sufficient number of people, particularly in the upper levels of society, and all the uprisings failed. The elite generally remained loyal to the dynasty and to the existing sociopolitical order and worked on their behalf against the rising tide of opposition.

In the early nineteenth century, too, the West, just entering an era of high imperialism, began major aggression against China. The Occident used the growing internal weakness of its prey and its own immense military superiority to exact special privileges and territories from the Qing. The Western pressures added to the burdens of the government and the problems of society. This situation not only aroused hostility to the West but also encouraged the opposition by providing it with an added reason for attacking those in power. At the same time, however, various groups began to find Western ideas and techniques useful for their struggles within China, and, for the first time in history, the nation began to come under significant Western influence.

The internal problems that began to manifest themselves at the turn of the nineteenth century grew out of the very success of the Qing Dynasty and of the junxian order. Both had reached an apogee in the mid-eighteenth century and, perhaps simply for this reason, were bound to decay, as had earlier dynasties and social systems. Life had been reasonably good for over a hundred years and, in the long run, for almost a thousand. The populace was educated and sophisticated. It had firm expectations of a decent standard of living, political justice, and the possibility of social advancement. When such expectations had been frustrated earlier, an aroused people quickly demanded political change. Now, on the basis of an opposition tradition with considerable experience and with problems more serious than any hitherto experienced, a crisis developed that was to bring down not only the dynasty in power, but the junxian order itself.

To be more concrete, one major result of the success of the junxian system in the long run and of the good society of the Qing in the short run was a rapid growth in population. In 1700 China already had two hundred million people and in 1800, three hundred million. By 1850 the population climbed to over four hundred million, having doubled on a very large base in the course of 150 years.[1] Population growth had been a crucial factor toward the close of various dynasties and at earlier turning points in Chinese history, most notably in the great eras of change in the middle Zhou and in the late Tang. Now it was the single most obvious cause of the growing difficulties and contradictions within society.

By 1800 or so, given the existing technological and scientific levels, population began to outstrip resources. Agriculture remained the most important sector of the economy, and yields per unit of land remained high. However, yields per person started to drop sharply. As a result, there were simply less and less to go around and increasingly fewer opportunities and possibilities for fulfilling the basic needs and expectations of the society and its people.

In this situation, life grew difficult and insecure. Income dropped, and opportunities for education and advancement closed down. For those lower on the social scale, the situation could lead to extreme poverty and destitution; for those higher up, it meant tighter constraints on daily life and the possibility, always strong in junxian China, of downward social mobility. At the same time, in the freewheeling economic system of the time, such pressures led to sharp competition for what was available and, in many cases, to increasingly unethical behavior. Consequently, the problems not only affected economic matters but put a severe strain on all aspects of Chinese life, moral, political, and intellectual.

By the early nineteenth century, the comparative lack of dynamism and idealism in Confucian philosophy further compounded society's problems. Confucianism had long been the junxian orthodoxy and had contributed greatly to the success of the age. However, the materialistic atmosphere and secular flavor of the era had weakened the power of the philosophy to evoke deep commitment. At the same time, as the official outlook, Confucianism had often been used to emphasize the justice of the status quo, and this role had dulled its critical edge. As a result, the outlook was less able to encourage moral behavior in times of crises and was ill prepared to deal with the problems that began to face China in the early nineteenth century. In a general way, of course, Confucianism continued to help people to develop an integrated picture of the problems that beset them, just as it can help the historian to analyze the situation that developed. However, the Confucian contribution to Chinese society for the next 150 years or so came more from the general principles of the philosophy and from its inherent power as a social theory and its almost unconscious effect on people than from any specific vibrancy that it retained.

Just as difficulties began to affect Chinese life, the Qing Dynasty entered its own period of decline. The problems of the dynasty and the government were enhanced by what was happening in society and, in turn, contributed further to the slide. One should not exaggerate the problems in 1800. The Qing was to have its ups as well as its downs for some time to come. It remained in power for another hundred years and might well have lasted longer but for foreign pressures. Nonetheless, the signs of dynastic decline were beginning: a drop in the quality of emperors, financial difficulties, and corruption.

Chinese political theory, with its sharp sense of the ebb and flow of human events, expected poorer emperors and a decaying court toward the end of a dynasty, and this development had happened throughout Chinese history. One reason for the process in the junxian age was the immense power that the emperorship had attained. Society had few official checks on the ruler and even fewer on the doings of the imperial family and its vast retinue of harem ladies and eunuchs. Over the course of time, such members of the inner court and other imperial favorites were able to increase their strength. Emperors could come to the throne who were selected not because they were good but because they were weak in will and stamina and could be easily manipulated. The Qing had made a good start, but the process of degeneration began to become evident by the nineteenth century.

Long-lived emperors were associated with effective rule in Chinese history, and while this connection was not always the case, it had often been true. A graphic indication of the growing weakness of the Qing line, therefore, was the comparative brevity of imperial reigns in the nineteenth century. In the 150 years from the beginning of the dynasty through 1795 there were only four emperors. In the 100 years from 1795 to 1911, there were six. The last of the long-lived rulers was the famous Qianlong emperor, who reigned from 1736 to 1795. Under Qianlong the Qing reached its height, and he is generally considered to be one of the greatest emperors in Chinese history. However, in the latter part of his reign, he became prone to the machinations of unprincipled favorites and was increasingly ineffective. In these years the decline of the Qing began to become evident.

In addition to the problems at court, the prime difficulties of the administration in the late eighteenth century were financial. Simply put, the government was increasingly unable to meet its expenses. One reason for this problem was the fact that administrative costs always went up as a dynasty remained in power. Entrenched interests tended to develop, and efficiency went down. In addition, the Qianlong emperor had spent vast sums on military campaigns in central Asia.

These had done much to resolve China's problems beyond the Wall, but they had also put a tremendous drain on the national treasury. Finally, of course, the population rise meant that the government needed more money to carry out its tasks just at a time when the imbalance between people against resources left a smaller surplus for taxation. Tax increases were also a particular problem for the Qing. Early in the eighteenth century the dynasty had committed itself never to raise land taxes, and, in the laissez-faire atmosphere of the time, it was a promise difficult to break.

The comparative impotence of Confucian orthodoxy, the laxness at court, and the financial problems of the government all combined to encourage corruption, both in public and private life. In the eighteenth century, the most famous example of corruption in government was the career of Heshen, the favorite of the Qianlong emperor during the last twenty years of his reign. Heshen was

> a sycophant and manipulator extraordinary, who rose like a meteor in one year . . . to be a Grand Councilor and minister of the imperial household. Thereafter he got his hands on the principal posts in charge of revenue and personnel, betrothed his son to the emperor's youngest daughter, and entrenched himself in as many as twenty different positions at a time. Having the emperor's ear, he built up his clique of similarly corrupt henchmen all over the empire and levied a squeeze upon the whole officialdom. The private wealth attributed to him by his enemies . . . included 60,000,000 ounces of silver, 75 pawnshops, 70,000 furs, a gold table service of 4,288 pieces, and other items alleged to be worth a total of 900,000,000 ounces or, say one and a half billion dollars.[2]

Certainly this description is an exaggeration, but it provides a general sense of Heshen's scale of operations.

Such behavior at the top encouraged and, indeed, required similar behavior all along the line. Higher officials demanded expensive gifts and payments from subordinates in exchange for favors. In addition, the general economic pressures of the time encouraged the elite to corruption. Public service all too often became a way of solving one's financial problems. *Sheng guan fa cai*, "become an official and strike it rich," was the cynical way of putting it. Such misbehavior also put a further drain on national finances and added to the burdens of society.

For similar reasons corruption spread through society. In the struggle for success that had always marked the junxian system and that now became all the harsher because of the moral, political, and economic situation, honesty became increasingly costly and unpopular. Intense competition became the name of the game. This, of course, proved more burdensome to the average person than to the establishment, for the lower down one was on the social scale, the less able one was to resist official exactions or to profit from various forms of illegality. For example, to avoid the onus of an across-the-board tax increase, the government added various surcharges to existing rates. This semiformal approach lent itself to corruption, and the wealthy and powerful began to avoid their fair share of taxes and, in the classic manner, to shift the burdens to those lower down and less able to pay. This behavior, in turn, further reduced the funds available for the government and increased the atmosphere of moral decay and competitiveness.

As such problems developed, social services from education to crime prevention began to decline, with the burden again falling on the less affluent parts of society. A clear sign of the decline was flooding, a traditional indication that the central government and the local elite were not carrying out their responsibilities. Another sign was famine. To some extent caused by the population rise, famine was, more immediately, a product of the fact that those responsible for the welfare of society were not able to get food where it was needed or to distribute it fairly in a time of crisis.

Against this background of decay, social and political activism began to revive among the people. One sign of this was the expansion of private institutions and organizations aimed at helping the average person to deal with his problems collectively rather than individually. Such groups could range from clan organizations to religious societies. A particularly noteworthy example was the increased importance of local militia forces. Another was the growing power and spread of fraternal organizations such as the so-called secret societies. One such group was the Triads of South China. The Triads had traditionally been made up of transportation workers, merchants, and minor government functionaries. Now, the group began to organize farmers. The basic purpose of such associations was to provide mutual aid and social benefits to their members. However, they could also be caught up in the immoral atmosphere of the time. Local militia, for example, might prey on weaker neighbors, and fraternal organizations might engage in various forms of racketeering.

The most striking sign of social activism in the late eighteenth century, however, was the renewal of popular rebellion, as the first serious revolts in a hundred years developed. There was a Triad uprising on Taiwan and then an even more serious outbreak, the White Lotus Rebellion, which spread across Central and Western China between 1796 and 1804. As had happened so often in the past, the outbreak was organized around a powerful religious group, the Buddhist White Lotus Society. The direct spark for the unrest is said to have been injustices in tax collection.

The White Lotus Rebellion did not directly challenge the legitimacy of the Qing by seeking to claim the Mandate of Heaven for a new government. In this sense, it was simply the continuation of normal politics: bringing a bad situation to the attention of Peking. However, the need for rebellion to obtain satisfaction was a sure sign that the paths of communication between the average person and those on top were becoming blocked, as was inevitable in a time of excessive competition and corruption.

At the same time, the rebellion further contributed to the downward spiral of the administration and of society. The weakness of the government became clear as the Manchu Banner forces, the heart of the Qing army, as well as the standing army of Han Chinese, the so-called Green Banner army, could not quell the unrest. Both had grown ineffective as a result of the general tendency for armed forces to decay in the junxian era and of the immediate problems of the late eighteenth century. The rebellion was ultimately put down only through heavy reliance on local militia forces.

The White Lotus and other rebellions also cost money, putting an added strain on government finances and increasing the need for taxes with their attendant injustices. In addition, the growing unrest provided an additional and lucrative arena for corruption through the confusion it sowed and through various forms of military procurement. Heshen, for example, is said to have made considerable money out of the White Lotus Rebellion, and his exactions are counted among the reasons why the uprising dragged on for eight long years.

Finally, while the various outbreaks were generally aimed at alleviating local problems and bringing justice to society, in the short run they could directly contribute to the growing difficulties of the average person. They hurt economic life and public welfare and caused all sorts of dangers to well-being and security. Nonetheless, they were harbingers of things to come, of the time when the destitution of society and the desire for change outweighed all the disadvantages of rebellion.

In addition to popular unrest, another sign of the developing spirit of opposition was a gradual revival of critical attitudes within the elite, something that had not flourished since the late Ming and early Qing. In the Ming, as we have seen, there had been a powerful and effective opposition within the establishment. However, this had all but disappeared in the Qing, and, on the surface at least, upper-class intellectuals in the late seventeenth and eighteenth centuries busied themselves with philological problems and seemed to lose touch with broader sociopolitical concerns and with whatever remained alive of the opposition tradition among the people at large.

This background meant that most of the elite in the early nineteenth century remained, as they were to remain until much later in the century, wary and conservative. This attitude was also the case, of course, because the higher a person was in society, the less likely he was to be hard-pressed and the greater his stake in the status quo. Nonetheless, a few critical spirits began to emerge. At this opposition developed, it also began to organize itself, though, because of the Qing restrictions on such activity, only in a most informal manner through the formation of such things as poetry clubs and local educational institutions, groups that denied, or at least seemed to veil, direct political action.[3]

The opposition intellectuals of the early nineteenth century did not favor rebellion, and, in fact, the suppression of unrest was one of their major goals. This concern sprang from immediate self-interest and also from the fact that in the junxian age popular rebellion, with its egalitarian and revolutionary potentialities, had become threatening to the elite. The new thinkers were deeply critical of the moral and material decay they saw around themselves. They sometimes even showed sympathy for datong approaches[4] and particularly admired Gu Yanwu and the early Qing radicals. On the other hand, they remained moderate in approach and worked to reform the government and the establishment, to halt the downward spiral, and to revive a sense of effectiveness and idealism in society.

One aspect of elite opposition took the form of a reaction against the philological approach within Confucianism and a call for attention to the concrete problems of the nation. The role of intellectuals, the critics argued, should be to develop specific knowledge and techniques for handling such matters as taxation, education, water control, military preparedness, and a host of other areas of administrative practice and social concern. Among other things, they sharply criticized the character of the examination system, which, they said, had come to direct education and people's minds toward empty rhetoric and useless information. Overall, they succeeded in reviving the ''school of practical statecraft,'' which had been influential in the late Ming and early Qing but which had been overwhelmed by the tide of textual studies later on.

The other major manifestation of elite dissatisfaction was the revival of an interest in religion, which, of course, had long implied an opposition mentality and which continued to play a role in the popular discontent of the time. In the early nineteenth century, concern with religion among intellectuals arose generally from a desire for moral uplift and spiritual support beyond what was available in the Confucian orthodoxy. To some extent, religion also received a boost from the philological movement itself.

The scholars of the eighteenth century had found forgeries and later interpolations in some of the standard texts upon which official Confucianism rested. The textual criticism could not overturn the general structure of Confucian theory; however, like the junxian atmosphere within which the philologists worked, it contributed to a certain loss of idealism in the orthodox outlook and to the search for alternatives. At the same time, partly because of the problems with the existing texts, the scholars had moved back to studying those from the Han Dynasty. This shift brought the more religious Confucianism of the Han to the attention of critical thinkers of the early nineteenth century. Others went even further and began to think seriously about Buddhism.

THE OPIUM WAR AND WESTERN IMPERIALISM

Western pressures on China started just about the time that the nation's internal difficulties began. The background to the onslaught was the growing disrespect for China as the eighteenth century closed and the nineteenth century dawned and, more generally, the rise of imperialism in the nineteenth-century West. The first results of this situation were British attempts to resolve certain problems of trade and relations with China in ways that violated Chinese laws and the nation's position of international equality. These attempts led to confrontation and, eventually, to combat: the Opium War of 1839 to 1842 and another conflict, sometimes known as the Second Opium War, from 1856 to 1860. The overwhelming foreign victories in both wars and the treaties that came into existence as a result established the basis for Western power in China for the next one hundred years.[5]

As we have seen, active Chinese trade with the Occident reopened in the sixteenth century as an appendage of the commerce that had developed between Ming China and Southeast Asia. Trade was on a relatively small scale, but the Western side soon faced the problem that had plagued all foreigners who had traded with China in the past: she wanted far fewer goods from them than they wanted from her. As a result, a balance of payments problem developed, and the Western countries were forced to ship silver to China to make up the cost of what they bought.

By the eighteenth century England was far and away the most important Western nation involved in the trade, whose volume had also increased tremendously. Tea had become immensely popular in Britain, and she took huge amounts from China, in addition to substantial quantities of silk and porcelain. As usual, there was no product that the English produced that could pay for what they imported. England sent woolens and various specialty items such as clocks and also carried raw cotton from India and luxury goods from Southeast Asia; nevertheless, the British also had to ship vast and ever increasing amounts of silver bullion to China. This was the basic problem the English faced at the beginning of the nineteenth century.

The other British problem was also related to questions of trade. In line with Chinese practice in dealing with foreigners, business with Britain and other Western nations was considered to be an aspect of international relations as well as a commercial activity. As a result it was closely supervised. The methods used were basically a continuation of the practices developed for the trade with Southeast Asia. By the late eighteenth century, this control took the form of the so-called Canton system. The Chinese government limited the trade to one port, Canton, and licensed a conglomerate to handle the Chinese side of the business. It established fixed times for the trade and did not allow the foreigners to travel freely in China. Peking made no great effort to fit the trade into the tributary framework, though a few Westerners went to the capital and did the prescribed ritual, presumably to obtain the added benefits and connections that could come from sending a tribute mission.

By the late eighteenth century British merchants, in their frustration over the trade imbalance with China, also began to chafe at the limitations of the Canton system. They believed that if they had freer access to the Chinese market, their problems would be solved. As a result, they began to seek solutions, to find new ways of relating to China. This quest, however, took place within the context of the growing disrespect for China.

As we have noted, the new attitude developed because the West was undergoing rapid material, social, and intellectual change but was doing so within the context of older traditions. One of the most momentous results of this situation was imperialism. Imperialism grew out of the new technological power and commercial potentialities of the Occident. At the same time, however, it also rested on the military effectiveness and the religious and evangelical fervor of still powerful fengjian attitudes. Finally, it was fueled by a belief in transcendent progress, which led to an intense feeling of superiority to the rest of the world.

Through the eighteenth century, English trade with China was handled by the East India Company. It was a firm dating back to the seventeenth century and tended to represent older, Enlightenment views. In addition, the company had a monopoly over the English side of the trade and so did not particularly mind the restrictions of the Canton system, which tended to support its own position. As silver continued to flow out, however, and the new era dawned, the company began to show signs of dissatisfaction. More importantly, its monopoly over trade began to fade, and private British merchants were increasingly active at Canton. These merchants were deeply representative of the new Western spirit and became the spearheads of imperialism in China.

The first major sign of the new era was a growing belief among the Westerners that Chinese law did not have to be obeyed and that China did not have to be treated as the equal of the Western nations. The foreigners decided, for example, that their nationals who committed crimes there should not be subject to the jurisdiction of Chinese authorities. Through the eighteenth century, Westerners accused of crimes were routinely judged and punished by Chinese officials. Now the foreigners refused to hand over their compatriots, arguing that Chinese law was unjust, though, in fact, it was only different and, in many cases, milder.

Nevertheless, given the ultimate pragmatism and flexibility that informed Chinese foreign policy, the Western demand to try their own people was negotiable. Chinese officials were not necessarily unwilling to allow foreigners on Chinese soil to be responsible, in the first instance, for their own good order and, indeed, had some historical precedents for doing so. However, constant tension developed as the basic condescension that informed the foreign demands became clear, for Westerners who committed crimes, even against Chinese, increasingly got off with sentences that were shockingly light by any standards, Chinese or Western.

One crime, in particular, quickly became the sorest point of contention between the two sides. The Westerners began to smuggle opium. Opium was illegal in China; however, the foreigners saw its sale as a way of redressing the balance of payments problem. Smuggling opium was, of course, an especially striking sign of the growing sense that China did not have to be treated as a civilized country, for the new English merchants who led the traffic and the Americans and others who followed suit were otherwise law-abiding men who would never have considered forcing opium into their homeland or another Western country.

Opium proved highly effective as a substitute for silver in payment for Chinese goods and by the 1820s had reversed the balance of payments in England's favor. The drug was produced in British territory in India. It found a ready market in China and commanded high prices. We do not know exactly why opium proved so marketable. The drug had been known at least since Tang times, but through the eighteenth century it had been used as a medicine and not very widely. It seems, therefore, that its new popularity came not only from the fact that the drug was available and habit-forming but also from the growing problems of Chinese society and life. The emotional and moral malaise of a people in a sophisticated culture fallen on hard times was probably not dissimilar to the use of narcotics among the more troubled segments of our own society.

The Chinese authorities also had as much trouble halting the flow of the highly valuable and comparatively compact drug as the United States has had in blocking the smuggling of narcotics. The corruption that was eating away at government and society sharply increased, of course, whenever people came into contact with the lucrative trade. From time to time, in order to stem corruption and raise taxes, Peking thought about legalizing opium. However, deep opposition to the dangerous drug and the fact that its purchase was costing China substantial amounts of money kept it illegal. The amount of opium smuggled in steadily increased in the first two decades of the nineteenth century; by 1820, sixty thousand pounds was arriving annually, and the figure kept climbing.

It was against this background that the foreigners, led by the British merchants, continued to work to end the restrictions of the Canton system. Though the opium, had, in fact, solved the balance of payments problem, the English wanted to legalize the drug traffic and to sell other goods, such as the burgeoning product of their cloth industry. At the same time, highly evangelical Protestant missionaries began to arrive in Canton. They were not particularly successful, and by the 1830s twenty-five or so missionaries had produced less than a hundred converts. The missionaries, too, felt deeply constrained by the travel restrictions of the Canton system and believed that abolishing them would turn China into an active and successful field for conversion.

Also at this time the British government became increasingly active at Canton. The monopoly of the East India Company had steadily weakened and was finally abolished in 1834. As the company gave up prime responsibility for British relations with China, the government stepped in. The end of the company's monopoly represented a triumph for the new independent merchants, and London was deeply under their influence as well as that of the missionaries. Aside from working to end the Canton system, the government was particularly concerned about matters of protocol and wanted relations with China to carry no hint of the tribute framework.

All three groups, of course, reflected the new imperialist attitudes and agreed that the West was a civilized and mature culture and that China was a barbaric and underdeveloped one. For example, even as one British diplomat emphasized the need for equal relations with China in terms of protocol, he made clear that China was not to be considered equal:

> No policy can be a good or successful policy in China which has not a special adaptation to the traditions, character, and prejudices of the nation, governors, and people; . . . there must be no *ko-towing* [*sic*] to them—the one besetting sin of the past—but rather an assertion in proper time and place, and with all temper and discretion, of the dignity and

rights of other nations immeasurably their superiors in all that constitutes a nation's worth, or a people's strength.[6]

An American diplomat put it even more bluntly when he wrote that treating China like an equal would be like

the treatment of a child as if it were a grown man. The civilized world, moved by philanthropic feelings, is too apt to consider any attempt to procure further advantages of trade with Eastern nations, though equally advantageous to them as to us, except by simple request, as unmannerly and unchristian. The sentiment is founded on a noble principle, but overlooks the childish character of the people with whom we have to deal, and whom it may be considered our mission to guide and enlighten.

The British merchants particularly emphasized that China should be forced to a laissez-faire policy in foreign trade. They did this partly because they did not see China as equal and were not concerned that under the common rules of international relations a country could set whatever terms of trade it wanted. Another reason was that their belief in free trade grew out of a developing junxian system in England that still coexisted with powerful fengjian attitudes. As a result, the British were beginning to react to trade restrictions of all sorts, but doing so in an ideological fashion that gave laissez-faire the character of religious gospel. For example, the sentiments of John Bowring, future minister to China, would have sounded as odd to Chinese ears of the time as they now do to our own more relaxed junxian sensibility:

That which nations have most earnestly to entreat from governments is, that latter would cease to honor them with any officious interference. . . . The best boon that they can give is to let the stream of commerce flow as it will; its tide is strong enough to bear away all impediments; and governments are but too much the victims of self-deception when they imagine that their decrees of prohibition or of encouragement do really produce the effects they contemplate. Those decrees are erected against and opposed to the natural tendency of things, and are in the end as absurd and ineffective as it would be to direct the winds by Order in Council or to manage the tides by Act of Parliament.[7]

Such views were, of course, particularly ironic because China basically had a laissez-faire economy and through the physiocrats may, indeed, have encouraged its development in the West.

Similarly, all the foreigners were deeply contemptuous of China's military weakness and proud of their own power to work their will if need be. As the German missionary Karl F. A. Gutzlaff (who distributed Bible tracts from opium boats) wrote, "All of China's thousand war-junks cannot withstand one small frigate."[8] And a British diplomat boasted, "What can an army of bows, arrows, and pikes and shields do against a handful of British veterans? . . . The batteries at the Bogue [the approaches to Canton] are contemptible."[9]

By the late 1830s England and China were on a collision course. Opium smuggling was now averaging four million pounds a year. From the Chinese point of view the situation was growing intolerable. Here were foreigners in China almost completely out of control: breaking the law, importing a dangerous drug, extracting Chinese wealth to pay for it, and encouraging corruption. They were also acting with increasing arrogance, pressuring for special privileges, and threatening force.

As usual, given the pragmatic character of Chinese foreign policy and the overall goal of seeking peace and stability in international relations, some of the outstanding issues might have been negotiable. Indeed, progress was made on protocol matters as representatives of the British government became more involved at Canton and Chinese officials understood their sensitivities to the language of tributary relations. However, no long-term improvement in relations was possible so long as the foreign lawlessness and opium smuggling continued. The behavior of the Westerners, of course, now made them seem like a new variety of barbarian: militaristic and desperate for Chinese goods. An appropriate response seemed increasingly in order.

This came in 1839 when Peking sent a special imperial commissioner to Canton to resolve the situation. He was the famous Lin Zexu. Lin was a leading figure in the reform-minded opposition and, perhaps for this reason, had powerful nationalistic leanings. He was also a particularly able man, scrupulously honest and with a strong sense of idealism and fair play. He came to Canton determined to end the opium traffic and to reassert Chinese authority.

Once on the scene, Lin tried to deal with the British using a combination of negotiations and pressure. Among other things, he studied Western international law and used its principles to emphasize that a nation had a right to control foreign trade and uphold its own laws. He composed two letters to Queen Victoria, putting the Chinese case. After rehearsing the benefits that England derived from trade with China, he wrote:

> I have heard that smoking opium is very strictly forbidden in your country; that is because the harm caused by opium is clearly understood. Since it is not permitted to do harm to your own country then even less should you let it be passed on to do harm to other countries. . . . Suppose that there were people from another country who carried opium for sale to England and seduced your people into buying and smoking it; certainly you would deeply hate it and be bitterly aroused. . . . [The merchants] spend rather few days in their own country but more time in Canton. To digest clearly the legal penalties as an aid to instruction has been a valid principle in all ages. Suppose a man of another country comes to England to trade, he still has to obey the English laws.[10]

Lin also moved directly against the opium traffic and the opium dealers, both Chinese and foreign. These efforts were to provide the English with an excuse for war and expansion in China. One of Lin's first moves was to demand that the foreigners hand over all the opium they had stored at Canton, which at the time amounted to over two million pounds of the contraband drug. The British merchants, seeing this demand as an unjust affront to their right to behave in

China as they saw fit, refused. Lin then put them under a mild form of house arrest pending compliance with his request. Eventually the merchants gave in under assurances from the resident British official that London would make China reimburse them for the supposedly illegal confiscation. Lin then destroyed the opium. By then British warships were on the way to supplement the handful of armed vessels already on the scene.

The immediate spark to war occurred when some drunken British sailors attacked a local temple and killed a Chinese villager. The English, as usual, refused to hand over the culprits and then sentenced the guilty men to brief terms of incarceration. Lin was outraged and ordered a halt to all trade. Intermittent fighting broke out, and Lin began to strengthen the military defenses of the Canton area and to organize and enlist the support of local militia forces.

In 1840 a large British force of armed vessels carrying ten thousand troops arrived. In the subsequent fighting China proved no match for England, which seized various strategic points along the coast and occupied several cities. One of the few Chinese victories took place when some militia troops outside of Canton successfully resisted a British incursion. In the course of the war, Lin was recalled and punished, and the power to deal with the English was placed in the hands of more accommodating officials. The fighting ended in 1842 with the Treaty of Nanking, which was soon followed by similar agreements with the other Western powers.

Taken together, these were the first of the so-called unequal treaties, which placed China in an inferior position in international relations for the next hundred years. The agreements opened four more ports to trade and abolished the restrictions on the manner and freedom of commerce within them. China ceded Hong Kong to England. Foreigners were placed under the legal jurisdiction of their own consuls, thus officially receiving the "right of extrality." The Western powers obtained a say in fixing Chinese import duties, paving the way for the nation's loss of tariff autonomy. China agreed to the concept of "the most favored nation," by which any privilege granted to one Western country would have to be granted to all. The opium question was swept under the carpet, though it was informally understood that China would not interfere with the traffic.

Neither side was satisfied with the terms of these first treaties, and for the next fifteen years Chinese officials and local groups worked in various ways to resist the opening of the new ports and to reassert their authority over the foreigners. The Westerners wanted even more privileges. War broke out again in the middle 1850s, and, once more, China was badly defeated. An Anglo-French expeditionary force took Peking in 1860, burned the imperial summer palace, and dictated a new set of treaties.

These agreements put the finishing touches on the system of unequal relations. Opium was legalized, a step that, among other things, led to its production in China, something that the land-poor country could hardly afford. China's rivers were opened to foreign ships, including gunboats. Missionaries received the right to live and proselytize anywhere in the country. More towns were opened for trade, some in the interior of the country rather than on the coast. Such treaty ports, as they came to be known, eventually existed all over China.

Within some of these towns the Westerners gradually assumed the right to open "concessions." Concessions were areas where the privilege of extrality turned into complete foreign control over part of a Chinese city. Chinese officials were excluded from authority, and both foreigners and Chinese lived, essentially, as they would have in a Western colony. The first of these concessions developed in what was to become the most important treaty port, Shanghai.

MASSIVE REBELLION

As if to confirm the old adage about the interrelationship between foreign problems and internal chaos, the two continued to go hand in hand; for now, just as the West was gaining a foothold in China, the nation's internal difficulties began to assume massive proportions. From the 1840s through the 1860s a great wave of popular rebellion swept across the land and almost succeeded in toppling the Qing Dynasty. The most famous and important of these uprisings was the Taiping Rebellion, which spread over South and Central China from 1850 to 1864. It was a mammoth event, one of the largest popular rebellions in Chinese history, and almost certainly bigger than had ever taken place anywhere else in the world.

The basic reasons behind the Taiping uprising and the other rebellions were the general problems of the nation: increasing poverty, natural disaster, alienation, frustrated ambition, and a government too weak and corrupt to tackle the problems effectively.[11] In addition, each uprising had its own special set of causes, depending on local circumstances and the sorts of people involved.

The immediate impetus to the Taiping Rebellion was the dissatisfaction of a minority group in Southeast China, in the provinces of Guangdong and Guangxi, where the revolt began. These were the so-called Hakka, or guest families. The Hakka were descended from people who had come from North China in the late Tang and Song. They remained, however, comparatively unassimilated into the local society, spoke their own dialect, and had some special customs. They also suffered discrimination at the hands of the local majority, and conflict between Hakkas and others was often a spark for political and social conflict. Hakkas provided the basic cadre for the rebellion in its early stages, and discrimination against them was an important source of discontent.

In addition to the special circumstances of the Hakkas, the Western presence at Canton, the chief seaport of Guangdong, added fuel to local problems. The government had suffered a loss of prestige among the nationalistic people of the South through its easy defeat at the hands of the foreigners. In addition, the shift of trade to other ports in the aftermath of the Opium War resulted in commercial dislocations in the area and added to its economic woes.

The founder of the Taiping movement was a Hakka, Hong Xiuquan. He was from a farming family of moderate means. However, as a child he showed considerable intellectual promise, and his relations scraped together the money to supply him with a good education, one that aimed ultimately at degree-holding status. This would have placed a heavy responsibility on him to succeed even in the best of times, of course, and the problems of the age made such pressures all the greater. Not only did the economic situation mean that it was harder to provide a child with an education, thus increasing what was expected of him, but the rise in population made it harder to succeed. For example, despite the fact that there were more than twice as many people as in the early Qing, the examination quotas had not been enlarged.

Hong managed to become a schoolteacher, an honorable but low-paying job. However, he was repeatedly frustrated in his attempts to obtain a degree. He took the exams three times without success, in 1833, 1837, and 1843. It is significant and exemplary of the lurking danger that frustrated social mobility could pose for the system that the other major organizer of the rebellion, Feng Yunshan, was also an unsuccessful candidate for degree-holding status. Later in the century, when broad dissatisfaction among the elite joined the misery of the laboring majority, the whole system would come tumbling down.

The exams that Hong took were held in Canton. During his first trip there in 1833 he heard a Christian missionary preaching and received a number of Bible tracts and sermons. Hong, we are told, glanced at them, put them away, and forgot about them. After his second failure in 1837 he seems to have had a nervous breakdown. He took to bed, the later stories said, for forty days and forty nights, often in delirium. In his illness Hong had dreams in which he was carried to heaven, where he met an old man. The old man said that the human race had forgotten him and forsaken him and was worshipping demons and perverted spirits; he called Confucius evil and told Hong to combat him and his demon followers. At another meeting with the old man Hong met a middle-aged man whom he called "elder brother." In Hong's delirium his family heard him say things like "Slay the demons! Slay the demons!"

Hong recovered from the illness. As before, he continued to teach school; however, he displayed an added dignity and sense of purpose and felt himself the recipient of some divine commission as yet unclear. At this time he took the new name Xiuquan, which means "accomplished and complete" and may also allude to the lowest examination degree, the one for which Hong was trying, the xiucai, "accomplished talent." Whatever else was on his mind, Hong was still interested in passing the exams, and he took them for the third and last time in 1843.

After this failure he chanced upon the Christian tracts that he had earlier received. After he looked at them, his dreams fell into place. He decided that the old man was God, the Heavenly Father of the Christians, that the middle-aged man was Jesus Christ, and that he, Hong, was the younger brother of Christ.

His divine commission was to destroy Confucianism, to slay the demon Manchus who dominated China, and to bring the nation to the true Christian faith and to a perfected society.

Hong began to preach and to gain followers, though he emphasized religious matters and kept his political dreams to himself. In the mid–1840s he founded the God Worshippers Society, primarily a religious group and Hakka fraternal organization. However, as social problems continued and the society gained cohesion, it became increasingly military in character, a local militia for the protection of poor Hakkas. As it grew in size, Hong began to make explicit his anti-Qing views and his plans for an uprising, attracting still more followers.

The God Worshippers openly proclaimed rebellion in 1850 in the hamlet of Jintian. By this time Hong had an army of twenty thousand. They began to march north, and as they moved, they attracted increasing non-Hakka support, though the leaders continued to be from the minority. In general, the uprising remained a movement of farmers and other workers, though it also attracted scattered elite support. Hong's followers met with great success as they went, their triumphs abetted by their own military effectiveness and the misery of the people they encountered, as well as by the incompetence of the government officials and armed forces along the way.

In 1851, on the march, Hong officially announced the establishment of a new political order, the Taiping Tianguo. Literally, this means ''Heavenly Kingdom of Great Peace'' and implies the salvation of the world in a Christian sense. As we have seen, however, taiping (Great Peace) was also a synonym for datong, and so the new government was also proclaiming that it was the Heavenly Kingdom of the Great Community. Hong styled himself the Tian Wang, or Heavenly King.

In 1853 the Taiping forces captured Nanking on the Yangtze River in central China, the second most important city in the country and formerly one of the capitals of the Ming Dynasty. By this time the organization had two million members. The Taipings renamed Nanking (literally Southern Capital) Tianjing (Heavenly Capital). The Yangtze valley and, most importantly, the densely populated and economically powerful area near the mouth of the river remained the heartland of the kingdom until the end. From here the new government launched forays and expeditions in all directions. One daring thrust almost reached Peking. Rebellions were going on at the same time in other places, but the Taipings themselves entered sixteen of China's eighteen provinces and captured six hundred cities at one time or another.

Perhaps the most striking thing about the Taipings was their fanaticism, which was grounded in several factors. One was clearly the character of Hong himself. To put it bluntly, he may have been, and in all likelihood was, seriously unbalanced mentally. Such individual factors, of course, influence history and can do so basically. However, the fanatic spirit of the movement had other and more general roots as well.

The most important was that the Taipings were in uncharted waters historically, for in the nineteenth century China was not merely at the end of a particular dynasty but also at the close of the junxian era. In historic times, it was a time comparable only to the first transition from fengjian to junxian in ancient China and, to a lesser extent, perhaps, the final triumph of the junxian system in the late Tang and Song. In addition, the Taipings were committed to establishing the Great Community. This goal had long been a feature of the junxian opposition, but those explicitly committed to setting it up had rarely, if ever, come to power. As a result, the Taipings were operating in an unprecedented historical moment and working to create a new and untried social order. This sort of situation can easily breed extremism.

Finally, the movement took place in a time of increasing chaos and misery, an era of crisis involving hundreds of millions of people. This situation encouraged a desire to transcend the past and fed the dream of starting from scratch at building a new cultural order. Such times and attitudes do not encourage moderation. Such feelings were particularly powerful because for the two hundred years of the Qing, a conservative elite had been committed to the status quo, and the opposition had rested almost entirely on the average citizen. This was still the situation in the mid-nineteenth century and meant that the Taipings had both long-term and immediate reasons for a fanatic hostility to the existing system and those who benefited from it.

Contributing to the fanaticism of the Taipings and, in addition to it, the most striking thing about the movement was that the rebellion was the first major example of borrowing from the West in the Chinese revolution. In the future such borrowing would assume massive proportions, and the influence of the Occident on the rebellion is paradigmatic of what was to occur later. Most importantly, the Taipings did not assimilate things randomly but, as might be expected, absorbed aspects of Western culture that could support their basic needs and goals within China. What they borrowed is understandable if one bears in mind that the West possessed new and unprecedentedly effective forms of production, was moving from fengjian to junxian, and had become fervently committed to the notion of transcendent progress.

Overall, in the nineteenth and twentieth centuries, the new industrial and scientific techniques of the West were of interest to China because they suggested ways of alleviating the nation's grave economic problems. The still powerful fengjian side of the Occident (and in some cases even tribal characteristics, which were relatively vibrant as compared to China) could support the datong ideal of supplementing the junxian system with the strengths of the past and provide examples of traditions and attitudes that had long been lost in China. Finally, the Western faith in progress, the fervent belief that the past could be transcended and a new order created, had great appeal for Chinese revolutionaries, troubled and disillusioned with their own society and values and eager to begin afresh.

These elements are already evident in the relationship between the Taipings and the West. For them the most important import was the idea of transcendent change. This was the basic way in which the Occident contributed to the fanaticism of the movement, particularly as the message was delivered by the fervent, evangelical, and exclusively minded Protestant missionaries of the mid-nineteenth century. In addition, fengjian aspects of Western culture helped to provide the Taipings with their spiritual drive, discipline, and effectiveness in the field of battle. Overall, science and technology were not of great interest to the movement; however, toward the close of the rebellion, some leaders also began to urge attention to such matters.

Aside from the particular fanaticism of the Taipings and the fact that they came under Western influence, the rebellion was squarely in the tradition of popular opposition as it had developed in the junxian era. Thus, the uprising was religious, anti-Confucian, nationalistic, and committed to the datong.

The role of Christianity was very similar to the part that Buddhism and other traditional faiths had played in earlier rebellions, particularly those inspired by a belief in the coming of the Maitreya, the Buddha of the paradise on earth. Indeed, there were outbreaks based on Maitreya Buddhism in the nineteenth century. However, like all Chinese outlooks, this belief may have been infected and hence weakened by the humanistic skepticism of junxian China. This possibility provides the likely reason why the major rebellion of the time emerged from a Christian group and also helps to explain why other great outbursts in the middle of the century were inspired by Islam, another faith comparatively unaffected by Chinese ways.

Like the influence of earlier religions, the Christianity of the Taipings contributed to the movement's belief in the possibility of fundamental change and to its zeal, organizational coherence, and sense of mission. It provided a baseline for opposing the Confucian orthodoxy and gave a boost to the notion of human equality. In particular, the most important concepts that the Taipings found in Christianity were monotheism and the redeeming nature of Christ on earth, which translated into the idea of God, the unique Father, and of Hong Xiuquan as his son, the new messiah who followed Christ to establish the good order on earth under the protection of the Lord.

Hong wrote:

> It seems to me that though the people of the world are many, they are all created by God and born of God. Not only are they born of God, they also depend on him for growth, and for their clothing and food. God is the Great Father, common to all people on earth. Death, life, calamity, and happiness are all in his hands. . . . If, out of anger, God should one day cut short your spiritual breath and life, would you be able to talk with your mouth, see with your eyes, hear with your ears, hold with your hands, walk with your feet, or make plans with your minds? Surely you would not. Let me ask again, is it possible, even for a moment, for the whole world not to receive grace from God? Certainly not. From this it will be seen that God is unmistakably present to give men protection.[12]

Elsewhere he wrote:

God is omnipotent and the son born to him could not be injured by the serpent. Behold I testify to the truth myself. In former times Melchisedec was I, and after the Elder Brother [Christ] had ascended, the child born of the sunclad woman was myself also: now the Father and Elder Brother have come down and brought me to be the lord especially to exterminate this serpent. Lo! The serpents and beasts are slain and the empire enjoys Great Peace. It is fulfilled.

The Taipings also emphasized the Ten Commandments, Sabbath, and baptism. They had the Old Testament attitude toward idols and rival beliefs and spoke a lot about heaven and hell, angels and devils. Their intense exclusiveness and sense of right and wrong gave added power to their nationalism, for they attacked the Manchu government not simply as barbaric but as the work of devils and imps who were blocking the work of God and the triumph of righteousness.

Hong wrote:

China is a spiritual continent, and the barbarians are devils. The reason China is called a spiritual continent is because our Heavenly Father, the Lord on High, is the true spirit who made heaven and earth and the mountains and rivers; therefore, in former times China was designated the spiritual continent. . . . Before Father descended to the earth, China belonged to Father, and yet the barbarian devils stole into Father's Kingdom. This is the reason Father decreed that I should come to destroy them.[13]

In addition to bolstering nationalism, the religion of the Taipings also gave them an unusually powerful baseline for attacking Confucianism. A Taiping book recorded that God said to Hong:

"These are the books left behind by Confucius, and also the books you read when you were in the world and even you have been spoiled by studying them." Then the Heavenly Father reprimanded Confucius, saying, "Why did you instruct people in such a way as to confuse them so that they do not even recognize me, and your name has become greater than mine?" At first Confucius still wanted to argue with God, but later he became silent, having nothing to say. . . . Seeing that everyone in the high heaven pronounced him guilty Confucius stealthily crept off and tried to go down into the world, thinking of escaping with the devil leader. But the Heavenly Father sent the Lord and the angels chasing after Confucius, and had him bound and dragged before Him. God was very angry and told the angels to flog him. Confucius appealed to Jesus for mercy. Thereupon, the Heavenly Father . . . allowed him to stay in heaven and enjoy happiness, thinking of his past merits, which balanced up his sins. But he was prohibited from going back to earth.[14]

The end of this story suggests that, at some level, the Taipings were respectful of the beneficial impact that Confucianism had on Chinese life, and they did, in fact, extol such things as the datong portions of the *Book of Rites*. On the whole, however, they strongly opposed the philosophy and all other traditional thought. Thus, in one decree reminiscent of the book burning of the Qin Dynasty, they even ordered that at present the books on the true doctrine are three in number, namely *The Sacred Book of the Old Testament*, *The Sacred Book of the New Testament*, and *The Book of Heavenly Decrees and Proclamations* [of the Taiping government]. All the works by Confucius, Mencius, and the philosophers of the hundred schools should be committed to the flames.[15]

In response both to the moral decay they saw around themselves and to the specific teachings of the missionaries, the Taipings were very puritanical, if not always in practice, at least in theory. Indeed, one of the particular appeals of evangelical Christianity was that its critique of China was often in harmony with that of Chinese radicals. The rebels banned alcohol, tobacco, and opium, and they established strict rules for relations between the sexes. Such policies, like so much of Taiping practice, were also aimed at bolstering the military effectiveness of the movement.

Military might was essential to the uprising from beginning to end, and the fighting power of the Taipings was extraordinary, especially as compared to the general weakness and corruption of most armies in late junxian China. Their power, of course, rested to a considerable degree on the vigorous traditions of warfare to which their religion gave access: the tribal and fengjian sides of Old Testament and European culture. The Taipings marched into battle singing hymns, zealous and disciplined, in a manner reminiscent of the Puritan armies of Oliver Cromwell. Above all, they too had the strength that came from the certainty of God's support.

As one Taiping book said, God

ordered the Savior, the Heavenly Elder Brother Jesus to take command of the heavenly soldiers and the heavenly generals and to aid the Heavenly King, and to attack and conquer from Heaven earthward, layer by layer, the innumerable demons. After their victories they returned to Heaven and the Heavenly Father, greatly pleased, sent the Heavenly King down upon the earth to become the true Taiping Sovereign of the ten thousand nations of the world, and to save the people of the world. He also bade him not to be fearful and to effect these matters courageously, for whenever difficulties appeared, the Heavenly Father would assume direction and the Heavenly Elder Brother would shoulder the burden.[16]

As might be expected, given the name of the new order, support for the Great Community was also an important feature of Taiping thought and organization. First of all, the Taipings stressed that society should relate like one family and were particularly fond of the passages to this effect in the *Book of Rites*, passages that had been particularly influential in establishing the datong tradition. Christian notions of the fatherhood of God and the brotherhood of man, of course, bolstered such ideas, and it is likely that the special emphasis that the Taipings placed on these aspects of Christianity came partly from the need to justify a familial view of society and, in fact, of the world.

''Speaking separately,'' a Taiping decree said, ''the world is composed of ten thousand countries; but speaking from the standpoint of unity, there is only one family. . . . All men in the world are brothers, and all women are sisters. How can it be right for us to entertain selfish distinctions between this and that, how can it be right for us to entertain the idea of mutual annihilation?''[17]

Second, the Taipings had the egalitarian ideals that formed an additional part of the datong approach. Their concept of social organization was inspired by the *Rites of Zhou*, which, like the *Book of Rites*, had exerted a particular influence on the tradition. In the Taiping plan, all families were grouped into units of twenty-five under a civil-military official, and these, in turn, were to be organized into larger and larger units reaching into the thousands. Within each unit there was to be communal control of property. In addition, all land was to be graded by quality and evenly divided among families. Besides farming, each family was also expected to do another sort of productive labor, such as handicrafts. All produce from the land and other work was to go into a central treasury and then be distributed according to need. As one Taiping book put it, ''Since we were all born of the same father of souls, why should there be any distinction between you and me or between others and ourselves? Where there are clothes, let us wear them together; where there is food, let us enjoy it together.''[18]

One particularly democratic aspect of the movement was its concern for women's rights. This was in line with the tradition of popular opposition, which sometimes gave a more equal place to women than was common in junxian China. In addition, it grew out of Hakka customs, which were also more egalitarian than the norm. The Hakkas may have had such traditions because they began migrating to the south in the late Tang and so maintained certain attitudes of that era, a time when the status of women was higher than it was to become later on. Western attitudes toward women, which were also more like those of the late fengjian age, supported this outlook, as did the democratic aspects of Christianity with regard to gender relations.

As in the equal-field system of the Tang, women received land under Taiping law on the same basis as men. Foot binding, which had never taken hold among the Hakkas, was forbidden. Women also fought in the Taiping armies: ''When revolution broke out in Jintian, all members of the God Worshippers joined with their families, so there were many women with the army. . . . They were good at using firearms and were dead shots. The morale of the Qing army was often broken by their presence.''[19]

Women could even sit for the examinations that the new regime established and take up official posts. It was reported that once ''more than two hundred women came to take the examinations. Fu Shanxiang, daughter of Fu Huai of Jinling came out first; her essay, in which she refuted the idea [that female servants are] 'difficult to teach' . . . met with great approval from the Heavenly King.''[20] The theme of the examination refers to one of the few statements in the Confucian *Analects* that can be construed as sexist.

Despite the egalitarian and democratic thrust of Taiping thought, there were some serious limitations in the degree to which the Taipings carried out their desires or even wished to carry them out. The socioeconomic program, for example, was put into operation only in Nanking and in some rural areas nearby. These were the only places that the rebels controlled steadily for many years. Elsewhere, though, they did establish administrative and tax procedures that were more honest and efficient than what the Qing had been providing.

A more serious problem in regard to democracy is that the Taipings established a strongly hierarchical political system in which the rulers were a class by themselves, with power and perquisites like those of a ruling dynasty. For example, while enjoining celibacy on others, Hong and his fellow leaders had vast harems. One reason for such disparities in Taiping behavior sprang, perhaps, from contradictions in the concept of the Great Community between the notions of society as a great family and the notions of egalitarianism. The former image suggested a patriarchy with a strong sense of hierarchy, and this influenced Taiping behavior. More concretely, the concept of an all-powerful ruler with vast privileges had been a part of the Chinese system for so long that sheer inertia kept it in place, and alternatives were not readily evident. Later, one of the greatest contributions of the West to the Chinese revolution would come when Western liberalism was understood as a way of reviving earlier and more democratic approaches toward governance. Indeed, near the close of the rebellion, at least one leader, Hong Rengan, began to sense such possibilities in Western thought.

Finally, in line with the third feature of datong thought, the Taipings were also concerned with combining the best in the past into a new synthesis and, specifically, bringing together the benefits of fengjian and junxian. This concern is evident in their sociopolitical structure. Thus, Hong the supreme ruler was called a *wang*, "king," in the style of the fengjian Xia, Shang, and Zhou Dynasties, rather than huangdi, "emperor," in later junxian fashion. In addition, Hong enfeoffed various other kings, including some who were to be given control over different parts of the country. Other efforts to restore fengjian approaches can be seen in the use of the local political and economic units derived from the *Rites of Zhou*, in efforts to reinstitute a sense of hereditary class, and, of course, in the hostility of the Taipings toward the marketplace, and in their military and religious spirit.

Nonetheless, the circumstances in which the Taipings found themselves also created problems for implementing this aspect of the Great Community. Most importantly, as we have noted, their intense hostility to the status quo coupled with Western influences generally made them aim at a complete break with the Chinese past, transcending it rather than using it creatively. As a result their revitalization of earlier approaches was more intuitive than it might otherwise have been and probably less effective, compounding the already immense difficulties that they faced from sailing in uncharted historical waters.

Ultimately, the Taiping rebellion failed to achieve victory. One reason for this failure was excessive decentralization within the new government. The various kings ran their own administrations and were constantly bickering and competing with one another and with Hong. In addition, Christianity, an untried religion, was difficult to translate into an effective political philosophy. Several of the kings claimed divine revelations equal to those of Hong and used them as weapons in their internecine battles. The culmination of such problems came in 1856, when a bitter struggle broke out among the leaders in Nanking. Hong survived, but most of the original founders of the movement and thousands of their followers slaughtered one another. The Heavenly Kingdom lasted eight more years, but the rebellion had lost its momentum.

The more basic reason why the Taipings failed, however, was that they were never able to gain significant support within the elite and virtually none at all among degree-holders. Most of the influential people in society felt that their basic interests lay with the government and the existing system, not with the opposition and most certainly not with fanatic revolutionaries bent on overturning the entire social order. At the same time, the average member of the elite was repulsed by the anti-Confucianism of the Taipings and by their Christian beliefs. From the point of view of the upper echelons of society, Christianity was simply a superstitious religion, inappropriate and dangerous as a guide to social action.

THE ELITE HOLDS FIRM: THE TONGZHI RESTORATION

The overall response of the establishment to the crisis of mid-century China goes by the name of the Tongzhi Restoration. The idea of a *zhongxing*, "restoration," reviving a dynasty after a period of breakdown and the trauma of major rebellion, was a hallowed one in Chinese tradition. There had been famous restorations in the Han and Tang dynasties. The name for the restoration of the 1860s comes from the young emperor who ascended the throne in 1862 and was given the reign title Tongzhi. In retrospect, the Tongzhi Restoration was not simply an attempt to save the Qing Dynasty but also the last cohesive effort to reform and preserve junxian China. A classic work on the period is, appropriately enough, called *The Last Stand of Chinese Conservatism.*[21]

The best symbol of the restoration was its leader, Zeng Guofan. Zeng was a model of orthodox Confucianism, a man of great personal honesty and rectitude. As Mary Wright wrote in *The Last Stand*, Zeng's diary bore testimony to his "sternness and austerity." As "a young man he had evidently enjoyed 'opium, women, and improper talk'; in his early thirties he dropped opium completely, but continued to censure himself for lapses on the other two counts. . . . He wrote his brother that he feared he might be spending too much time in calligraphy and study at the expense of more direct duties: writing memorials and investigating officials."[22] Though a high official, Zeng often wore shabby old clothes; he was frugal and avoided ostentation. In a sense his character, the best that orthodox Confucianism could produce by that point, bore testimony to the populist spirit that affected even the most established members of society after a thousand years of the junxian system.

Nevertheless, Zeng emphasized the hierarchical side of Confucianism. Like any Confucian, he understood the importance of public welfare and a sound political order to maintaining a good society and heading off rebellion. However, he laid greater stress on the fact that China's crisis had developed because of a breakdown in social stratification. Disregard for social "differentiation," he wrote, "in the end results in disorder in the empire, indeed until beasts are led to consume human beings."[23] Zeng's immediate purpose was to put down rebellion. Then he wanted to restore the quality, morale, and effectiveness of the elite and, in particular, of the degree-holders. In this way he hoped to revive the government and to bring stability and health to society.

The basic technique that Zeng and the restoration used to suppress unrest was the creation of armies made up of local militia units under the control of local degree-holders. These armies varied in size, but the hallmark of the movement became great provincial forces. For example, Zeng's own rise to prominence in the 1850s and 1860s rested initially on the army that he welded together from local corps in his home province of Hunan.

In the Hunan army, which served as a model for others, Zeng stressed the morale of the troops. Initially, at least, they were fairly paid. They were indoctrinated with the values of honesty and loyalty that Zeng himself represented. They were, of course, also heavily educated in the need to quell rebellion, but this need was not envisioned simply in terms of battling the enemy. The Hunan troops were also supposed to win the support of the people through their good behavior. For example, there were strict rules, not unlike those of the Taipings, forbidding looting and violence against noncombatants, both long-standing traditions among government troops.

Further to strengthen their armies, Zeng and the leaders of the restoration began to arm them with modern, Western weapons. At the time of the Opium War, Western military hardware had made a deep impression on some officials, including Lin Zexu. The restoration, however, was the first major instance in the nineteenth century in which the elite began to borrow from the West, and the foreign influence fits the general pattern of Sino-Western interactions.

The interest grew out of the exigencies of internal politics, in this case the desire to put down rebellion. At the same time, modern weaponry was a product both of the powerful fengjian tendencies within the Occident and of its new developments in science and technology. The faith in transcendent progress, the aspect of the West that had held so much appeal for the Taipings and would continue to influence the opposition, did not, of course, make an impact on the elite at this time, for it was still basically on the side of the status quo.

The government imported weapons and established a few modern arsenals. The foreign military hardware gave the armies that received it a great advantage over the rebels, still armed, for the most part, with outdated Chinese arms. In addition, the armies of the restoration also recruited some Western soldiers. One of these was the famous "Chinese Gordon," who later died at Khartoum at the hands of the Mahdi and became one of the subjects of Lytton Strachey's *Eminent Victorians*. Gordon's "Ever-Victorious Army" helped to defend the area near Shanghai from Taiping onslaughts. Such direct Western assistance was not the basic reason why the government forces defeated the Taipings, though it proved of some significance in the last stages of the war.

The Taiping Rebellion ended in 1864 with the fall of Nanking. By the end of the decade all the other important rebellions were also quelled. However, the broader reforms at which the restoration aimed did not succeed. The downward slide in which society found itself had simply gone too far. At the same time, widespread rebellion, as always, exacerbated the government's problems. Most importantly, however, the restoration failed because it depended for success on the very group that, at least in the short run, was the least affected by the nation's difficulties (except insofar as they faced the danger of revolution) and the most likely to be implicated in the problems themselves.

The desire to improve the quality of the ruling elite was, in some ways, contravened from the start by what was happening in the Manchu imperial family. Here, at the top of society, things grew increasingly worse. The ascension of the Tongzhi emperor had been engineered by his mother, Cixi, through a bloody coup. As the empress dowager, she continued to dominate the court from then on. Her power violated one of the prime rules of the Qing, that the imperial harem should not interfere in politics. When the Tongzhi emperor died in 1874, supposedly through dissolute behavior encouraged by his mother, the empress again controlled the succession. She chose her three-year-old nephew, who came to the throne as the Guangxu emperor. His accession was again illegal in that it violated prescribed rules of succession in terms of generations, but it assured that Cixi would retain control.

The empress dowager was effective at wielding power, but she was an unethical person, with a reputation for corruption and decadence. She was not alone. Prince Gong, the most important Manchu official in the 1860s and for many years thereafter, was also a talented administrator but widely known for financial peculation. As a result, there was no real example of honesty and integrity where Confucian theory said they were most essential, at the top.

Still, Zeng and his fellow reformers tried. They were constantly searching for honest and talented men to bring into public service. Among other things, they created extra-bureaucratic coteries of administrators, who became their personal secretaries. This step not only aimed at improving the government but was also meant to relieve the employment crisis among the nation's degree-holders and, hence, to raise their morale and commitment.

Zeng also tried to improve the chances for success among people who sought degree-holding status but who had grown poor as a result of the general decline in living standards and the chaos of rebellion. The restoration government gave out monetary relief and revived the system of higher education. At the same time, it reestablished the examinations where they had been disrupted and increased the quotas of those who could pass. Such policies, however, proved to be mere palliatives and, in any case, affected only a very small group, even of the social stratum that was involved.

One of Zeng's particular concerns was to limit the sale of degrees and of government positions. A small-scale traffic in titles and office was a long-standing practice going back to the beginnings of the Qing. In the freewheeling atmosphere of junxian China it was considered a reasonable way of raising funds for the government and of creating an alternate way to attain a degree or a job. However, as the government became pressed for money, it had increased the sale and given out more significant positions, reaching a point where the enterprise was considered a serious impediment to administrative effectiveness. Those who bought their jobs tended, for obvious reasons, to be more corrupt than the norm. The sale also hurt the morale of all those who sought positions through the regular path of the examinations and further limited their opportunities for employment. This situation was the reason that the restoration was particularly concerned about such problems. However, as a result of the government's insatiable need for money and the added costs of war and chaos, far from a reduction in sales in the 1860s, things became even worse.

The chief arena in which the government needed immediate reform and to which the restoration paid particularly close attention was on the local level. There the magistrate and his staff of subordinates handled the bulk of actual contacts with the people. Administrative decay and corruption on the local scene, often with the connivance of powerful elite families, were a major cause for rebellion. Unjust taxation, for example, had become a particularly serious problem.

The restoration could do nothing substantial on this front, however, in the face of deeply entrenched special interests that, in fact, often included the very people whom the reformers relied upon and were trying to help. Indeed, as with so much else, things, in general, seemed to become worse. For example, local magistracies were often for sale after the Taiping Rebellion. In addition to encouraging corruption, this situation meant a rapid turnover of personnel and a lowering of standards. At the same time, it gave local notables, permanently on the scene, greater opportunities for mischief.

With the failure to restore the quality of local government went the collapse of any attempt to reform taxation. There was some temporary improvement in places, but unjust practices quickly returned. The powerful evaded their fair share, and surcharges were collected all along the line. When the restoration leaders established a new tax on commerce, the *likin*, partly to relieve the pressure on farmers, it quickly became a notoriously corrupt scourge on economic life.

Overall, when Zeng looked over his accomplishments, he was deeply discouraged. He had not improved the quality of the degree-holders: "One might happen to run across" good men, he wrote, "but they cannot be found when one looks for them."[24] He had not improved administration: "There was not the slightest improvement in local government in my jurisdiction and I am extremely ashamed." Eventually, Zeng himself came in for criticism. One friend wrote that he was no longer "strong enough in his hatred of evil, gradually becoming inured and flexible instead of retaining an upright and uncompromising spirit."

5

The Fall of the Qing

INTRODUCTION: THE TRIUMPH OF THE OPPOSITION

From the 1870s onward, with the failure of the Tongzhi Restoration, disillusionment with China's problems spread ever more widely through society. Most significantly, important segments of the elite began to form an open and organized opposition. Such activity had, hitherto, been limited largely to popular groups with a laboring constituency. As a result, for the first time since the closing years of the Ming Dynasty, a single great movement for change began to form. In 1911 this movement overthrew the Qing, the junxian order, and the imperial system. By 1949 it resulted in the establishment of the People's Republic of China. The last decades of the nineteenth century and the early years of the twentieth are, therefore, of immense importance and represent one of the major turning points in Chinese history.

As members of the elite began to organize themselves against those in power, they generally did so as reformers and radicals, not as advocates of revolution or of datong ideals. Indeed, their activities still sprang, to some extent, from the fear of popular rebellion. Nonetheless, like everyone else, they felt increasingly insecure economically and disenfranchised politically. At the same time, they were deeply troubled by the general decline in standards and morality within society and were unalterably opposed to imperialism. For these reasons elite and popular dissent began to blend with comparative rapidity, testimony not only to shared problems but also to the weak class lines of the late junxian era and to long-standing traditions of opposition, dating back indirectly to the ancient era and directly to the Song.

One initial aim of the elite radicals was to bring greater democracy to the authoritarian and highly centralized structure of the Qing imperial system and to solve their own problems and those of the nation by working to relegitimize the notion of an open and organized opposition. Their other goal was to heighten nationalism and to unite the Chinese people against internal breakdown and foreign aggression. Both of these purposes, however, brought them closer to the popular movement for change, for not only were democracy and nationalism also associated with this opposition, but, by their very nature, they were aims that worked to reopen channels of communication among different levels of society. As a result, by the 1890s, though radicalism in the upper echelons of society still opposed rebellion, its most dynamic representatives had become increasingly sympathetic to datong approaches and advocated reforms that called for revolutionary change. This, in turn, set the stage for the reunification of the opposition, which developed by 1911.

As the elite turned to radicalism, it came under increasing Western influence. In general, this did not yet encompass the notion of transcendent change and of a total break with Chinese tradition as it had for the Taiping rebels. On the other hand, like the leaders of the Tongzhi Restoration, those involved soon showed a deep interest in Western science and technology. At the same time, they grew to appreciate the suggestive possibilities that Western thought and institutions presented for trimming the excesses of the junxian order with the benefits of the past and, thus, supporting the ideals of the Great Community. As a result, by the early twentieth century, the impact of the West had become immense and the next generation would espouse a sharp break with the Chinese past.

THE SELF-STRENGTHENING MOVEMENT

The first major indication that a sense of crisis was brewing within the elite was the so-called Self-strengthening or Foreign Affairs Movement of the 1870s and 1880s.[1] The Self-strengthening Movement was basically aimed at creating a national effort, led by the government, to introduce Western industry and communications into China. Its leader was Li Hongzhang, a former aide to Zeng Guofan, who had risen to prominence during the battles against the Taipings. In 1870, Li became governor-general of Chihli (since renamed Hebei), the strategically placed province in which Peking is located. He remained in the post for twenty-five years and from there presided over the efforts at economic development.

The self-strengtheners generally represented the highest levels of the Chinese government, and Li himself was probably the most powerful official in the nation. At the same time, they often seemed narrowly concerned with China's foreign problems. The movement, therefore, cannot properly be called part of the developing opposition. Nevertheless, those involved were deeply aware that China stood at a crucial turning-point in her history and by no means advocated a simple continuation of the status quo. "An exhausted situation leads to change," they were fond of quoting from the *Yijing*, "and this change then leads to success."[2] As a result, their work had something of a critical flavor and, in particular, showed a basic dissatisfaction with the laissez-faire economic arrangements of the junxian era.

In the short run, the Self-strengthening Movement grew out of the Tongzhi Restoration and the intellectuals of the early nineteenth century who had revived the school of "practical statecraft." More broadly, however, it looked back to early phases in the development of the junxian system, when fengjian influences were still strong and the government had assumed a far more active role in economic life than it did later on.

Thus, the most famous slogan of the movement, "Enrich the State and Strengthen the Military," is particularly associated with the Qin Dynasty, which had brought the ancient junxian phase to completion, and with Wang Anshi of the early Song, the beginning of the later junxian era. Indeed, the term *self-strengthening*, itself from the *Yijing*, had first been used in its economic sense in the Song, when an official concerned with border defense used it to suggest that the government initiate economic policies aimed at resisting the nomad incursions that were then engulfing the nation.

In a similar vein, the immediate goal of the self-strengtheners was to meet the Western onslaught by encouraging the material developments that had made the Occident a threat to China. As Xue Fucheng, a leading figure in the movement, wrote:

> Western nations rely on intelligence and energy to compete with one another. To come abreast of them, China should plan to promote commerce and open mines; unless we change, the Westerners will be rich and we poor. We should excel in technology and the manufacture of machinery; unless we change, they will be skillful and we clumsy. Steamships, trains, and the telegraph should be adopted; unless we change, the Westerners will be quick and we slow.[3]

And Li Hongzhang put such hopes by writing:

> The method of self-strengthening lies in learning what they can do, and in taking over what they rely upon. Moreover, their possession of guns, cannon, and steamships began only within the last hundred years or so, and their progress has been so fast that their influence has spread into China. If we can really and thoroughly understand their methods—and the more we learn, the more improve—and promote them further and further, can we not expect that after a century or so we can reject the barbarians and stand on our own feet?[4]

In addition to their foreign concerns, the self-strengtheners also hoped that economic development, by raising the living standards of the people, might also provide a way of solving China's internal problems. Another common theme of the movement was *fu min* or *li min*, to enrich the people, to improve their livelihood. It was for this reason, for example, the Xue Fucheng called Western technology and the possibilities it presented for human progress "a most wonderful phenomenon in the universe."[5] Overall, however, the self-strengtheners were not broadly concerned with reform aside from their desire to involve the government in economic development. They had little or no interest in directly attacking the injustices of society or its rampant corruption and debilitating moral vacuity.

Indeed, like the Tongzhi Restoration, a final purpose of the movement was to strengthen the Qing government so as to keep down rebellion. There was, in fact, a noticeable decline in popular unrest in the 1870s and 1880s. This was, to some extent, simply a matter of timing. One wave of rebellion had been defeated, and another had not yet gathered force. In addition, the death and desolation of the vast mid-century revolts may have reduced population pressures and left unused resources available for exploitation. However, the fact that, from the restoration onward, those in power had foreign arms that gave them a tremendous edge over rebels also played an important role. The self-strengtheners, deeply committed to social order, worked to maintain the advantage.

The Self-strengthening Movement did succeed in opening a few modern arsenals, factories, and mines and in establishing some railway and telegraph lines. However, it made almost no dent on China's basic economic problems, let alone in improving the life of the people or resisting imperialism. The plans failed partly for sheer economic reasons: China's huge, poverty-stricken population left little surplus available for investment. In addition, manpower was cheap and, at least in the short run, depended on traditional ways of doing things for employment.

In addition, there were difficulties in administering the program. These sprang to a considerable extent from the powerful laissez-faire traditions of the late junxian era. There was little experience with economic activism on the part of the government and often little support for it, a situation made all the worse by the corrupt character of the late Qing bureaucracy and the general problems of society.

The self-strengtheners found it difficult to raise taxes for their projects, and considerable tension developed in their efforts to find an effective relationship to the private sector. As a result, businessmen complained repeatedly about excessive interference on the part of officials or lack of support from them. At the same time, the officials involved were often accused of peculation or protecting their bureaucratic bailiwick rather than helping development. Li Hongzhang, in particular, earned a reputation for voracious corruption. Such charges were partly the product of those who, viewing the Self-strengthening Movement from within the laissez-faire traditions of the time, could see an effort to "enrich the state" only as an effort to enrich government functionaries. Nonetheless, the accusations seem to have had considerable bases in fact.

Though the Self-strengthening Movement represented those in power and failed to make a direct impact on China's problems, it contributed to the general sense that the nation required fundamental change and even to the datong direction that elite opposition was eventually to take. Critics of the existing order built on the accomplishments of the movement in paving the way for the acceptance of public effort on behalf of economic progress. At the same time, they picked up the idea that the West could provide inspiration for such effort, not only in terms of new techniques but also as examples of governments actively committed to developing and maintaining effective and powerful societies.

THE ELITE JOINS THE OPPOSITION

The Qingyi Movement

In the 1870s and 1880s, while the self-strengtheners were influential, an opposition movement proper began to flourish within the elite. The movement grew out of the literary associations and schools with which critical intellectuals earlier in the century had sought to veil their political purposes. Now for the first time in the Qing, such groups began to coalesce into a coherent and important political force. The new grouping took the form of a qingyi movement. *Qingyi* literally means "pure discussion" and can more properly be understood as "critical elite opinion."[6]

Qingyi movements were a well-known form of political activity and had existed at several times in the past, particularly those marked by grave problems at home and, typically, a threat from abroad. The notion implied loyal and seriously committed members of the elite, often intellectuals and students, working outside of the centers of power for changes in incorrect and ineffective policies. It also implied, as it did in this case, that those involved formed a coherent political opposition locked in a power struggle with the officials who dominated the government.

The first qingyi movement had taken place in the waning years of the Han Dynasty, and the most recent had developed at the end of the Ming as the elite portion of the massive political and social upheavals that marked the close of that dynasty. The Ming example provided a particular model and inspiration to the qingyi of the nineteenth century. A major reason, of course, why the Qing government had forbidden organized political opposition and the elite had, for the most part, gone along, was because of the revolutionary implications of the late Ming situation. The revival of qingyi was, therefore, a clear indication of the profound disillusionment growing within the upper levels of society and of their comparative lack of concern with the broader danger that organized political activity could entail. And, in fact, the movement displayed the basic compatibility between elite radicalism and popular discontent in the late nineteenth century and provided a clear sense of why the two would recombine into a single, great opposition movement.

The qingyi drew inspiration from all the problems of China, domestic and foreign. However, its most direct stimulus to action came from the increasingly difficult economic issues that confronted the elite (as they did the average man)—problems of getting ahead and even of maintaining a person's status and that of his family. The situation was particularly burdensome for those who had aspirations toward the life of a degree-holder but were not wealthy, and this group provided the spearhead of the movement; for it had now become still more difficult to pass the examinations and to obtain suitable employment if one did.

Quotas for degrees had been enlarged during the Taiping Rebellion and the restoration. However, the increases had gone almost entirely to areas that could make substantial financial contributions to the government and so had benefited only a few wealthy places. In addition, the rise in the sale of degrees heavily favored those who remained prosperous. As a result, it has been estimated that two-fifths of those who received the highest degree came from the richest province, Jiangsu, and of the 1,450,000 degree-holders, more than a third had obtained their status through purchase.[7] Thus, the examination system, one of the bastions of the junxian system, had itself become a virtual marketplace.

In addition, for those who did obtain a degree, the chances of finding a good job were often poor. The depressed economic situation limited all forms of activity. In particular, the chances for a successful career in government, traditionally the most prestigious and often the most lucrative form of employment for the upper elite, were not good, for the continued and widespread sale of office limited the number of positions available. At the same time, many young men had moved ahead quickly in the mid-century era of rebellion and restoration and still monopolized the best jobs.

As a result, those involved in the qingyi tended to be men in their thirties and forties, youthful from the Chinese point of view. If they had degrees, the men obtained them through the regular route of examination rather than purchase. If they were in the government, they held lower-level positions and had close links with dissatisfied members of the elite on the outside. Only a handful of qingyi figures were high officials or important local notables.

Because the nation's problems were great and their own chances for influence were slim, the qingyi adherents particularly emphasized the need to expand the group that provided inputs into government policy and, ultimately, to replace those in power with their own followers. What they advocated was a *shifeng*, a spirit of vigorous political dedication and activity within the upper echelons of society. They saw themselves as the beginning of this spirit and wanted to expand it to others.

Such a shifeng would, of course, have increased the size of the movement and its own influence. At the same time, it contributed to a democratic thrust in the qingyi. Indeed, one of its frequently proclaimed goals was "to unite those above with those below" and so to bring all the people of China into a grand national effort to solve the nation's problems. This goal was one reason why the movement marked a step, however tentative, in uniting elite and popular opposition to the status quo.

In foreign affairs, the qingyi was extremely militant and opposed everything Western save, perhaps, for weaponry, which could be used against the foreigners themselves. One of their special heroes was the famous general of the Song Dynasty, Yue Fei, who had suffered martyrdom for his fervent criticism of those who were appeasing nomadic invaders. Such intense nationalism, which was closely linked to the democratic implications of the movement, was the other thing that moved it closer to the popular opposition. "What the barbarian has always feared," one qingyi member wrote, is "the consolidation of the hearts of the Chinese people."[8]

By 1890, the concrete political program of the qingyi movement stressed the need to allow all degree-holders to write memorials directly to the throne and for the elite, as a whole, to become involved in political life. At the same time, it pushed for a host of specific policies ranging from calls to clean up corruption to demands for educational reform and a halt to the sale of degrees and offices. In times of confrontation with foreigners, as with France in 1884 and Japan in 1895, the qingyi represented the war party. In everything it did, of course, the movement worked to take over the reins of power.

The immediate political targets of the qingyi were the high officials, including Li Hongzhang, the self-strengtheners, and, ultimately, the empress dowager herself. The movement attacked this establishment as corrupt, pragmatic, and even decadent. From the opposition point of view it was certainly unfit to lead the great national revival that the country required. One reason the qingyi was so hostile to Western influences was its sense that the self-strengtheners were emphasizing economic innovation as the key to China's problems precisely in order to avoid the consequences of broad-based politics and fervent nationalism. As a qingyi partisan wrote, "The superiority of China over foreign lands lies not in reliance on equipment, but in the steadfastness of the minds of the people."[9]

Through the early 1890s the movement had only limited success. One member later reported:

> The construction of palaces and parks went on, and the graft and corruption of the officials continued unchecked. Sun Youwen and Li Lianying [two creatures of the empress, the latter a notorious eunuch] dominated the government, while the officials not only kept their mouths shut but suppressed the expression of public opinion. The lower officials had to offer bribes, while the high officials, as soon as they left the court, indulged themselves in drinking and banqueting in the company of prostitutes and actors. . . . Under these conditions not only was political reform out of the question, but even the old form of government and its discipline were trampled upon.[10]

The Reform Movement of 1898

In the middle of the 1890s, however, radicalism within the elite began suddenly to increase in prominence. At the same time, it continued to move steadily closer to popular outlooks and also developed a positive attitude toward learning from the West and, indeed, came under profound foreign influence. In 1898 a leading group of reformers even came to power in Peking, and though their period of success was extremely brief, it marked the first time that radicals had achieved political victory in the late Qing and provided clear testimony to the explosive situation developing in the country.

At the most general level, the new political configuration resulted from the accumulation of earlier problems for which those in power seemed to have no solution. Among other things, popular rebellion was again on the rise, and by the mid–1890s there was endemic unrest in virtually every part of the country. In addition to providing evidence of the ineffectiveness of the government and threatening the elite directly, the revolts continued to make China easy prey to foreign aggression.

Indeed, the most immediate reason why radicalism soared after 1895 was that imperialism reached a crescendo. For most of the next decade, China became the chief object of the Occident's drive to control the world, and Japan began to join in the effort. All the elements of the unequal treaties continued to exist, and new features of foreign penetration developed, including direct seizures of Chinese territory. The beginning of the new wave of foreign pressure was marked by a disastrous war with Japan in 1894–1895. In the fighting the Chinese forces, armed with modern weapons and including a new navy that the self-strengtheners had created, were quickly overwhelmed.

The massive defeat was particularly striking and particularly humiliating because Japan was an East Asian nation that, in the previous thousand years, had received much of its higher civilization from China. Japan won basically because in the latter part of the nineteenth century, during the course of the famous Meiji Restoration, she had begun a dynamic transformation from fengjian to junxian. In this process, the internal tendencies of Japanese historical development had been important. At the same time, the West, by its own aggression against Japan, had proven both a stimulus to change and an extremely appropriate model, for the two cultures were both roughly in the same place in terms of fengjian and junxian. As a result, by the 1890s, Japan resembled the West in many ways. She had highly effective armed forces based on a lively military heritage, equal and extremely dedicated citizens, and a growing industrial base. She had also developed an imperialist ethos, which led to her moves against China.

In the Treaty of Shimonoseki, which ended the conflict, Japan annexed Taiwan, and, for the first time in the Qing, China lost a province to a foreign power. Japan also exacted a heavy indemnity and added new features to the system of unequal treaties. Among other things, these gave foreigners the right to open industrial enterprises in the treaty ports. The other imperialist nations soon joined in, and the famous "scramble for concessions" began.

The Western powers exacted economic privileges, including options for mines and railways. In 1897 and 1898 they began to carve out spheres of influence, some covering whole provinces, where they planned to assert political and economic control. They also seized Chinese territory on long-term leases that made the areas indistinguishable from colonies. For example, Germany took Jiaozhou Bay in the province of Shandong and established the colony of Kiaochow and the city of Qingdao. It also claimed the entire province as its sphere. Russia,

France, and England proceeded in a similar fashion elsewhere. China, it seemed, was on the verge of "being carved up like a melon," to use a common image of the time. In this situation, the need for drastic reform became evident not only for internal reasons but for survival of the nation itself.

The most striking and significant example of the spreading radicalism of the late 1890s is the group that came close to power in the summer of 1898 and that came to be called, appropriately enough, the Reform Movement of 1898.[11] The Reform Movement grew directly out of the earlier qingyi opposition and remained rather elitist in approach. It was unsympathetic to violent change and tried to work within the existing system as far as possible. Nonetheless, it greatly sharpened the democratic tendencies that had only been implicit earlier. It also made an open commitment to the ideals of the Great Community and advocated broad changes in many areas of Chinese polity and life. As a result, it marked an extremely important step in the unification of elite and popular discontent and in the progress of the Chinese revolution.

As might be expected, the Reform Movement remained extremely nationalistic. However, it changed the attitude of the qingyi toward Western civilization. The reformers became the first substantial group in the elite to appreciate what the West had to offer beyond science and technology and, in particular, found inspiration for many of its datong goals in the still vibrant fengjian and tribal traditions of the Occident. As a result, the reformers were deeply influenced by the West and Japan and led the way in advocating not only the material culture of the Occident but also its thought and institutions.

The organizers of the Reform Movement of 1898 were among the most talented members of the generation that had grown up in the era following the great rebellions. A number of them did well in the exams, even in the tough competition of the time, and they were often fine scholars, philosophers, and artists. We have no statistical study of their background as a group; however, they seem to have come from ambitious families that, at the moment, found themselves in difficulty. In this sense, they continued to typify the general decline in the security of the elite, the phenomenon that, besides imperialism, was the prime impetus to the new upper-class radicalism. In addition, many of the important figures in the movement and of the opposition from then on came from southern China, probably because this was the part of the country where nationalism had, traditionally, been strongest and where Western pressures and influence were often most powerful.

The leader of the Reform Movement was Kang Youwei. Born near Canton in 1858, he came from a degree-holding family with a long tradition of public service. However, when Kang was six, his father died, and the family fell on hard times. Nonetheless, Kang received a fine education, became a prolific scholar, and eventually passed the highest level of the examinations. Kang's second in command was his pupil, Liang Qichao. Liang, who was also from the Canton area, came from a family that had been farmers for generations until his grandfather succeeded in obtaining a degree. Liang's father, however, repeatedly failed to pass the exams and continued to work the fields. Liang also became a famous scholar, a degree-holder, and, ultimately, one of the most influential figures of the early twentieth century.

As a young man, Kang Youwei studied with his grandfather and then with a well-known teacher who shared some of the radical proclivities of the time. Nonetheless, the curriculum aimed basically at preparation for the exams and emphasized orthodox Neo-Confucianism. As a result of the arduous work and the slim chances for success Kang, in his twenty-first year, had an intellectual crisis in which he grew disgusted with what he was learning, the official heritage of the junxian age.

As he later wrote:

> I remarked to my teacher, "When it comes to principles and techniques, Han Yu [the pioneer of the Confucian revival in the Tang] is shallow and superficial. The writings of the great literary figures of the Song, Ming, and the present dynasty are vague, empty, and lacking in substance." . . . I gradually grew weary of books and began to conceive new ideas. Of what use, I asked myself, were the works of such scholars of the school of philology as Dai Zhen, whose books filled my teacher's house?[12]

Kang's experience, not unlike that of Hong Xiuquan, the founder of the Taiping movement, was not uncommon in young men preparing for the exams, for they were infused with a deep need and pressure to succeed, particularly if they came from a family that depended on them for prosperity. Kang's crisis, however, was less severe than Hong's had been, perhaps because his family background was, ultimately, more secure. In typically radical fashion, he also turned to religion, but it was to Zen, the highly sinicized form of Buddhism that had earlier lent support to Wang Yangming in his own disillusionment with the junxian orthodoxy.

"I abruptly abandoned my studies," Kang wrote, "and the reading of books, locked my door, and refused to see friends. I sat alone to cultivate my mind. My schoolmates thought my behavior was strange because our teacher stressed practice and scorned Zen and none of us studied it." Nonetheless, Kang persisted. "Sitting quietly by myself, I would suddenly come to the realization that the universe and its myriad things were all part of me. A light dawned within me, and believing that I was a sage, I would be happy and laugh; then, thinking of the suffering of the people in the world, I would be sad and cry." Kang soon returned to Confucianism; however, he now had a mission in life, to become a sage, and one in the datong spirit of Wang Yangming.

It was shortly after his personal crisis that Kang visited Hong Kong for the first time. It was, by then, a flourishing Anglo-Chinese city, and he wrote that he saw "the elegance of the buildings of the foreigners, the cleanliness of the streets, the efficiency of their police. I was impressed by the organization and administration of the foreigners, and I realized that we must not look upon them as barbarians as our older and more conservative people have done."[13]

Books on Western history, thought, and science were by then widely available, particularly through an active missionary press. Kang bought and read some and began to develop a broad sympathy for Western culture. His outlook, in general, remained within the Chinese tradition. However, the Occident made a far greater impact on him than on earlier elite thinkers and did much to help structure his attitudes toward reform and his ideals for the future.

It was in the 1880s and early 1890s that Kang worked out the theories that would have a profound impact on the radical movement. His ideas were deeply influenced by the opposition tradition of the junxian age, by men like Zhang Zai of the Song and, of course, Wang Yangming. Liang Qichao reported that his teacher found Wang's work "direct, clear, sincere, lively, and useful" and "adopted it as the guiding principle of self-cultivation and student instruction."[14] In the short run Kang also showed the impact of all sorts of nineteenth-century thinkers, especially those who had returned to an interest in religion and Han Dynasty Confucianism.

However, in his profound disillusionment with the status quo and his sense that no real solution to China's problems was possible within the decayed framework of junxian life and thought, Kang often avoided acknowledging a debt to post-Tang China. Instead, he approached the task of reinvigorating the datong tradition within Confucianism through a comprehensive effort to elevate the status of Confucius himself and of the ancient era of fengjian and early junxian in which the master had lived.[15]

He argued that really valuable knowledge had been developed only in the period of the Three Dynasties, the Warring States, and the early Han. He said that the texts from these eras were closer to Confucius's own time and that many had, in fact, been written or edited by the master himself. He conceived Confucius to be a radical reformer and even a revolutionary and claimed that the orthodox versions of the classics and other ancient works were later forgeries. By turning in this direction, Kang fitted into the long-standing tradition that envisioned the datong as a grand ideal that would blend fengjian and junxian. At the same time, of course, Kang's position allowed him to circumvent the traditions of the previous thousand years and to legitimize borrowing from the West.

From Kang's point of view, the most important classical text was the famous chapter in the *Book of Rites* that described the Great Community. Here, Kang felt, was to be found not only the inspiration for the datong but also Confucius's prediction that it would some day be established. The original texts upon which Kang based his ideas had presented the datong as a decline from an idealized tribal age and as a goal for the future. Kang, like earlier radicals, and now also under the impact of the West, emphasized the latter interpretation.

It was in this way that he understood three ages that had been mentioned in the ancient texts and that he took as describing successive eras of "Disorder," "Ascending Peace," and "Great Peace," that is, taiping or datong, all building on the past to create and, in a sense, to recreate the Great Community. He wrote:

> When I came to read the *Liyun* chapter [of the *Book of Rites*], I was greatly moved and exclaimed, "Herein are to be found the successive changes of the three ages of Confucius,

and the real truth of his great way." . . . This text represents the esoteric words and true teaching of Confucius. It is a precious record without superior in any country, and a divine recipe for resurrecting all sentient beings throughout the world.[16]

To support his argument that Confucius stood at a crossroad in history in which he was able to summarize the descent from the past and the ideals for the future, Kang liked to quote the well-known passage from the *Analects* where Confucius alludes to the Three Dynasties and says, "The Shang perpetuated the civilization of the Xia; its modifications and accretions can be known. The Zhou perpetuated the civilization of the Shang, and its modifications and accretions can be known. Whatever others may succeed Zhou, their character, even a hundred generations hence, can be known."[17]

Kang went even further in his homage to Confucius and to the outlook of the ancient period. He said that the master had not only made clear the dynamics of history but should also be venerated as the founder of a religion.

Heaven, having pity for the many afflictions suffered by the men who live on this great earth, caused the Black Emperor to send down his semen so as to create a being who could rescue the people from their troubles—a being of divine intelligence, who would be a sage-king, a teacher for his age, a bulwark for all men, and a religious leader for the whole world. Born as he was in the Age of Disorder, he proceeded, on the basis of this disorder, to establish the pattern of three ages, progressing with increasing refinement until they arrive at the taiping.[18]

There seems to have been at least as much pragmatism as sincerity in this evaluation of Confucius, for Kang personally understood Confucianism to be a humanistic philosophy and even said that it was superior to Christianity because "it swept away divine authority."[19] Nonetheless, the approach provided an opening to the popular opposition with its religious orientation and, more generally, fit into the datong tradition, which sought to reinfuse the junxian system with the spiritual vitality of the past. Religious Confucianism had, in particular, been a common view in the Han, an era that Kang especially admired and that had recently received renewed emphasis among critical intellectuals.

On this score, as in so many areas, the West provided Kang with an excellent example of vibrant fengjian institutions that had grown weak in China. Thus, the Occident still clearly displayed the power of religion and its value in fostering the morals, social cohesion, and overall success of a culture. As Kang wrote:

Christians honor heaven, love mankind, tend the soul, and repent sins. . . . Only the contemporary Chinese have . . . no devout respect for their own religious foundations and separate themselves from the perfection to be obtained from religion. Even uncivilized tribes have their religion, and in comparison with them we Chinese live carelessly from day to day like irreligious animals. Do our four-hundred million countrymen really wish to be satisfied with the situation?[20]

Kang Youwei's ideas contained much that was true, and they were also deeply indicative of the dynamics of the nation as the Qing Dynasty and the junxian system drew to a close. At the same time, they provided support and a source of commitment to Kang and his immediate followers as they worked to remake China. Overall, however, his general theories probably hurt the cause of the Reform Movement more than they helped. His faith in Confucianism as a religion probably smacked of rebellion to many members of the elite not yet ready for revolution, and his claim that the orthodoxy rested on spurious texts met with bitter opposition and today is generally considered wrong. Nonetheless, Kang's philosophy is highly significant as one of the last attempts to revolutionize China under the banner of Confucianism and may yet turn out to be the springboard to the re-creation of a vibrant and progressive tradition of Confucian thought.

As he developed his ideas, Kang Youwei continued to make his way through the examinations and also began his political life. On the national level he joined the qingyi. He emphasized the need for an open and active opposition within the elite, something rather typical of the movement, and learning from the West, which was more unusual. He also founded a school in his hometown to spread his ideas and organized what he claimed was the first anti–foot binding society in China. Kang's concern with the plight of Chinese women, like that of the Taipings before him, was inspired both by the opposition tradition and by the West; it was also a harbinger of the future when the revolutionary movement would place great emphasis on women's rights.

The Reform Movement of 1898 emerged on the scene as a distinct political force in the spring of 1895. Kang and Liang Qichao were in Peking, along with thousands of other candidates, to compete for the two hundred or so places open for the highest degree. It was, however, also the time of the humiliating peace negotiations with Japan. Kang responded by organizing a mass meeting among the examinees who sent a militant petition to the throne asking that the peace treaty be rejected and that China fight on. He later called the gathering, among the very crème de la crème of the younger generation of degree-holders, "unprecedented in the Qing Dynasty,"[21] and Liang later characterized it as "the beginning of a broad-based political movement in China."[22] The petition failed, and Kang passed the exam. This not inconsiderable success might eventually have led to an influential position in the government; however, the reformer rejected the minor post he was offered (second-class secretary in the Department of Weights and Measures of the Board of Public Works) and opted to remain in opposition.

For the next three years, with rebellion in the air and imperialism at an unprecedented level, the political situation in China became very fluid. Li Hongzhang, his leadership and the whole Self-strengthening Movement discredited by the war, fell from power. Meanwhile, the reformers worked to expand the size of the radical movement and to bring it to power. They continued to direct their activities mostly toward the elite, but their actions and plans looked toward participation by all citizens and, in the long run, even to datong goals.

Taking off from the gathering of 1895, the main thrust of their efforts was to encourage the formation of political clubs, periodicals, and educational institutions. Even the qingyi had never called for formal and public groups working to assume political power, and given the restrictions on such activity, which had hitherto been obeyed by the upper levels of society, the call to organize was nothing short of revolutionary. As Kang wrote, "The spirit of China has been dispersed for a long time and the elite, cautioned by prohibitions dating back to the Ming against forming political associations, have not dared to congregate for discussions."[23] And Liang put it more bluntly by saying that the establishment had come to "hate parties as an enemy and to view societies as criminal."

The broad response that met the reformers' call for organization provides a striking expression of the disillusionment that was by then rampant in the upper echelons of society. Kang and Liang founded their first group, the Society for the Study of National Strength, shortly after the Japanese war. Its support came mostly from the qingyi, though the name of the group also beckoned to former self-strengtheners, who themselves were looking for new political directions. Thereafter, organizations sprang up in every part of the country.

Some groups were run by the highest levels of the local establishment and were extremely moderate. Others were more obviously radical. There were organizations representing specific places, such as the Suzhou Study Association and the Guangdong Study Association. Others had names like the Mathematics Academy, the Datong Translating Society, the Agricultural Study Association, the Society to Protect the Nation, the Humble Trades Primary School, the Understand the National Shame Society, the Liaoning and Peking Elementary School for Manchus, *Current Affairs* (a newspaper), the Society for the Study of Women's Issues, the Datong School, the Confucian Study Association, and so on.[24]

The reformers saw the sheer act of organizing the opposition as the prerequisite for everything else they hoped to achieve. Overall, their most important goal was to curb the excessive authority that the emperorship had attained in junxian times. Long a target of political critics, this power, in the form of the Qing Dynasty, had been used to block democracy in the previous 250 years and had prevented the revival of the broad and united movement for change of the late Ming.

In a famous essay on organization written in defense of the renewed political activity, for example, Liang Qichao linked the evils of autocracy directly to the general crisis in China's junxian order and to the nation's hapless international position.

> The ruler treats the government as if it were his private property, the officials treat their positions like private domains, the farmers hold fields privately, workers consider their enterprises private, merchants consider their profit a private matter. . . . As a result, within a group of 400,000,000 people we have 400,000,000 separate countries, that is to say, no country at all. So those who govern well know that it is absolutely essential for the ruler and the people to form part of one group, together, and that this knowledge is the essence of their common humanity and of good administration. Seeking unity and not

division, cohesion and not fragmentation is the art of forming a community and the key to becoming a powerful nation.[25]

Similarly, Kang Youwei, in good Confucian fashion, saw the bad example of the ruler as the fulcrum of China's problems and, in particular, of the lack of democracy and the oppression of women.

Coming down to the present, ministers of state, kneeling in abject submissiveness before the sovereign are so awed by his majestic presence that they dare not speak out. Wives, downtrodden and repressed, remain untutored and unenlightened. . . . I am afraid all these are merely results of convention; they do not accord with the highest principles of justice and reason. Now, according to the nature of things, whatever is put under excessive pressure will inevitably break away.[26]

And he predicted that "at the end of one hundred years all this will change. The sovereign will no longer be exalted nor the subject looked down upon, and men and women will be regarded as of equal importance."

Like the radicals of the early Qing, the reformers frequently attacked the power of the emperor by citing precedents from the tribal era and from the ancient fengjian age of the Three Dynasties. For example, Tan Sitong, another important figure in the movement and perhaps its finest political philosopher, contrasted the situation in earlier times with the junxian order of the Qin and of the more immediate past when he wrote:

For the past two thousand years, the ruler-minister relationship has been especially dark and inhuman, and it has become worse in recent times. The ruler is not physically different or intellectually superior to other people: on what does he rely to oppress four hundred million people?

At the beginning of the human race, there were no princes or subjects, for all were just people. As the people were unable to govern each other and did not have time to rule, they "joined in raising up" someone to be the prince. Now, "joined in raising up" means not that the prince selected the people, but that the people selected the prince; it means that the prince was not far above the people, but rather on the same level with them. . . . When it is said that they "joined in raising up" the prince, it necessarily means that they could also dismiss him.[27]

Things were more hierarchical "in ancient times," he continued, but still,

loyalty meant actually being loyal: If the subordinate actually serves his superior faithfully, why should not the superior actually wait upon the subordinate also? Loyalty signifies mutuality, the utmost fulfillment of a mutual relationship. How can it be maintained that only ministers and subjects should live up to it? Confucius said, "The prince should behave as a prince, the minister as a minster." He also said, "The father should behave as a father, the son as a son, the elder brother as an elder brother, the younger brother as a younger brother, the husband as a husband, the wife as a wife." The founder of Confucianism never preached inequality.

Tan, it should be noted, concluded with a suggestion that the four cardinal Confucian relationships that he had just mentioned (prince-minister, father-son, elder brother-younger brother, and husband-wife) should be subordinated to the fifth, that between friend and friend. In this way he may have been suggesting a way of reconciling the apparent contradiction in datong ideals between a society organized like a great family and democracy, a contradiction that, among other factors, had left the Taipings open to the paternalistic attractions of autocratic power. He wrote:

> The world, misled by the conception of blood relations, makes erroneous distinctions between the nearly related and the remotely related, and relegates the relationship between friends to the end of the line. The relationship between friends, however, not only is superior to the other four relationships, but should be the model for them all. When these four relationships have been brought together and infused with the spirit of friendship, they can well be abolished.

At every point in their political work, the reformers drew inspiration from the West and from Japan. They were deeply impressed by the possibilities that Western science and technology held out for solving China's economic problems. They did not advocate a complete break with the Chinese past but nonetheless were eager to import the dynamism and sense of possibility that infused the Occident.

Overall, however, the most significant impact of the West came through its fengjian side, through the vibrancy of institutions and values that had disappeared in junxian China and whose revival had, in line with datong ideals, long been a goal of the opposition. These included the powerful and effective religious faith of the Occident, which, as we have noted, Kang Youwei sought to instill in China. It also meant an active role for the government in economic life and, of course, emulating the military vigor that so marked the West.

Above all, though, the reformers most admired liberalism, which was the predominant ideology in the West's transition from fengjian to junxian and, under similar circumstances, had recently begun to play a major role in Japan. There were, of course, aspects of the outlook that held little or no appeal. Significantly, these were the parts that were crucial in the fight against the fengjian order in the Occident, things like laissez-faire economics[28] and a deeply secular spirit. The reformers, after all, were working to transform a decaying junxian system by blending in the best of the past, not to firm up the status quo.

It was precisely for this reason, however, that they were deeply attracted by the political aspects of liberalism: broadly based and decentralized authority, governments responsible to the people, and rulers bound by explicit constitutional restraints and parliamentary bodies. These institutions retained a powerful imprint from the Jews of Mosaic times, the ancient Greeks, and the northern European peoples, tribal or near tribal eras when so much of the West's political theory was first developed. At the same time they kept alive the dispersal of political power and the limitations on kingly authority associated with the aristocratic traditions of the West's recent fengjian past. As a result, political liberalism presented a perfect complement to the long-standing desire within the opposition to revive China's analogous but more distant and, as a result, more obscure traditions. De Bary, indeed, has persuasively argued that this position, earlier exemplified by such men as Huang Zongxi and Gu Yanwu, should itself be called liberalism.[29]

Thus, in the 1890s, Wang Kangnian, one of the leading advocates of democracy and learning from the West wrote:

> Chinese who discuss governmental systems speak only in terms of governing the people by the ruler. In the West, however, there are democratic countries and also countries governed jointly by the ruler and the people. Chinese scholars are surprised and consider it strange. Nevertheless, what is strange about it? In ancient times all who discussed government always gave consideration to the people.[30]

And he continued with evidence from various classical texts to prove his point.

Kang Youwei made a similar point about liberalism, particularly as practiced in the United States. He wrote:

> In ancient times the fengjian system was in use and the governance of the people was intelligent. Later generations could not continue to implement the system. As a result, it faded into the past and into disrepair. . . . Now local autonomy is really the fengjian of the ancients. But the ancient world was the Era of Disorder and only one person was enfeoffed in each area; this led to constant problems of war and bickering, so the system declined. Now we are in the era of Ascending Peace. The mass of people must, so to speak, be enfeoffed. Citizens should be allowed to govern themselves. Parliaments should be given heed. Everyone should be allowed to plan for the common good. Then the profit from land will be greatly expanded, industry will progress, customs will become beautiful and talent emerge. This is the system in America where the states and counties permit self-rule, the fengjian of the aristocrats of old now applied to the people of a whole large country.[31]

Beyond their general arguments against the existing order and their efforts to legalize an organized political opposition, the reformers also elaborated a concrete program for national renovation. Their proposals, which still aimed basically at an elite constituency, were not fundamentally different from what the qingyi had advocated, save for the interest in learning from the West. However, in every respect, what the reformers wanted was more democratic and beckoned more directly to the popular opposition.

For example, in political matters they demanded that all citizens be permitted to write directly to the throne. In educational affairs they sought to de-emphasize the examination system and to involve the government in establishing a system of public schools that would open up greater opportunities to the general public, including women. Their military program called for a nationwide militia armed with modern weapons to supplement the national army. Given the rebellious atmosphere in the country, this proposal may, in a sense, have been their most radical one. The Reform Movement, however, did not specifically call for the equalization of land. Kang and the other leaders supported the idea in principle, but the redistribution of property was, apparently, still not a sufficiently popular cause with the elite to risk making an issue of it.

In foreign affairs, the reformers were fervently nationalistic and anti-imperialist. They stressed that the radical program was necessary to unite the nation and to save it in the face of the heightened foreign pressures. At the same time, they advocated policies that would rid China of every slight to her national sovereignty. They took particular aim at the unequal treaties. Kang Youwei called the system of agreements the ''extreme national disgrace'' and spoke harshly of the earlier officials who had acquiesced in its creation.[32]

Between 1895 and 1898, as the reformers worked to establish a broad political movement, they did not shun working on the inside for power. They tried to win the support of high officials and addressed memorials to the throne urging the emperor to act decisively and even draconically to solve the nation's problems. This approach was a compromise with autocracy and somewhat in contradiction with the democratic aims of the movement. However, it promised faster results and, the reformers could hope, might lead to a constitutional monarchy eventually, for the emperor seemed to support their cause.

The ruler in the late 1890s was still the Guangxu emperor whom the empress dowager Cixi had placed on the throne as a child in 1874. In 1888 he had officially taken over the reins of government, a move that actually meant that he entered into an uneven competition for authority with his great-aunt. He soon turned to the qingyi for support because he wanted new men in the government loyal to himself rather than to the empress and her followers. He found the reformers congenial partly for the same reason. In addition, he was, like them, a young man and seems to have developed a sense of his responsibility to save the dynasty and the nation in their hour of peril. Nonetheless, he remained a weak personality, skittish and with a deep sense of dread and subservience toward Cixi.

In 1898 came the foreign seizures of Chinese territory that seemed to foreshadow the disintegration of the country. At the same time, there were power shifts in the imperial family, most notably the death of Prince Gong, a longtime ally of the empress. These events gave the emperor and the reformers the chance for which they had been waiting. On June 11 began the famous Hundred Days of Reform, in which Kang and his followers had their brief taste of power. In the course of the summer, the emperor issued a storm of decrees, many of them in line with the radical program. He also worked to consolidate the political position of the opposition.

By August, he was replacing high officials loyal to the empress with his own followers, including reformers like Tan Sitong. Cixi decided to act. She was fearful that if things continued in the same direction much longer, she would lose all influence. At the same time, she worried that the power of the Manchus and of the Qing Dynasty would not ultimately be strengthened by what was happening but would collapse. In September, perhaps in response to moves on the part of the reformers, she began to organize a coup. A more resolute and mature emperor might have thwarted her plans, but Guangxu proved helpless.

The coup came on September 21. The empress placed the emperor under arrest in the palace. Kang Youwei and Liang Qichao fled to Japan, a price on their heads. Six of their supporters, however, were caught and summarily executed. The group, enshrined afterward as the *liu junzi*, the Six Virtuous Men of 1898, included Tan Sitong and Kang's brother, Kuangren. Tan had a chance to escape but, the stories say, instead organized a daring effort to rescue the emperor with the help of experts in the martial arts. At his execution he behaved with great bravery and proclaimed that he welcomed death because no real progress was ever possible unless men were willing to sacrifice their lives for it.

Despite the setback to radicalism represented by the failure of the Hundred Days, the momentum of the opposition proved inexorable. In 1899 a major popular uprising, the famous Boxer Rebellion, began in North China (the movement practiced the martial arts as part of its discipline, hence the odd English name). At its start the revolt may, as usual, have been both revolutionary and nationalistic.[33] As it developed, however, it took a somewhat peculiar turn but one symptomatic of the ever increasing conjunction of elite and mass discontent.

It dropped its opposition to the government and developed the motto "Support the Qing and expel the foreigners." The dynamics of the shift included encouragement from the court, which, after the coup, seems to have come under the influence of qingyi members who had not followed the reformers and deeply hated the West. In any case, the empress came to view the Boxers as an effective way of uniting the dynasty and the people and of expelling the imperialists.

In the spring of 1900 the Boxers and allied groups began attacks on missionaries and other foreigners in North China and also on Chinese converts to Christianity. Ultimately, they killed many hundreds of people. In May, the foreign diplomats in Peking, growing fearful of the unrest, sent for additional forces from the coast. An expedition of two thousand soldiers began to move inland. In response, the Chinese government openly sided with the people, sending its best divisions to the front. Together, they drove the expedition back in what was probably China's greatest military victory against the West until that time.

Meanwhile, bands of Boxers entered Peking, and on June 20 the famous "siege of the legations" began. The next day China declared war on the imperialist powers, though the government worked indirectly to prevent the beleaguered diplomats from being overrun. The Western nations and Japan responded by preparing a far larger expedition to take the capital, raise the siege, and put down the unrest. There was some hard fighting, but on August 14, Peking fell and Cixi and her prisoner, the emperor, fled the city. Now it was the foreigners' turn to loot and kill, and they eventually did so with both greater efficiency and in greater numbers than had the Boxers. They restored order, and by the end of 1900, there were forty-five thousand troops in North China, and Russia occupied Manchuria.

In the long run, the Boxer Rebellion brought some benefits to China. The uprising was an example, however symbolic and foolhardy, of what coordinated activity on the part of the government and the people was capable of achieving, a lesson not lost on the Western powers. Foreign diplomats and military men began to realize that China could no longer be freely bullied without fear of dangerous and costly retaliation. In the short run, however, the incident was a disaster and marked a nadir in China's international position.

As part of the humiliating peace settlement, China was forced to pay a heavy indemnity, which the nation could ill afford in view of its massive internal problems. In order to extract the money, the foreigners increased their grip on the nation's economic resources. Many people were punished for their role in the uprising, and a number of high officials and local leaders were executed. Russia remained in control of Manchuria, and Peking was under semioccupation.

THE REVOLUTION OF 1911

It was clearly a time for a fresh start, and in this atmosphere a demand for broad-ranging change spread with great rapidity. Indeed, the most striking feature of the last decade of the Qing is the degree to which the status quo lost support at all levels of society and within virtually every political grouping. At the same time, elite and popular opposition continued to blend and to grow very close. Most importantly, rebellion and revolution, hitherto supported mainly by laboring people, now grew ever more appealing to the upper echelons of society. The culmination of ten years of political ferment was the Revolution of 1911. It was in many ways the product of elite politics but had very wide support and, given its profound character, was a surprisingly bloodless event.[34]

The breadth of dissatisfaction becomes most evident in government policy during these years. A so-called Qing or Manchu reform movement came into being and implemented changes that often went beyond what the radicals of 1898 had promulgated only a few years earlier. The Qing reform developed partly to meet the demands of the nation and partly because the government, ultimately made up of the same sorts of people as society in general, also felt the need for drastic action. The most influential official of the decade was the former qingyi leader, Zhang Zhidong. In 1898 he had turned his back on the reform movement, but now he adopted its program and was able to win the support of the empress.

It should be noted at the outset, however, that the Qing reforms did nothing to save the dynasty and, indeed, may have hastened its end, for the government found itself in the common dilemma of regimes trying to stave off revolution—they implement policies that do not really resolve basic grievances but, rather, serve to whet the appetite for change and to strengthen the opposition. Thus, the Qing was unable to end the widespread poverty, social injustice, and immorality that were the basic stimulus to rebellion and, barring that change, could not solve China's other great problem, imperialism. In addition, in the highly charged nationalism of the time, the fact that the imperial family was Manchu rather than Han Chinese made everything the rulers did suspect and, ultimately, unacceptable.

Most directly dangerous to the government was the fact that its reforms steadily transferred authority from Peking to provincial and local groups. Such decentralization of authority was, of course, basic to the radical program. As one influential magazine wrote:

> Uniting the hearts and spirits of the people and the government and of different levels of society must begin locally . . . then the familial spirit of fengjian will replace the evil dictatorial style of junxian. If this process moves from the districts and the prefectures to the provinces and from the provinces to the whole nation, we will create a commonwealth with good government and attain the glorious benefits of the datong.[35]

Nonetheless, in an era of rapid change, such views not only were idealistic in intent but also displayed the political interests of their advocates and could provide support to any group opposing the government and seeking independent power.

Perhaps the most striking reforms that the government adopted were in the field of education. Peking encouraged and supported the formation of new schools, many of them open to women as well as men. The curriculum in these institutions aimed to keep up with the times and shifted from an emphasis on Neo-Confucian orthodoxy to broader learning both in the Chinese tradition and in Western knowledge. At the same time, increasing numbers of young people went abroad to study. In 1905, the examination system, the fifteen hundred-year-old mainstay of the junxian order, was abolished, and the new schools began to spring up all over the country. By then there were over ten thousand students studying overseas, the vast majority in Japan. Though these educational changes were revolutionary in their implications, they aroused only minimal controversy.

This somewhat surprising consensus existed partly because of the almost universal desire for change within the nation. However, it also developed because the reforms brought a welcome reduction in the power of the government. When the examination system worked effectively, it not only had been a means for certifying talent but, with its central direction and its emphasis on official learning, also had been a powerful prop for the authority of Peking. On the other hand, the new schools were generally in the hands of the local elite, and their course of study encouraged unorthodox ideas. At the same time, since the schools often mixed people from different backgrounds and social strata, they provided the opposition with a convenient setting for political organization. Students who went abroad, of course, were open to even more iconoclastic influences and were even freer of governmental restraints. Since such students often came from influential backgrounds and moved into important positions when they returned home, they presented a particular danger to the Qing.

Similar and even more serious problems developed in another great area of change, military reform. From the Taiping Rebellion onward, there had been various attempts both by rebels and by the government to emulate the martial ethos, weaponry, and organization of the Western nations and Japan. Through the Self-strengthening Movement, military development on the part of the government often aimed at putting down rebellion. By the late 1890s, however, as a result of the increased imperialist pressures and the new political atmosphere, it was assumed that the prime mission of the armed forces was to oppose foreigners. Military reform, therefore, continued to be an integral part of the radical program. After the Japanese war a few Western-style battalions had been formed, and some were among the units that joined the Boxers against the foreign invasion of 1900.

In the final decade of the Qing, military reform moved ahead quickly. By 1910 Peking had succeeded in fashioning a large army structured along Western and Japanese lines. It was well trained, well armed, and comparatively well paid and had high morale. In addition, military service became popular and, what was particularly striking, for the first time since the late fengjian era of the Tang, an honorable career for the sons of the elite. The foreign powers were aware of the new situation, which, to some extent, contributed to controlling their rapacity. At the same time, though, the new armed forces ultimately helped local power at the expense of the government and, indeed, become something of a military arm of the opposition rather than of Peking.

Thus, the new military units were actually regional forces under only the general direction of the central government. The enlisted men, the noncoms, and the lower commissioned officers were all native to the areas where they were stationed, and they enjoyed close ties and good relations with the local populace. Like the new schools, the units mixed people from all walks of life and became excellent foci for political organization and for uniting elite and popular opposition. As a result, by 1910, the army was a stronghold of local authority, infiltrated and often dominated by various groups hostile to the government.

A third great area of reform was also in line with the radical program but further weakened the hold of Peking. This was the movement toward a liberal political system. In 1906, under intense pressure, the Qing began to move toward restructuring the basic governmental form of the nation. In 1908 it agreed to a nine-year program for the creation of a constitutional system. In 1909 provincial assemblies convened for the first time, and in 1910 a national assembly met with representatives from these lower bodies.

Needless to say, almost all the groups were under the domination of powerful local notables with close ties to the army. They were eager for influence, and the crucial issue between the various assemblies and the central government quickly became how to divide up power. Such legitimized official authority in local hands had not really existed since fengjian times and did much to hasten the end of the Qing.

The government even made some strides in combatting imperialism and national poverty, in a sense the two most concrete problems facing the country.

However, here the failures were more striking than the successes and so contributed to weakening the hold of the dynasty. With its new army developing and nationalist zeal sweeping the nation, Peking supported and, where necessary, mobilized a "rights-recovery" movement to reverse the high tide of foreign aggression that had begun in the 1890s. As a result, China regained some control over her sovereignty and her basic economic resources. For example, the German sphere of influence in Shandong never attained the importance for which the Germans had hoped and by 1907 meant little or nothing.

But the accomplishments in anti-imperialism were comparatively minor when compared to China's continued position of inferiority in international affairs. The unequal treaties still existed. The foreign concessions and the leaseholds, essentially imperialist colonies spread all over the country, were still in place, and the foreigners retained considerable economic power. In 1905 Japan defeated Russia in war, took over and then expanded the latter's grip on Manchuria, and proved impossible to dislodge. Such continuing problems served to inflame nationalism more than the successes of the government did to harness it. At the same time, they turned Han Chinese ever more sharply against the Manchus, who were increasingly clumped, psychologically at least, with the "foreigners," whom they could not oust.

In economic improvement the story was essentially the same, though the results proved even more disappointing. From the national point of view, the basic idea was to emulate Japan's rapid and successful development, to assuage poverty, and to resist imperialism. Some projects were begun, and foreigners could now find themselves in competition with the Chinese government and Chinese businessmen for control of industrial and commercial opportunities. However, as in the era of the self-strengtheners, fundamental economic and social problems continued to plague China's efforts and made it impossible to copy Japan.

In particular, when Japan began its modernization drive in the 1860s, she had a population one-tenth that of China and an agricultural system that may have been less efficient overall.[36] As a result, the nation could more easily raise agricultural production and use the surplus capital to support industrialization. More importantly, since Japan, like the West, was modernizing at the same time as she was moving from fengjian to junxian, she could copy the latter's sociopolitical approaches and military techniques with comparative ease, thus assisting social stability and national defense and allowing economic development. A similar process was impossible for a China in a declining junxian era, in uncharted waters historically, with a steadily weakening government and endemic unrest, and under constant foreign pressure. Japan's progress was by no means easy or assured, and for China to have emulated her example would, under the circumstances, have required nothing short of a miracle.

Not only did the hopes for economic development prove nugatory, leaving an impoverished populace and the image of a decaying society, but they also contributed directly to political tensions. There was often open and bitter competition between the government and businessmen, with the latter frequently tied to powerful elements on the local scene who wished to profit from the new opportunities. Since such businessmen were generally in direct competition with foreigners, they often became particularly nationalistic and suspicious of Peking. For example, because major projects such as railways and mines were expensive and capital was short, the government sometimes turned to foreigners for loans. Such loans, unlike those in the past, were, for the most part, carefully drawn to preserve China's sovereignty and economic independence. Nonetheless, they opened Peking to charges of truckling to the imperialists.

Once it became evident that the reform program was undermining the authority of the Qing, the government began to reemphasize the centralization of power. In some ways this was a logical corollary of everything else Peking was trying to do. For example, a strict national budget and higher taxes were necessary for many of the innovations of the decade, and, in general, effective executive authority on the national level could not be abolished without grave consequences for the security and prosperity of the country. However, all plans for recentralization, of course, ran directly against the main current of the time and only served to aggravate tensions.

As the government pursued its troubled course of reform, the opposition grew ever more powerful, often benefiting from what the Qing was trying to do. One of its leaders was Liang Qichao, who, from his exile in Japan, wrote voluminously and with great influence. To the extent that mature members of the elite became radicalized as a result of propaganda rather than their own experiences, it was probably through the writings of Liang.

The chief purpose of his efforts in these years was to deepen and spread the commitment to nationalism among the upper classes. At the same time, he worked to introduce Western concepts and theories into Chinese political discourse. From the point of view of later developments, one of the most important of these was socialism (*shehuizhuyi*), which Liang equated with the idea of datong. This connection was reasonable since both concepts place great stress on a sense of community and on the equalization and public management of wealth.[37] The terms were soon widely associated, providing a harbinger of the future, when the radicals of the next generation would operate almost entirely within the framework of Western outlooks.

Other important figures included such people as Huang Xing, who led the way in uniting popular organizations and the army, and Qiu Jin, the female revolutionary who died a martyr's death at the hands of the government. However, the person who came to symbolize the Revolution of 1911 in Chinese eyes and to be enshrined ever after as the ''Father of the Chinese Republic'' was Sun Yat-sen.

Sun was a professional revolutionary whose single-minded purpose was to overthrow the government. All his writings and activities were aimed at this goal and, in particular, at uniting and strengthening the opposition by bringing together the elite and popular movements for change. Sun was not personally responsible for the revolution and, when it came, was not even its leader in any clear sense. Nonetheless, precisely because he was a practical politician, selecting whatever ideas and techniques he found useful, he caught up and expressed the spirit of the age better than any other individual.

Sun's youth and education, which provided the possibility of links to all levels of society, prepared him well for his future tasks. He was born in 1866 into a farming family living near Canton. His uncle had fought with the Taipings, and Sun always looked back with sympathy on that great popular rebellion. He received his primary education in his hometown, but when he was fourteen, he went to live with a brother who had emigrated to Hawaii. Sun received his advanced education abroad and in the foreign colonies of Macao and Hong Kong, eventually obtaining a Western medical degree. He began his political activities in the 1890s in the Macao-Hong Kong area.

As a result of his background he was able to develop close ties to mass organizations such as secret societies and local corps that were providing the spearhead of popular opposition. At the same time his medical degree and his intimate knowledge of the West provided access to influential members of the elite and put him in touch with the latest intellectual trends. By 1894 Sun had helped to organize a revolutionary association, the Society to Revive China. In 1895 it made an unsuccessful attempt to seize the city of Canton. Sun fled abroad with a price on his head and, except for brief, illegal visits, did not return to his homeland until 1911.

During these fifteen years of exile he wandered over the world organizing support for a revolution in China. Among other things, he worked to mobilize the now sizable community of overseas Chinese on behalf of the opposition, and they became his chief financial support. His base of operations was Japan, which was close enough to China to allow him to maintain links to activities at home and also gave him access to the ever increasing number of influential students who came there to study.

In 1905, in Tokyo, he helped to found the *Tongmeng Hui* or United League. Its express purpose was to bring together popular groups, the army, and students into a single revolutionary organization. It was for the league that Sun first enunciated his famous "Three Principles of the People," the *San Min Zhuyi*. The three principles were essentially political slogans. As a result, they provide an excellent summary of the attitudes within the opposition just before it succeeded in overthrowing the Qing and also a clear sense of the degree to which popular and elite attitudes had blended.

The first of the principles was *minzu zhuyi*, nationalism. For Sun nationalism meant partly what it implied to the elite opposition, that the Chinese people would have to unite to solve their problems and to resist imperialism. In one particularly vivid image, similar to Liang Qichao's complaint that junxian China was made up of millions of tiny nations, Sun said that the Chinese people were nothing but a "sheet of loose sand," so disunited and competitive had they become.

However, as for the Taipings and the popular tradition in general, another crucial aspect of nationalism for Sun was anti-Manchuism. He stressed that people should oppose the government not simply because it could not solve China's problems but precisely because it was not in the hands of Han Chinese. After 1900, anti-Manchuism was also becoming increasingly popular within the elite, and now Sun made it one of the central rallying cries for a broad-based revolution.

The second of Sun's principles was *minquan zhuyi* or democracy. Once more, for Sun, democracy meant partly what it had to the reformers of 1898 and to earlier elite radicals: limitations on the power of the ruler, the ideal of a free and open political life. However, to him it also meant that China should become a republic rather than a constitutional monarchy as most of the reformers had wanted and as Liang still advocated.

We have no adequate study of how the concept of republicanism took hold. A nonhereditary ruler had, of course, disappeared from China in tribal times, the era associated with Yao, Shun, and Yu. As a result, when, after fifteen hundred years of the fengjian order, political theory began to be written down, there was little or no vibrancy left to the idea. Indeed, as far as we know, no traditional Chinese thinker ever openly advocated republicanism, though many idealized the transmission of power through merit represented by the early sage rulers. Sun's inspiration, therefore, seems to have come largely from the West and, in particular, the United States. The idea, however, was in harmony with the overall datong sympathy for curbing autocracy by reviving ancient ideals.

At the same time, we may speculate, the demand for republicanism was also something that could help to unite the opposition and that may, conceivably, have had some popular roots. Electing local leaders had sometimes been a feature of junxian China. As a result, spreading the system to the national level may have had a special appeal to the average person who, when it came to politics, was less likely than a member of the elite to think in terms of Peking and the emperor. Furthermore, republicanism represented the deeper alienation from the dynasty and all its works that typified those lower down the social scale. After 1900, opposition to the imperial system seems to have spread rapidly, and when the revolution came, it was in the name of a republic.

Sun's third principle was *minsheng zhuyi*, people's livelihood, a concept he associated with both the datong and socialism. Above all, people's livelihood meant economic equality, and Sun was deeply impressed by the notion of a single tax on landed property, an idea derived partly from traditional sources and partly from the writings of the American socialist Henry George. In his commitment to the redistribution of wealth, Sun was again working to bring popular demands into the program of a united opposition. Popular revolutionaries, as exemplified by the Taipings, had long advocated such goals. On the other hand, elite radicals, as late as the Reform Movement of 1898, despite their general sympathy toward datong ideals, did not push economic equality in their practical politics.

Sun himself did not emphasize his third principle as much as he did his other two, sensing perhaps that the elite portion of his constituency was still not fully amenable to redistributing property and was more likely to support a revolution in the name of nationalism and democracy. Nonetheless, every member of the United League took an oath to "drive out the Manchus, restore Chinese rule, establish a republic, and equalize land rights,"[38] and Sun thereby not only firmed up his support within the laboring majority but raised socialism to a new level of prominence among all those who opposed the dynasty.

From 1905 onward, the United League and other groups engaged in revolt after revolt. Assassination attempts began against members of the imperial family and high officials, and the army was increasingly infiltrated with revolutionaries. By 1908, whatever chance the government and the dynasty had for avoiding collapse began quickly to evaporate. In that year, the empress dowager, for fifty years the unscrupulous but effective leader of the imperial family, passed away. A few hours before her death the Guangxu emperor perished mysteriously, almost certainly on the orders of Cixi.

The new emperor was a child of three, who was given the reign title, Xuantong. In 1909 Zhang Zhidong, the leading Han official in the Qing reform movement, also died. In the next year the various popular assemblies began to verge on open disloyalty, and there were repeated mutinies in the army. What power remained in the central government passed into the hands of a small band of disheartened Manchu noblemen totally unable to deal with the growing crisis.

The immediate spark to the revolution came in the fall of 1911 with a clash between Peking and powerful local figures in Sichuan Province. The government wished to build a railway down the Yangtze River to Hankou in the neighboring province of Hubei and to do so with a foreign loan. The local people wanted to build and finance the line themselves. Open defiance developed against officials on the scene, and the army did not intervene. In October, in nearby Wuchang, an uprising broke out in an army unit with ties to the United League. The Revolution of 1911 was on.

With amazing speed province after province, led by the local assemblies and the army, declared its independence of Peking. In December Sun Yat-sen returned from abroad and, in a meeting of his followers was elected president of China. On January 1, 1912, he officially proclaimed the establishment of the Republic of China. On February 12 the Qing Dynasty and the Xuantong emperor bowed to "the Mandate of Heaven . . . manifested through the wish of the people" and abdicated in favor of the new government.[39] The Chinese imperial system had come to an end, and the junxian system now entered upon its final agony.

6

Disunity, the Nationalists, and the Communist Victory

OVERVIEW; DISUNITY

The Revolution of 1911 was followed by an era of chaos that lasted until the Communist victory of 1949. Interrupted only briefly by the unifying efforts of the Nationalist government, these years were generally a period without real central authority, of internal conflict, of renewed foreign pressures, and, with the Japanese invasion of the 1930s and 1940s, of full-scale war and occupation. Overall, it was probably the worst disorder that China had known since the tenth century, the time between the Tang and the Song dynasties, when the nation made the final transition from fengjian to junxian. The era of disintegration in the twentieth century, of course, marked the end of the junxian era.

The eventual establishment of the People's Republic was a product of a unified movement, blending elite and popular discontent that had been forming for the better part of a century. Indeed, during this era, the distinctions among the various levels of society, increasingly vague as a result of the long-term impact of the junxian system, became virtually meaningless in the face of social breakdown and confusion. The Chinese people seemed to form one vast opposition movement, poor and disenfranchised, facing a small handful who controlled things. The victory of the disaffected took the form of a great uprising not dissimilar to the rebellions of the previous thousand years. It not only opposed the junxian order but was also nationalistic and marched under the banner of a non-Confucian ideology with messianic overtones.

At the same time, however, the Western impact on the revolution expanded greatly, assuming a larger role, overall, even than the Christianity of the Taipings. Above all, those involved were entirely won over to the notion of transcendent progress, of making a complete break with Chinese tradition. As a result, they not only de-emphasized or ignored all connections between their movement and the past but also came to view Chinese history and Chinese problems from a Western point of view and to describe what they were doing in Western terminology. Western thought of all sorts was influential. However, the most important became Marxism, which in this era eclipsed not only Confucianism but other traditional outlooks as well and became the leading ideology of change.

In the decade following 1911, it soon became apparent that the fall of the Qing had not really done much in a positive sense toward solving China's problems of internal decay and foreign aggression.[1] The revolution had made an important contribution toward uniting the opposition and clearing the ground for change; new developments were in the air. However, it proved easier to bring down the existing system than to establish a new one. Things, in fact, seemed to become worse.

Suddenly the nation found itself rent of its moorings. Gone were not only the mandate for the Qing but also the mandate for the hoary imperial system, and for the junxian order that had structured society for over a thousand years. In this situation the decentralizing tendencies that had contributed to the fall of the dynasty came to the fore. There was no clear way of enforcing political legitimacy, and dominance passed into the hands of those who had the power to seize it, generally military men or those who could hire them.

In 1912, in the name of national unity and order, Sun Yat-sen resigned the presidency of the republic in favor of Yuan Shikai, the leading general of the new armies of the late Qing. Yuan managed to maintain a tenuous sort of authority through his ties to military subordinates around the country, but his power was weak, and in 1915, trying to hold things together, he declared his intention to become emperor. This effort to establish a new dynasty proved to be an ignominious failure that garnered virtually no support and led to immediate rebellion. Yuan died a few months later.

Things then fell apart completely. Various generals came into control of different parts of the country. These were the infamous warlords, and the era from 1916 to 1928 is often called the Warlord Period in twentieth-century China. For the most part, the warloads were men without particular long-term goals who controlled, at most, a province or two. Some were better than others, but they were generally out to get what they could, which was a secure base and the possibility for occasional forays beyond.

There was no real central government. Peking became the plaything of various nearby generals. Whoever dominated it would declare himself to be the government of China, but this had no standing internally and precious little effectiveness internationally. An analogous situation developed locally, though because of the breakdown in unity we know less about it. Power often came into the hands of a coalition of the rich and influential, backed by minor military men. These local figures, like the warloads higher up, developed a bad reputation as a group of petty tyrants, rapacious in their behavior and uninspired by higher ideals.

In this situation, as might be expected, life for most people became terrible. All the earlier difficulties associated with the unfavorable balance of people and resources continued, together with the attendant immorality, injustice, and competition, and such problems now became all the more serious because of the breakdown of political order and the rise of militarism.

The different levels of "government" all clamored for funds, and the demands on the people became increasingly burdensome, random, and unfair. The constant warfare also brought the depredations of battle. Warlord armies, in particular, became notorious for marching across the landscape, despoiling fields, robbing and looting, and leaving a wake of destitution behind. At the same time, with no central government, interregional cooperation for the sake of public welfare all but disappeared. Systems of water control broke down or were wantonly destroyed for military advantage. Often food could not be shipped where it was needed. Flood, famine, and misery became the hallmarks of the age.

There were few constraints on those in power. On the local level such groups as militia units, fraternal organizations, and clans became one method of protecting people or raising rebellion. There was also an increase in the influence of faith sects, which, in the classic pattern, could provide solace to the embattled citizen and a basis for political organization. On the national level, Sun Yat-sen and other leaders of the revolutionary movement that had overthrown the Qing tried to reunite the opposition and to wrest power from the warlords. However, they had little success aside from the rebellion against Yuan Shikai's imperial pretensions. Overall, like the warlords, no one in the opposition could find the key to restoring order. Even worse, in the unhappy and competitive atmosphere of the time, various local organizations and revolutionaries could even turn to exploitation of the status quo.

With the collapse of central authority, imperialism became aggravated, further contributing to the nation's woes. To some extent, the Western powers were too preoccupied with fighting one another after 1914 and the start of World War I to pressure China. However, Japan more than moved into the breach. When the war started, Japan entered on the side of the Allies. She immediately seized the German colony of Kiaochow and the other German holdings in Shandong, and the province now joined Manchuria as a Japanese sphere of influence. In Shandong, Japan was able to develop far more power than the Germans had ever had. Then in 1915, she presented the notorious Twenty-one Demands, which, if implemented, would almost have reduced China to the status of a Japanese protectorate. They were partly rejected but, nonetheless, greatly increased Japanese economic and political influence.

In 1916, partly in response to the Japanese moves, China also entered the war on the Allied side, chiefly to be in a favorable position to press the Western powers for the return of the German holdings in Shandong. At the same time, the nation was impressed by Woodrow Wilson's supposed message of the self-determination of peoples and hoped that the peace could lead to an end to China's unequal position in international affairs; however, the Versailles Peace Conference in the spring of 1919 dashed all hopes. Not only did China remain bound by the unequal treaties, but the Western leaders allowed Japan to retain control of Shandong.

THE MAY 4TH MOVEMENT AND THE BREAK WITH TRADITION

It was in this extreme situation of *neiluan* and *waihuan*, internal chaos and foreign disaster, that an effective movement for change began to reemerge in the late teens and early 1920s. The most significant manifestation of the new revolutionary tide was the momentous New Culture Movement, or May 4th Movement, as it is more commonly known. As the former name implies, the basic thrust of the movement was to make a critique of Chinese society, past and present, and to lay the foundations for establishing a new way of life.[2]

The movement had much in common with the coalition that had brought down the Qing. There was, however, at least one major difference, for in the May 4th era the united opposition, like the popular tradition of the past, turned on Confucianism for the first time. Instead, the so-called May 4th generation began to find in the West more ideological guides to social analysis and political change and adopted the goal of achieving a sharp and transcendent break with Chinese tradition.

Overall, the New Culture Movement lasted for about ten years, from 1915 to 1924. Its other name, the May 4th Movement, derives from a great student demonstration in Peking in the spring of 1919. The demonstration was precipitated by the betrayal of China at the Versailles Conference, which was then in session. It was also a protest against the warlord clique running the capital, a disreputable cabal that had taken bribes in exchange for China's acquiescence in the Shandong settlement. As a result, the May 4th events became a perfect symbol of outrage at the most immediate problems of the nation—warlordism and imperialism—and of their interconnection.

The May 4th Movement began among intellectuals centered around Peking University, a school that was originally established during the Hundred Days of Reform of 1898 and that flourished in the new educational atmosphere of the early twentieth century. As usual, we do not have a good statistical study of those who organized or joined. However, it would appear that family background and status were no longer the most important factors. Instead, the chief characteristic of the participants was youth.

The famous founders of the movement were all young by Chinese standards, in their twenties or thirties, and their immediate followers, students in the first instance, were even younger. The most senior figure in the founding group was Chen Duxiu, 37, who established the famous magazine *Xin Qingnian*, *New Youth*, which became the most influential journal of the era. He came from a prosperous family and became a follower of Kang Youwei and Liang Qichao in his late teens. Other celebrated figures included the literary reformer Hu Shi, who was 25, the writer Lu Xun, 35, both from impoverished elite families, and the philosopher Li Dazhao, who was 27 and from a farming background.

In addition to youth, the most striking thing in the makeup of the movement was the degree to which women were involved. Women were prominent in all activities of the time and in significant numbers. Partly because the female activists tended to be students and, therefore, especially young, there were no women as important at the time as some of the men involved. However, many women who participated, such as the writer Ding Ling, later went on to become famous and highly influential.

After the May 4th demonstrations, the New Culture Movement attained great notoriety. It spread to every corner of the land and began to attract the support of people in all walks of life. However, in every group, the youth and the women seem to have retained a particularly prominent position.

The reason why the youth, both male and female, now became the spearheads of the revolution was partly a reflection of the long tradition of student activism in China. At the same time it was a consequence of the comparative decline of family background and status as decisive factors in creating dissatisfaction and in determining a person's political behavior. The Three Bonds of Confucian social theory (between father and son, husband and wife, ruler and minister) refer, among other things, to three basic variables in history: age, gender, and status. Now with status all but meaningless, because of both the long-term character of the junxian system and the more immediate chaos, it would seem logical for age and gender to come to the fore as crucial variables.

More concretely, by Chinese tradition and Confucian theory, youth were considered to be in a subordinate position when it came to wisdom or access to influence. Women also occupied an inferior place and, of course, had been the most repressed group in the junxian era. For these reasons, youth and women were most prone to alienation from the old order, the ultimate outsiders. As a result, once the revolution took the form of insiders versus outsiders, with the latter in the vast majority, youth and women were particularly able to understand and to sympathize with the situation and to move into positions of political leadership.

Finally, the young, both male and female, were active because of their educational background. They were the first group that had grown up and received an education after the abolition of the examination system and the restructuring of the nation's schools in the waning years of the Qing. They were, in fact, the products of such changes. For this reason their training was far less orthodox than that of the generation of Kang and Liang. At the same time, they also had a thorough grounding in Western knowledge, both from the curricula of the new schools and, often, from study abroad. For example, all the important leaders of the movement had been students overseas. Such foreign influences, of course, strengthened the iconoclastic outlook of the generation and encouraged it to political activism.

The critique that the New Culture Movement made upon Chinese society was not much different from what had been developing within the opposition for the past hundred years. Basically, it saw the nation and its people as poor, corrupt, and repressed. As Chen Duxiu wrote in the opening issue of the magazine *New Youth*, "The strength of our country is weakening, the morals of our people are degenerating, and the learning of our scholars is distressing. Our youth must take up the task of rejuvenating China. The purpose in publishing this magazine is to provide a forum for discussing the ways of moral cultivation of the individual and the methods of governing the state."[3]

What made the movement significant, aside from the fact that it marked a revival of organized revolutionary activity on a nationwide scale, was the reason that the May 4th leaders found for the unhappy situation that surrounded them. They decided that China's problems did not arise from the specific shortcomings of the Qing, nor even of the junxian order, but rather grew out of the deepest recesses of Chinese culture, out of the whole style and attitudes of society taken as a whole and in all periods of history. They began to speak of the entire past as a unit, traditional as opposed to modern, from which a sharp break was both necessary and possible.

In other words, the May 4th generation now fully adopted the Western idea of transcendent progress. More precisely, for a hundred years the Occident had seen China as backward, stultified, and immoral. At the same time, there was little sense that the nation stood at a particular point in historical development; rather it was viewed as basically worthless and in need of a general revolution in culture at the most fundamental level. The May 4th generation, trained in Western attitudes from an early age, found such ideas extremely appealing.

The basic reason for this appeal was simply the accumulation of frustration and anger with the continued problems of China. The more alienated a person was, the more likely he was to take a holistic and totally negative attitude toward the past and to wish to break with it completely. Thus, the Taipings, the products of an unhappy minority and representing the broader problems of China's laboring majority, had tended toward such views. The attitudes of the May 4th generation arose from similar feelings.

The group represented the pent-up frustrations of youth, of women, and, more broadly, of all outsiders suffering under the heel of chaos, warlordism, and imperialism. At the same time, they had seen the ostensible success of the opposition in 1911, of a revolution committed to nationalism, democracy, and socialism, yet China was still in a terrible situation. As a result, angry and disillusioned even with the progressive legacy of the previous generation, they easily moved to the idea that the nation's problems lay at a far more fundamental level than simply a particular dynasty or sociopolitical system and that Chinese tradition needed to be attacked on all fronts.

It was as the May 4th thinkers adopted Western outlooks and began to search for the basic problems in Chinese culture that they turned on Confucianism. Their opposition to the philosophy, of course, marked a sharp break with the political avant-garde of the previous generation, such as Kang Youwei and even

Sun Yat-sen. At the same time, it gave the movement a particular significance by removing the last bar to a unity of the elite and popular traditions of change.

Overall, the hostility of the New Culture leaders to Confucianism grew out of the same cause that had impelled earlier rebels to oppose the philosophy. It was too historically and practically minded to easily provide the driving force for rapid revolutionary change, and, of course, it had no place at all for the now widespread desire for a total and transcendent break with the past. In addition, as the junxian orthodoxy, Confucianism was implicated in the problems of China stretching back several hundred years and even continued to be used in an extremely debased and fatuous fashion by warlords and others in power to defend the lopsided and immoral hierarchy of insiders and outsiders that developed after 1911. Finally, the fact that the latter were now represented by the young and by women contributed directly to their opposition to a philosophy that had helped to place them in a position of subordination.

In their critique, the May 4th thinkers stressed the conservative side of Confucianism, which, under the influence of the West, they said represented feudal values. The word they used for feudal was fengjian. This was a reasonable translation and, in many ways, not inappropriate to describe one side of Confucianism, which had originally developed in the late Zhou as the fengjian system was, for the first time, just beginning to give way to the junxian.

However, the fact that the new intellectuals now took fengjian in a pejorative sense provides a striking example of their growing alienation from the past; for in the full junxian era from the Song Dynasty onward and continuing as recently as ten or fifteen years earlier, fengjian had, of course, been seen as a lost ideal, the revival of whose strengths was a prime goal of critical thinkers, a term laden with the most positive overtones. As we shall see, with the introduction of Marxism, such alienation in terms of vocabulary was to reach a point where any dialogue with earlier Chinese social theory and, in particular, with the nation's radical and liberal traditions was to become impossible.

In any case, in attacking Confucianism, the leaders of the New Culture Movement emphasized its concern for order and hierarchy rather than its call for virtue and education. They said the philosophy held everything in a fixed and static position, blocked the human potential of all people, and made them outsiders in their own nation and the collective victims of a dynamic and advanced West. In particular, of course, they stressed that Confucianism prevented the full development of the young and of women, thereby transmitting the problems to everyone perpetually.

As Chen Duxiu wrote in a famous critique of the philosophy:

> In China the Confucianists have based their teachings on their ethical norms. Sons and wives possess neither personal individuality nor personal property. Fathers and elder brothers bring up their sons and younger brothers and are in turn supported by them. . . . Confucius lived in a feudal age. The ethics he promoted is the ethics of the feudal age. The social mores he taught and even his own mode of living were the teachings and

modes of a feudal age. The objectives, ethics, social norms, mode of living, and political institutions did not go beyond the privilege and prestige of a few rulers and aristocrats and had nothing to do with the happiness of the great masses.[4]

As for what Confucianism did to women, he wrote:

When people are bound by the Confucian teachings of filial piety and obedience to the point of the son not deviating from the father's way even three years after his death and the woman obeying not only her father and husband, but also her son, how can they form their own political party and make their own choice? The movement of women's participation in politics is also an aspect of women's life in modern civilization. When they are bound by the Confucian teaching that "To be a woman means to submit," that "The wife's words should not travel beyond her own apartment," and that "A woman does not discuss affairs outside the home," would it not be unusual if they participated in politics?

There were thinkers in the May 4th generation and afterward who defended Confucianism, though it ceased to be the mainstream of practical political thought. One of the most imaginative was Liang Shuming, who, building on the datong tradition, worked to apply the philosophy to the problems around him. His basic views were similar to those of Kang Youwei, in that he saw the Neo-Confucian orthodoxy as China's basic intellectual problem and as a deviation from the true essence and highest ideals of Confucianism. However, given the situation of the nation and the political needs and dissatisfactions of the revolutionary movement, he was unable to convince many people that the philosophy was still acceptable.

For example, Hu Shi answered Liang and, by implication, the entire previous generation by writing, "Because the cannibalistic rules of propriety, laws, and institutions for the last two thousand years have all hung out a signboard of Confucius, this signboard of Confucius—whether it is from the old shop or counterfeit—must be crushed and burned!" What characterized this era, he argued, were China's "unique treasures":

eight-legged essays [a rigid form of composition required on the examinations], bound feet, eunuchs, concubinage, five-generation households, memorial arches for honoring the chastity of widows who did not remarry, hellish prisons, and law courts filled with instruments of torture. . . . In the span of seven or eight hundred years of the prevalence of Neo-Confucianism not even one Neo-Confucian sage or worthy recognized that binding young girls' feet was an inhuman and barbarous act.[5]

Strictly speaking, much that Hu criticized could not legitimately be blamed on Confucianism; however, his list indicated that the philosophy had, at least, been compatible with injustice and shows what it was up against because of its role as the junxian orthodoxy.

On the surface then, the May 4th thinkers, brought to the edge of despair by the plight of the Chinese people and the Chinese nation, turned on their own cultural heritage. However, it is necessary to emphasize, particularly for Western readers, that, as they did so, they themselves bore testimony to the greatness and resiliency of that culture; for they criticized their own society and its history harshly and without tears and bravely uncovered its deepest problems and contradictions. Indeed, they were even unafraid to find inspiration for their critique in a foreign culture. The West, whose views they so often espoused, has not seen such an era for a long time.

As a result, even in the attack that the May 4th thinkers made upon Confucianism, the historian can see that they were contending with the philosophy from the point of view of its own highest values, for in criticizing its concern for order and hierarchy, they were, unconsciously perhaps, following the injunctions of its dynamic and democratic side. This was the side that said that any human agency, be it a ruler, a society, or an outlook, that ceases to produce and maintain virtue and justice is no longer worthy of respect. What was being proclaimed, in essence, was that Confucianism itself was now in that position.

The rather subtle relationship between the May 4th Movement and the past is best exemplified not so much in the political essays of the time but rather in fiction and, particularly, in the work of Lu Xun. It was Lu Xun's insight into the deepest concerns of those around him and into the broad drift of his age that came as close to the Confucian attributes of a sage as one could ask and that made him the finest author of twentieth-century China and one of the greatest of any time or place in history.

Lu Xun was born Zhou Shuren into an elite family that soon found itself in difficult economic straits. In 1901 he received a scholarship for study in Japan; his purpose was to pursue a medical career. While overseas, however, he had a famous moment of insight that turned his mind from science to political affairs. During the Russo-Japanese War he saw a newsreel from the front lines in Manchuria. It showed Japanese troops executing a Chinese prisoner accused of being a Russian spy. Standing around watching the execution were Chinese onlookers, who seemed unconcerned and, indeed, to be enjoying the spectacle. Lu was horrified. Here was a Chinese citizen suffering execution on Chinese soil at the hands of a foreign power fighting another foreign power for control of that soil, and here was a group of his fellow countrymen observing the scene with amused interest. With such social atomization abroad in the land, Lu decided that it was foolish to become a doctor, to save senseless material for public executions or for watching them. He decided, rather, that what China needed was a doctor of the spirit.

Lu returned home in 1909, taught, supported the Revolution of 1911, and then joined the Ministry of Education. In typical fashion, he became increasingly disillusioned with the results of the revolution and eventually decided to become a writer. His first story, "A Madman's Diary," appeared in *New Youth* in 1918 and created an immediate sensation. It set the tone for his later work and encapsulated the complexities and ironies of the May 4th era.

The story takes the form of the diary of a man who, seeing the competitive and repressive character of the society around him, goes mad. What he decides is that everyone is trying to eat him; in Chinese, *ren chi ren*, "people eating people," is also an equivalent of our image of a dog-eat-dog society. The madman is particularly distracted by the fact that even the members of his own family, that supposed repository of Confucian virtue and mutual concern, are out to devour him.

At one point, looking for solace, he turns to a book on Chinese history. What he finds "scrawled all over every page are the words: 'Virtue' and 'Morality.' " However, as he studies the pages more closely, he begins to see "words between the lines, the whole book being filled with the two words—'Eat People.' " Thus, he accuses Confucianism of something that, by its own standards, is considered to be one of the greatest of improprieties, insincerity. The diary ends with the famous lines, "Perhaps there are still children who have not eaten men? Save the children."[6]

In another piece, Lu took direct aim at Confucianism and its role, again in an ironic and horrifying way. The pathos of the great story "Kong Yiji" is universal. However, its deepest sadness comes if one imagines readers steeped in Confucian values. It takes place in the late Qing and is about an old man with scholarly pretensions who has repeatedly failed to pass the examinations. He is called Kong Yiji, and his name alludes directly to Confucius, whose family name in Chinese was, of course, also Kong.

Kong Yiji lives a hand-to-mouth existence doing odd jobs, generally as a tutor or secretary. At the same time he is a pathetic and stupid figure who feels very superior and acts with great arrogance toward the workers with whom he mixes at the local bar. Ultimately, he is a harmless person, but they respond to him in a brutal and insensitive fashion. He becomes the butt of their jokes and even the disdain of the young people whom he tries to instruct in a bit of esoteric knowledge.

In other words, Kong is a person with abstract claims, in a Confucian sense, to respect on the basis of age and education, but he has been left helpless and poverty-stricken by a system where only power and money count. At the same time, his character alludes to Confucianism itself and the sorry image that the philosophy had developed, especially among the young. To drive the point home, the narrator of the story is a boy who helps around the bar, one of the youngsters whom Kong has tried to teach.

Eventually, Kong Yiji is accused of robbing some books from a rich man and has his legs broken. But even now, there is no sympathy or understanding for the old man, because of both his arrogance and the fact that he has perhaps brought the calamity on himself. Most importantly, however, the callousness is a reflection of the profound atomization of the surrounding society. At the end, Kong comes into the tavern dirty and disheveled, like the most pathetic beggar, pushing himself along on a plank with wheels, for he can no longer walk. "Warm a bowl of wine," orders Kong, and the boy continues:

At this point my employer leaned over the counter, and said: "Is that Kong Yiji? You still owe nineteen coppers!"

"That . . . I'll settle next time," replied Kong, looking up disconsolately. "Here's ready money; the wine must be good."

The tavern keeper, just as in the past, chuckled and said, "Kong Yiji, you've been stealing again!"

But instead of protesting vigorously [as he used to do], the other simply said, "You like your joke."

"Joke? If you didn't steal, why did they break your legs?"

"I fell," said Kong in a low voice. "I broke them in a fall." His eyes pleaded with the tavern keeper to let the matter drop. By now several people had gathered round, and they all laughed. I warmed the wine, carried it over, and set it at the doorway. . . . Presently he finished the wine and, amid the laughter and comments of the others, slowly dragged himself off by his hands.

Kong does not return, and the narrator cares as little about him as does anyone else:

A long time went by after that without our seeing Kong again. At the end of the year, when the tavern keeper took down the board, he said, "Kong Yiji still owes nineteen coppers!" At the Dragon Boat Festival the next year he said the same thing again. But when the Mid-Autumn Festival came, he did not mention it. And another New Year came round without our seeing any more of him.

Nor have I ever seen him since—probably Kong Yiji is really dead."[7]

And so the story ends.

MARXISM

The spread of Marxism in China was partly a result and partly a cause of the dominance of Western thought in the May 4th era and of the decline of Confucianism. In 1921, Li Dazhao and Chen Duxiu took the lead in organizing the Chinese Communist Party, and in the following decades Marxism became the preeminent outlook of Chinese thinkers and revolutionaries. Not everyone adopted the philosophy, of course, but it became the central focus of social analysis and controversy even for those who did not, and, in one way or another, almost all political activists came under its influence.

From the point of view of Chinese history and of the Chinese social theory we have been employing, one can say that Marx's philosophy of socialism, like that of the Chinese datong thinkers of the ancient era and of post-Song times, grew out of a sense that the junxian system opened up possibilities for a highly successful society, but one that, at the same time, was itself open to grave injustices. Marx, of course, did not use the word *junxian*, but rather the word *capitalism* to designate the era involved. In addition, he believed that the crucial element in the rise of the system was the development of industry. Indeed, the importance of industry to the Marxist scheme of things is the major reason why, despite the general similarities between the two concepts, junxian cannot simply be translated as capitalism.

It is worth noting, however, that if Chinese history is used as the baseline, one would say that the West entered junxian roughly at the same time that industry developed and that it was for this reason that Marx and other Western thinkers believed that technology was the crucial variable that allowed the full establishment of centralized nonaristocratic government, a market economy, and civilian and secular values. It would seem, though, that the latter can triumph (and, indeed, go into decline) without the former, or, to put it in Marxist terms, that capitalist relations of production can develop without capitalist means of production.

Marx emphasized that capitalism was not only producing undreamed of wealth and a new sense of human potentiality but also developing social and economic contradictions that would eventually and of necessity bring down the system. In particular, he argued that the urban working class, the proletariat, would soon come to outnumber all other people at the same time as it grew increasingly poor, sophisticated, and revolutionary. Eventually, it would seize control of society, abolish capitalism, and establish socialism or communism.

Marx did not spend much time describing socialism, focusing instead on capitalism and why it must fall. His overall understanding of the concept, however, was surprisingly similar to datong. This similarity was, most likely, a coincidence or a result of parallel historical circumstances and the fact that both socialism and datong ideals represent a critique of junxian society. Conceivably, however, it may also, to some extent, have been a product of Chinese influences on the eighteenth-century Enlightenment, an era that Marx greatly admired, or of the fact that he had an interest in the Taiping Rebellion.[8]

Thus, Marx's most famous definition of communism was that it was a system where each person would produce goods according to his ability and receive benefits according to his need. This notion was essentially the same as the fundamental feature of the Great Community, that all people would relate as though they were part of a single family. Thus, in a family, members contribute what they can, which is often disparate, depending on their age and gender; nonetheless, they all receive what they need. As in the Chinese tradition, another part of the Marxist image of socialism was democracy. Marx believed that all people were basically born equal and should, ideally, be involved in all aspects of life, from economic production to governance.

The third element in the datong ideal was that it would blend the best in past systems. As a thinker in the nineteenth-century West, Marx was a firm believer in the notion of transcendent progress and had a powerful feeling that communism should and would represent a complete break with the past. Nonetheless, though Marx saw capitalism as a higher stage of human development than feudalism, like Chinese radicals, he sometimes displayed a respect for the coherence, honor, and faith that he saw in feudal times and that presented a marked contrast to the anomie and morally hollow interactions of capitalism as he understood them. Even more important, Marxism itself, like other Western outlooks of recent centuries, has a powerful fengjian side, which, in the usual fashion, was one of its major appeals in China. Most significantly, of course, both socialism and the datong tradition oppose a market economy and call for the equalization and public ownership of property, and it was for this reason that Liang Qichao and others had already begun to equate the two.

By the time that the May 4th generation became interested in Marxism, it had undergone a number of changes and additions. From the Chinese point of view the most important were those introduced by Lenin, and the outlook that took hold in China is commonly recognized as a form of Marxism-Leninism. The chief contribution of Lenin was to assert that a socialist revolution was possible in a society without much industry. He still believed that the urban proletariat was the key group in the transition to socialism, but he also suggested an important, if subsidiary, task for peasants. In addition, Lenin developed the notion of a vanguard party, the Communist Party, which would lead the revolution. He argued that such a group, well organized and properly conditioned, could carry out many of the historic tasks that Marx had assigned to the proletariat. Finally, Lenin supported a theory of imperialism that argued that the Marxist revolution had not occurred in the industrial nations because overseas expansion had given capitalism a new lease on life, exporting its problems, so to speak. At the same time, he asserted that the colonial peoples had been held back in their own socioeconomic development by the economic consequences of imperialism.

The May 4th thinkers turned to Marxism because it was the preeminent revolutionary and socialist ideology of the modern West. Other Occidental outlooks that had proven influential, the Protestantism of the Taipings and the liberalism of the late Qing, might be supportive of China's revolution and its datong component, but Marxism seemed even more appropriate. At the same time, the Russian Revolution and the various Communist movements in Europe at the close of World War I also did much to bring the outlook to the attention of Chinese activists and to convince them of its truth and inevitable triumph.

Not only did Marxism seem to have great power, but, as we have seen, its general sense of socialism was also surprisingly close to the ideal of the Great Community. At the same time, the problems of capitalism as seen by Marx were basically the same as the ones that Chinese radicals made in their own critique of China's decaying junxian system: social atomization, widespread poverty, the repression of human potentiality, and a hollow, amoral atmosphere. A major reason why liberalism lost influence in the 1920s and 1930s in the face of Marxism was precisely that it seemed tied to the capitalist system.

A further reason why Marxism-Leninism proved influential was that it fitted perfectly into the powerful nationalism of the May 4th era. In addition, though the opposition in China had, in the face of foreign imperialism and the weakness of Manchu rule, long since adopted the nationalism of the popular tradition, it seems to have retained something of the culturalist, cosmopolitan ideals of the elite. Marxism also appealed to such attitudes and in this sense helped to seal the unity of the revolutionary movement. Thus, Marx and Lenin were not particularly nationalistic and stressed that the socialist revolution would be a proletarian victory that would transcend national boundaries. At the same time, however, the Leninist theory of imperialism argued that the continued viability of capitalism in the West and Japan rested on overseas expansion; the international revolution, therefore, required a powerful nationalism and drive for equality on the part of the oppressed nations.

The link between liberalism and the very countries that were exploiting China was, of course, a related factor in the appeal of Marxism-Leninism. This connection was made particularly vivid for the May 4th generation by the differences between the East Asian policies of the new Soviet state and those of the Western countries and Japan, for just as the latter were swindling China at Versailles, the Bolsheviks were behaving very differently. In the famous Karakhan Proposals of 1919 they electrified Chinese patriots by announcing:

> Every nation whether large or small should have complete autonomy. We proclaim that all secret treaties made before the revolution with China, Japan, or the allies are hereby abrogated. . . . We hereby renounce all territory obtained through aggressive means by the former Russian imperial government in China, Manchuria, and elsewhere. . . . In short, we hereby renounce all special privileges formerly obtained by Russia in China. . . . If the Chinese people as a result of our proposals wish to become a free people and escape the evil fate of becoming a second India and Korea as has been planned for her at the Paris Peace Conference, we fervently hope that the Chinese people will make common cause with the peasants, workers, and Red soldiers of the Soviet Union and fight for their freedom![9]

In the future, there was tough bargaining on specific Russian privileges, and Soviet leaders often used Chinese politics for their own ends. However, in the following decades Chinese revolutionaries generally considered Russia to be on the side of national liberation and social progress for their country and felt a concomitant sympathy for Marxism.

Beyond its revolutionary and socialist values, victory in Russia, and support for nationalism, Marxism-Leninism also shared the general attributes that made Western thought appealing to China in the nineteenth and twentieth centuries: those that arose from the Occident's faith in transcendent progress, its transition from fengjian to junxian, and the development of science and industry.

Marxism's powerful sense of transcendence is evident in its fervent belief that capitalism was doomed to destruction and would be replaced by a new system that would be totally unique in human experience and would free all people from the burdens of the past. This belief was, of course, particularly attractive for the May 4th activists, who were so desirous of breaking completely with a discredited history and remaking China at a fundamental level.

The fact that Marxism combines fengjian and junxian characteristics was also an important part of its appeal; though, as we have noted, it represents an aspect of the outlook that is least evident from within Marxism itself. Thus, the philosophy is basically a humanistic social theory that emphasizes its freedom from metaphysical causes. Nonetheless it also has a powerful prophetic and even messianic thrust in its approach to the evils of the contemporary scene and its certitude about the inevitability of socialism. This combination was deeply appealing to the revolutionary movement of the 1920s and 1930s, which had come to represent a blend of the rationalistic traditions of elite opposition and the religious ones of popular rebellion.

Thus, Li Dazhao could write of Marxism that

> not only the Russia of today, but the whole world of the twentieth century probably cannot avoid being controlled by such religious power and swayed by such a mass movement. . . . The revolution in Russia is but the first fallen leaf warning the world of the approach of autumn. Although the word "Bolshevism" was created by the Russians, the spirit it embodies can be regarded as that of a common awakening in the heart of each individual among mankind of the twentieth century.[10]

On the other hand, Chen Duxiu could assert that Marxism represented the only true "social science," a precise tool that could and should be used to take all other outlooks and "analyze them one by one and offer rational explanations."[11]

Similarly, Marxism, through the Leninist concept of the party, supplied the organizational benefits that religion had provided to earlier rebellions in the form of dedicated and zealous congregations of believers. In addition, though it was envisioned as a civilian organization that ultimately aimed at social equality, the structure of the Communist Party also transmitted the military effectiveness of the West and even something of its still vibrant belief in the duties and obligations of a selfless aristocracy. These characteristics not only made a connection with the datong tradition but also provided a highly appropriate way of dealing with the militarization and chaos of Chinese politics after 1911. As a result, Lenin's notion of a vanguard of dedicated and disciplined revolutionaries who would lead the people to socialism proved appealing not only to those who formed the Communist Party but also to Sun Yat-sen, who in 1923 reorganized his Nationalist Party, the Kuomintang (Guomindang), along Leninist lines.

As Sun wrote:

> The Russian Revolution took place six years later than that in our country, and yet after one Revolution the Russians have been able to apply their principles thoroughly; moreover, since the revolution the revolutionary government has daily become more stabilized. Both are revolutions: why have they succeeded in Russia, and why have we not in China? It is because the Russian Revolution owed its success to the struggle of the Party members: on the one hand the Party members struggled, on the other hand they were aided by military forces, and so they were able to succeed. Therefore, if we wish our revolution to succeed, we must learn the methods, organization, and training of the Russians; then there can be hope of success.[12]

Finally, Marxism's relationship to science and industry was of immense importance to its triumph in China. Marx, of course, saw an intimate connection between industrialization and socialism, though, assuming the former as a given, he did not concern himself much with the process of economic modernization. However, by the time Marxism became popular in China, the link had been transmuted into the ideological basis of Russia's technological development, and the philosophy was often particularly praised for its contribution along these lines. Lenin once defined communism as Soviet power plus electrification, a highly appealing approach to those who wished to socialize and enrich China's poverty-stricken agricultural society.

As should be clear, Marxism-Leninism was, from a wide variety of angles, highly appropriate to the needs of the Chinese revolution. However, once the philosophy became paramount among thinkers and political activists, it also brought problems in its wake. These problems sprang from the same source as Marxism's appeal, the fact that the ideology was a product of the nineteenth- and early twentieth-century West. As a result, in addition to its revolutionary side, the outlook also transmitted the imperialist attitudes of this era, including its contempt for the history and culture of non-Western societies. The most serious result of this situation in China was to encourage the Chinese Communists to elitist attitudes and dictatorial behavior toward their fellow citizens and so to negate one of the traditional goals of the opposition movement, the destruction of the authoritarian character of the junxian age.

First of all, the Western triumph in industry and its deeper antirural traditions prevented Marxists from appreciating the sophistication and revolutionary character of the Chinese people, the vast majority of whom were, of course, farmers. In the West's recent fengjian era, the serfs had been considered the lowest class, virtually animals. Even Marx had referred to peasants as "sacks of potatoes" and spoken of the "idiocy of rural life." Lenin, of course, gave rural people a greater political role. However, it was a deeply subordinate one, and socialism was envisioned as a dictatorship of the proletariat, which meant, in practice of their theoretical embodiment, the Communist Party.

Similarly, the transcendent character of Marxism led the already disillusioned May 4th generation to a denial of any relationship between their own movement and the past and to profound confusions in their understanding of Chinese history and society. This situation is most strikingly evident in what came to be the Marxist analysis of Chinese history. Since China had been and remained an agricultural society, the Communists asserted that virtually the entire Chinese past had been fengjian or feudal, including not only the Three Dynasties and the transitional period that followed but also the high junxian era of the previous thousand years!

Such theoretical nihilism, of course, made a clean break with the views of their forebears. However, it also created profound analytical confusion and, in particular, obscured the impact that a thousand years of the junxian system had made on Chinese society. In so doing, of course, it also destroyed any possibility of understanding the vibrant opposition tradition of that era, for infusing the junxian system with the spirit of fengjian had no meaning whatsoever if one claimed that the era had not been junxian but had, indeed, been fengjian all along.

Finally, because of its own origins in a society just at the beginning of a junxian age, Marxism, like the Christianity of the Taipings, sometimes transmitted excessively fengjian approaches. In economics it opposed not only laissez-faire but free enterprise of any sort, thus increasing governmental control of all aspects of life. Furthermore, the Leninist party structure brought with it not only a sense of aristocratic obligation and of military effectiveness but also a still powerful heritage of extreme elitism and regimentation. Finally, Marxism not only had great spiritual strength but also carried some of the sectarian traits of Western religion. It was committed to the notion that it had an exclusive insight into reality that no other perspective shared. It was prone to bitter, often metaphysical disputes with differing points of view and was, as a result, highly intolerant of those who opposed it.

The difficulties that such views brought in their wake included intellectual chaos and political miscalculation. For obvious reasons the full antipathy toward rural people that characterized Marxist theory could never really take hold in China; however, the Chinese Communists were to have many problems because of their particular fondness for urban workers. Similarly, the notion that China was just emerging from feudalism created a persistent inability to create a coherent Marxist interpretation of Chinese history or a satisfactory understanding of the current scene. It implied, for example, that the nation had sharp class lines, an error that often led the Communist Party into needless conflict with groups that might otherwise have been among its supporters. As we have noted, however, the most serious result of these attitudes was to strengthen the dictatorial rather than the liberal possibilities bequeathed from the past. The power of the former had indigenous roots as well: the long-standing imperial traditions of the junxian age, the chaos within the nation, and even the tensions in datong theory between patriarchy and equality. Marxism-Leninism, however, deepened the problems immensely.

Marxists could all too easily see themselves and their organizational instrument, the party, as a single ray of enlightenment in a bleak, feudal landscape, a landscape peopled by unhappy but unsophisticated peasants who could not lead a socialist revolution or create a socialist society. The need to bring salvation to such people, coupled with the Communist belief that they had the sole insight into truth, was, of course, far more conducive to dictatorial behavior and to a hierarchical relationship between the leaders and the led than to a frank recognition that China was in the midst of a great revolutionary upsurge with a long and powerful history, a significant socialist component, extremely broad support, and farmers and rural society long playing a crucial role.

THE KUOMINTANG AND THE COMMUNISTS IN THE 1920s

The triumph of the Communist Party from its creation in 1921 to the establishment of the People's Republic in 1949 was to prove an uneven story in which early failures were crowned by eventual success. These thirty years also saw the reign of the Kuomintang, the Nationalist Party of Sun Yat-sen, with whom the Communists alternately cooperated and contended, and also the Japanese invasion of China, a cataclysmic event that was to play a crucial role in helping the latter to victory.[13]

The Communist Party was founded with aid from representatives of the Comintern, the international Communist organization run from Moscow, and for its first fifteen years of existence was, for the most part, under the domination of the Soviet Union. Almost immediately after the party came into being, Russia ordered its members to join Sun's Nationalist Party. The reasons for this order were partly ideological: since China was a feudal country according to Marxist theory, what it needed was not a socialist revolution in the first instance but the creation of a middle-class government and capitalism. Sun and the Kuomintang, it was claimed, represented groups committed to such goals. At the same time, Russia was looking for allies in all parts of the world, and Sun, the most famous revolutionary in China, and his comparatively experienced Kuomintang seemed far more important than the fledgling Communist Party.

Sun himself was eager for an alliance because he, too, was looking for support in his never-ending struggle to regain influence and revolutionize China. As a result, at his base in Canton, he accepted the Communists into the ranks of the Nationalist Party and began to use Comintern advisers. With this assistance he restructured his party into a tight and effective Leninist-style organization and also set up the famous Whampoa Military Academy, which supplied the officer corps for a new and well-motivated Kuomintang army.

The commandant of the academy was Chiang Kai-shek. Born in 1887, Chiang came from a family of farmers and businessmen that had fallen on hard times when he was young. He studied military affairs in Japan before the Revolution of 1911 and then returned to work on and off with Sun Yat-sen. After the alliance with the Communists he was sent to the Soviet Union for further training and then returned to head Whampoa. The political commissar of the academy was a Communist, the twenty-six-year-old Zhou Enlai. Zhou was from an elite family that, like Chiang's and that of so many others, lost its wealth while he was growing up. Nonetheless, Zhou received a good grounding in Chinese learning. He went to France during World War I and there became a Communist.

As the uncontested leader of the Kuomintang and a hero to virtually every progressive faction in China, Sun Yat-sen was able to maintain the alliance between the Nationalists and the Communists with comparative success. As he built up his power, his goal was to launch a "Northern Expedition" from Canton that would overthrow the warlords and reestablish an effective republic. The

Communists served Sun loyally and did various sorts of organizational work to further his plans. In line with their Marxist ideology their greatest interest and greatest success lay in mobilizing urban workers and bringing them to support the Kuomintang.

Unfortunately, Sun was not to realize his dream of fulfilling the Chinese revolution; he died in 1925. After his passing, plans for the Northern Expedition continued. However, disputes began to break out within the Kuomintang, most importantly between the Communists and Chiang Kai-shek, who was working his way up to leadership of the party and using his military connections as a base. Early in 1926, just before the expedition was to begin, Chiang turned openly on the Communists in the Kuomintang ranks. He removed them from high office and barred them from further positions of influence.

At this point, many Communists felt that they should break with the Nationalists. Under Soviet pressure, however, they remained in the alliance. One reason for the pressure was the continuing theory, which was never officially abandoned, that China was a feudal society. More importantly, China had become enmeshed in Soviet internal politics. Joseph Stalin was just concluding his struggle with Leon Trotsky for the mantle of succession to Lenin, and the alliance between the Kuomintang and the Chinese Communists had become an issue of contention between them. Trotsky was generally associated with skepticism about the tie, and Stalin, with support for it. If the cooperation had ended in 1926, it would have been something of a delayed triumph for Trotsky, whose power in Russia was rapidly declining.

The Northern Expedition, reminiscent of the Taiping offensive seventy-five years earlier, set out from Canton in July 1926. The chief contribution of the Communists was to mobilize workers in the forefront of the advancing Nationalist armies. They organized in the countryside, but their emphasis continued to be on urban areas, most notably Shanghai, China's greatest industrial center. However, when Chiang's armies reached the city in the spring of 1927, he launched a second and far more serious coup against his allies. With their work done, thousands of Communists and their supporters were brutally executed and their organizations disbanded. For a short time afterward Stalin still harbored hopes that the alliance with the Nationalists could be salvaged. However, it soon became evident that this goal was impossible, and the Kuomintang and the newly independent Communist Party became bitter enemies.

THE NANKING DECADE

The Kuomintang armies continued to march north and took Peking in 1928. Chiang Kai-shek then established the seat of government of the Republic of China at Nanking, a former capital of the Ming and of the Taipings. He renamed Peking ("Northern Capital") Peiping ("Northern Peace"). The next ten years or so, until the full-scale Japanese invasion of the middle and late thirties are often called the Nanking decade of twentieth-century Chinese history. Chiang and his Nationalist government ultimately failed to retain control of China, and he and his efforts to do so have often received a bad press. Still, the Nationalist regime did make some progress toward solving China's problems.

One area in which Chiang did comparatively well was his effort to bring an end to warlordism. He bargained with the various generals, bribed them, and even used force as a last resort. As a result, by the middle thirties he had received the allegiance of many of the important warlords and was having some success in spreading the influence of the Nanking government to the provincial level. At the same time, he had, to some extent, brought under control the rampant warfare of the previous era.

The other task Chiang Kai-shek undertook with some success was combatting imperialism. He was a fervent nationalist and worked effectively against the unequal treaties. By the 1930s, the republic had regained tariff autonomy and considerable control over China's financial resources. Chiang had also ended the extrality enjoyed by Russia, Germany, and some of the smaller foreign powers and also substantially cut the number of foreign concessions in Chinese cities.

Despite such successes, however, Chiang had one very broad drawback that ultimately weakened the republic and made even the progress that it did achieve a rather shallow affair. This was that he had little or no feel for the Chinese revolution as a whole, for the intense opposition that had been building for over a hundred years to the social breakdown and moral vacuity of the junxian order. His attitude, then, related to a broader problem of the Nanking government, elitism and authoritarianism, a feeling that people needed to be led, a distrust of the average citizen, and a comparative lack of concern with the terrible problems he faced.

In the first instance, the reason for such attitudes seems to have been Chiang's lifelong involvement with the army. As the heir to Sun Yat-sen and the leader of the Kuomintang, he was not simply another warlord. However, he was not basically a civilian politician either or even a leader who could combine military power and revolution into an effective blend. As a result, he invariably thought more of controlling society from above than of reviving the nation by mobilizing the resources and energies of an aroused populace.

As with the Communists, the dictatorial character of the Kuomintang and its elitism were also a reflection of long-standing Chinese problems and of influences coming out of the West and Japan. However, in this era, the Communists were guarded against the worst political consequences of such failings by their basic commitment to revolution and popular mobilization. Similarly, though Chiang Kai-shek may have retained some residual loyalty to the goals of economic justice embedded in the official ideology of the Kuomintang, they seemed extremely low on his scale of priorities.

Eventually, as the general approach of the republican government became clear, its base of power grew more reactionary. It began to attract support and to rely for its authority on the small handful of people in control of society, of those committed in one way or another to the status quo. That is to say, in many ways, Chiang's regime became a part of China's problems rather than a solution.

As a result of the character of the republic and Chiang's flaws, the national unity that Nanking achieved was far from complete. Since it was built not on a broad popular movement but rather on negotiations between high military figures, the influence of the central government remained weak below the provincial level and often did not extend into rural areas at all. Similarly, Nanking's anti-imperialism was also limited and for the same reasons. In some ways, indeed, Chiang, a man who prided himself on his nationalism, was to become one of the saddest victims of imperialism.

Thus, Chiang's initial leverage against the unequal treaties had been a series of antiforeign movements that swept China in the wake of the May 4th Movement. These ranged from vast public demonstrations to violent attacks on concessions and other enclaves of foreign privilege. These movements made it increasingly costly for the imperialists to maintain their position and aided the government in its negotiations. However, as the revolutionary fervor of the Kuomintang subsided, Chiang no longer supported the use of mass politics to pressure foreigners, and he came to oppose the use of force against them to a degree far less than was demanded by most political activists of the time or even by the radicals of the late Qing.

Even more serious, just as the Nanking regime became associated with those in power rather than with outsiders, it also grew uncomfortably close to foreigners. By the middle 1930s the republic's base of power was in the coastal cities that were the center of Western influence. Like Sun Yat-sen before him, Chiang married into one of the great Shanghai families, the Soongs, and converted to Christianity. When Japanese aggression began, many in China felt that the government did not respond with sufficient fervor. Chiang eventually fought Japan and even ended the system of unequal treaties. He continued to be deeply influenced by the Leninist belief that imperialism was the prime source of China's problems. But the bitterness with which he frequently expressed his nationalism must have been increasingly fed by the knowledge that he had often been subtly co-opted.

In addition to limiting the immediate success of the Nanking government in national unification and anti-imperialism, the conservatism that overtook the Kuomintang also meant that the broader needs of the Chinese nation for a revival of moral authority in an effective political ideology completely eluded Chiang and his government. Nanking found no framework of thought that could rival Marxism-Leninism in popularity and that, despite its indirect influence on the Kuomintang and on Chiang himself, was not appropriate for the insider's position that the government claimed by the 1930s. Seeking a way out, the Nationalists, in the so-called New Life Movement, did create a warmed-over and highly authoritarian version of orthodox Confucianism. But it was, of course, utterly unrelated to the moods and needs of the country and held no appeal even for such men as Liang Shuming, who were trying to develop a radical Confucianism appropriate to the time.

Worst of all, however, Chiang's regime made no dent on the mass poverty of China and on the misery of the average person, the nation's most pressing problems. The countryside remained a disaster area, and life in the cities, except for those on top, was not much better. Many of the reasons for this situation were beyond the immediate control of the government: China's huge population, lack of capital, and political chaos; at the same time, the Great Depression of the 1930s was particularly hard on rural people the world over. Nonetheless, Chiang expressed comparatively little concern with the issue of economic injustice and was certainly unable to transmit what feelings he did have to the country at large. The reasons for his problems were, naturally, intertwined with all the shortcomings of the republic but were tied, most importantly, to the increasing reliance that it placed on those who were exploiting the nation's distress.

THE COMMUNIST VICTORY

While the Kuomintang was having its difficulties, the Communists were gradually developing tactics and outlooks that led to their eventual victory. In terms of concrete results, however, they emerged from the Nanking decade in an extremely precarious position. They were certainly far weaker than Chiang's government, and few observers would have guessed that they would ever defeat the Kuomintang, whatever the shortcomings of the Nationalist regime; and, indeed, their ultimate success was crucially advanced by the impact of the war with Japan.

After Chiang's coup of 1927, the Communists found themselves defeated and hounded, with no popular base to speak of. The great cities, in which the party had hitherto concentrated its activities, were in the hands of the Kuomintang, and the cadres who remained were forced underground. At the same time, various army units, led by Communists, were scattered around the country. All the groups faced a common problem of strategy because of the urban bias that dominated the party's thinking and the impossible political situation in the cities. One approach that found particular favor in the eyes of Moscow was to launch an uprising in a town or to have a loyal army unit seize one by assault. The hope was that the city thus controlled would provide a base for a gradual revival of Communist strength. All such attempts failed, however, often at considerable human cost.

The strategy that ultimately proved most effective was, not surprisingly, the one most appropriate to Chinese traditions and to the current scene. It developed among the armies in the countryside, the most famous of which was to become a force in the Southeast that collected under the leadership of Mao Zedong and Zhu De. Mao, who, of course, emerged as the preeminent figure in Chinese communism, was born in 1893 in Hunan Province. He was from a family of farmers and had received a sound education in Chinese and Western knowledge. However, unlike many important figures of the era, he had never studied abroad. Mao became involved in the May 4th Movement as a young man in his home province and in 1918 went to Peking, where, for a time, he became an assistant to Li Dazhao in the Peking University Library. He became a Marxist and attended the founding meeting of the Communist Party in 1921.

Perhaps because he was from a farming background and perhaps because his outlook was developed entirely within China, Mao Zedong became one of the Communists who, at a comparatively early date, recognized the central role that farmers were playing in the Chinese revolution. At the time of the Northern Expedition he had helped to organize a rural uprising in Hunan. In his famous report on the movement he wrote:

> In a very short time, in China's central, southern, and northern provinces, several hundred million peasants will rise like a tornado or tempest, a force so extraordinarily swift and violent that no power, however great, will be able to suppress it. They will break all trammels that now bind them and rush forward along the road to liberation. They will send all imperialists, warlords, corrupt officials, local bullies, and bad gentry to their graves. All revolutionary parties and all revolutionary comrades will stand before them to be tested, and to be accepted or rejected as they decide. To march at their head and lead them? Or to follow at their rear, gesticulating at them and criticizing them? Or to face them as opponents? Every Chinese is free to choose among three alternatives, but circumstances demand that a quick choice be made.[14]

The complex and colorful Zhu De had been born in 1886 into an elite family in Sichuan Province. He received an excellent education in Chinese classical knowledge, which may have contributed to his later sophistication in relating the Communist movement to the realities of China. In 1905 he sat for the imperial exams the last time they were given and then turned to local politics and military affairs. He joined the Kuomintang after 1911, picked up the opium habit, and ended up as something of a petty warlord in his home province. In 1922, after being defeated by another general, he went to Shanghai, conquered his drug habit, and sailed for Europe. There he studied Western philosophy and became a Marxist-Leninist.

In 1928 several military units under the leadership of Mao and Zhu gathered in a remote area on the border between the provinces of Jiangxi and Hunan. Like the starting point of traditional popular rebellions, the place was beyond the easy administrative control of higher governmental authorities, comparatively secure from attack and self-sufficient economically. There the Communists organized an administrative structure and developed their military power into what became China's Red Army. They also carried out a radical program of land redistribution. In 1931 the area was proclaimed to be a new state, the Chinese Soviet Republic.

The Communist strategy in Jiangxi was considerably more in harmony with the realities of Chinese politics than it had been earlier. Nevertheless, problems continued to plague the party because of its overly strict adherence to Marxism-Leninism and Russian practice. Most importantly, the Communists still believed that urban workers had to lead the revolution and that the party represented them. Since there were, essentially, no urban workers in the area, this outlook simply led to an increase in the self-importance of the party and to a dictatorial style in working with the local farmers. At the same time, the Communists' analysis of Chinese society as recently feudal or early capitalist encouraged them to see and even to stimulate intense social conflict rather than to make use of the broad-based dissatisfaction that existed. As a result, their program of land redistribution tended to be mechanistic and unjust and needlessly alienated and injured many decent people.

What eventually destroyed the Jiangxi Soviet, however, was not its internal problems as the Communists worked their way back, one might say, to an approach appropriate to China. Rather it was the power of Chiang Kai-shek, who, understanding the special threat that the Communists posed, made concerted efforts to dislodge them. Chiang and the nearby warlords launched a series of so-called Extermination Campaigns against the new Soviet Republic. At first these failed, but the noose tightened, and by 1934, after the Fifth Campaign, the Communist position became untenable.

The result was the famous Long March of 1934–1935. In October 1934, under cover of darkness and over a period of several weeks, one hundred thousand Communists, the Red Army and its followers, moved out. The difficult trek lasted a year and took the Communists a distance of six thousand miles to a new base in the distant Northwest. Only twenty thousand of the original group were there at the end, the rest dead or scattered. The Long March has remained one of the great sagas in the history of Chinese communism, and today all Chinese children learn of the rivers crossed, the mountains climbed, the deserts traversed, and the battles fought.

Despite the heroic character of the march, however, Mao and his followers recognized it for what it was, a desperate retreat that destroyed whatever progress they had made in Jiangxi. In the Northwest they wandered for a time, ultimately settling at Yenan (Yan'an), an out-of-the-way place in Shaanxi Province. The following decade is the famous Yenan period in Chinese Communist history, the era of the Japanese invasion.

Japanese imperialism had subsided somewhat in the 1920s, but in the 1930s, with the rise of militaristic and authoritarian government in Tokyo, aggression began again on a grander and more direct scale than ever before. As part of his anti-imperialist efforts, Chiang Kai-shek had begun to reassert Chinese control over the Japanese sphere of influence in Manchuria. He was making some headway, and so, in September 1931, Japan invaded. It conquered the area easily and early in 1932 established the puppet state of Manchukuo. Then it began to apply pressure to North China proper. In 1937 full-scale war broke out with Japanese attacks on Peiping and up and down China's coast.

In the face of the foreign attack and nationwide demands for an end to internal bickering, Chiang and the Kuomintang were forced into an alliance with the Communists. The unity, or "popular front" as the Communists put it, proved to be very shaky, and by the early 1940s sporadic fighting again broke out between the two sides. In the short run, however, the front gave the Communists some respite from Nationalist pressure as they established themselves in the Northwest. In the long run, it was the disparate effect of Japanese aggression on the Kuomintang and the Communists that, for the first time, tipped the balance of power decisively in favor of the latter.

Chiang's armies often fought bravely as they tried to defend China from the invaders. However, it soon became evident that they could not withstand the Japanese war machine. As a result, by the late 1930s, the republican government and the core of its armies were forced to evacuate their base of power in the cities of eastern China and retreat to the far West, to Chongqing (Chungking) in Sichuan Province. Once there, they still could not resist Japan in direct frontal warfare, and they were unable and probably unwilling to mobilize the people for a guerrilla strategy.

As a result, for the rest of the war a long stalemate developed between the Nationalists and Japan. In this situation the Kuomintang government, already a rather frayed affair, grew pessimistic, cynical, and corrupt. At the same time, pressed for money, it often exploited the local people under its control and began to print money with abandon. The results, including massive inflation, alienated the citizenry at all levels of society. American aid poured in but, under the circumstances, simply provided an additional arena for corruption. It also heightened Chiang's dependence, both psychological and material, on foreigners and further helped to separate him from his own people.

Significantly, the major success of the Nationalists during the war was in the area of foreign relations rather than internal politics, but it was nonetheless a signal one. Operating within the intricacies of wartime diplomacy, Chiang Kai-shek succeeded in bringing the unequal treaties to a full and final end. In addition, he received assurances that all territories that Japan had seized from China since the nineteenth century would be returned. Indeed, in formal terms at least, Chiang attained recognition for his country as a coequal partner with the other major powers fighting the Axis, and it was agreed that in the United Nations Organization, which was to be created after the war, China would sit on the Security Council along with England, France, Russia, and the United States.

In the meantime, the Japanese invasion allowed and encouraged the Communist Party to organize and lead a classic popular rebellion, and one that relied, for the most part, on farmers. When they arrived in Yenan, the Communists, of course, already possessed the requisite ideological zeal and organization, were committed to socialism, and were deeply nationalistic. Now they found themselves in a position where opposition to foreign invasion required them to gain as much support from the local citizenry as possible. At the same time, cut off from Soviet influence and with the failure of Jiangxi behind them, they were more able than ever before to come to grips with the practical realities of Chinese politics and of the Chinese revolution.

In the face of Japanese aggression, much of the dominant elite fled North China: warlords, Kuomintang officials, and local notables alike. However, though the Japanese army could move into an area, seize crops, terrorize, and kill, it could not establish an effective and stable system of control over a vast area of a hundred million people, most of whom were bitterly opposed to its presence. In this situation, the Communists emerged as the champion of Chinese resistance and also developed an authority that began around Yenan and gradually spread over much of the North.

The Communists were no more able to fight Japan with conventional warfare than were the Nationalists. However, their revolutionary outlook meant that they had no fear of resisting the enemy through organizing a broadly based guerrilla movement. They helped militia corps and other local organizations to protect their territory and also formed such groups into larger units that operated full-time over a wider terrain. At the same time, they enlarged and strengthened the Red Army for guerrilla work and also for major confrontations with the foe.

Such activities could not hope to liberate North China and had little impact within cities. However, in the rural areas that formed the bulk of the territory, they, to some extent, harried the Japanese forces and kept them off balance. More importantly, these activities mobilized the nationalism of the people, gave them hope, and, of course, brought them to support the Communist cause.

Building on their military activities, the Communists also worked to establish a governmental system in the North. As they did so, in line with their ideology and their desire for broad-based support, they worked carefully to bring outsiders, those who formed the vast bulk of the population, into the political process. To this end, they greatly increased the size of the party, the institution that provided what central authority there was, and tried to enroll people from all strata of life. As a result, the party came to include a large number of farmers and also a considerable representation from the elite, including intellectuals, who had fled the occupied cities and joined the cause. In their day-to-day activities, party cadres worked at establishing more equitable political relations among local people and organized auxiliary groups, such as women's leagues and poor farmers' leagues, which were given a role in decision making.

Finally, insofar as possible under wartime conditions, the Communists worked to improve the economic life of the average person and to equalize wealth. However, because the party was trying to maximize support and did not wish needlessly to alienate anyone who was resisting Japan, its policies were now based more on the actual situation in the countryside and less on theory than they had been in Jiangxi. The Communists put their major effort into making sure that what goods were available were fairly distributed and that people had some hope of surviving. They carried out a program of rent reduction and, even more importantly, did much to free farmers from usurious credit arrangements that had kept them in thrall for generations. The party also undertook a moderate program of land redistribution; however, unlike the past it did not do so with the aim of proving that intense social conflict existed or that it should be needlessly aroused.

Despite the practical, effective, and popular style that the Communists adopted during the wartime years, it should be stressed that they did not change their basic commitment to Marxism-Leninism, and the problems associated with the ideology continued along with the benefits. In theory, farmers and the elite were still an appendage to the revolution, and the party represented the proletariat. As a result, the dictatorial side of the movement remained firmly in place, and the party was especially hard on the intellectuals who found themselves in the liberated areas. On the whole, however, the Yenan period was, comparatively speaking, the least elitist and the most open in the history of Chinese communism, just as it was the era least influenced by the West.

As a result of the differences between the Communists and the Kuomintang during the war, when Japan surrendered in August 1945, the power of the two parties was the reverse of what it had been in the late 1930s. The Communists were spread over half the country at the head of a vigorous army and with considerable popular support. The Nationalists were isolated in a corner of the far West with few followers and a disillusioned and corrupt military. Chiang and his forces returned to the East, and for the next four years the two unevenly matched enemies fought for control of the nation.

There was tough campaigning, and some areas, including Yenan, changed hands. However, the Communists steadily expanded their territory. In the meantime the cities under Kuomintang control suffered a terrible hyperinflation that wiped out all vestiges of support for the republic. Chiang Kai-shek called for massive American aid, and though some was forthcoming, it could do nothing. In 1949, Chiang's government and the remnants of his armies fled to the island of Taiwan, which had returned to Chinese control with the defeat of Japan, and on October 1, Mao Zedong stood on the Gate of Heavenly Peace in what was again the capital city of Peking and proclaimed the establishment of a Communist state, the People's Republic of China.

7

The People's Republic of China

INTRODUCTION

It is far harder to be confident in discussing a contemporary society than it is to speak of history. Distance in time can reveal the main outlines of an era and clarify its major issues and directions of change. In addition, crucial facts about the immediate past are often difficult to obtain. We do not have archives or recourse to the host of private communications that are available from history. Finally, of course, it is far more difficult to be objective about current issues; our own prejudices and interests are far more apt to be directly involved.

Such problems are compounded when dealing with the People's Republic. Since 1949, China, after a thousand years of the junxian system, has been in a new phase of her history. As a result, using the past to clarify the present, the only means available, is particularly uncertain. At the same time, the difficulties of obtaining sound information are increased by the fact that for the past forty years Chinese society has been tightly controlled, and much that is significant and interesting has been unavailable to the Chinese people, let alone to foreigners. Finally, problems of objectivity are increased for Americans because for many years the United States and China had very poor relations, and the two nations still have profound political differences. Dogmatism is always out of place in understanding humankind and never more so than in the study of contemporary China.

When Mao Zedong proclaimed the establishment of the People's Republic of China, he had the active support of a vast number of his fellow citizens, the enthusiastic sympathy of even more, and the guarded hopes and well wishes of almost everyone else. The new government was the product of 150 years of revolutionary activity that had found increasing favor in the eyes of the Chinese people and of moral idealism and political opposition that dated back far earlier. At the same time, the Communist leadership seemed deeply committed to solving the problems that had fueled discontent for so long and that had, in many ways, become even worse in the years since the fall of the Qing: poverty, unrepresentative and ineffective government, national weakness, and a poor moral climate.

In facing these mammoth tasks, the new government not only had the benefit of historical ideals and the support of the Chinese people but also had the organizational strength of the Communist Party and the experience that it had garnered in the revolutionary struggles of the previous thirty years. At the same time, the leaders had the zeal and self-confidence that came from Marxism's faith in the inevitability of progress and the possibilities of creating a just and prosperous society.

On the other hand, they were also burdened by attitudes that had caused problems in the past and would become even more serious in the future. Thus, the authoritarian legacies of the junxian age and the pressing problems of the nation combined with Marxist-Leninist dogma to encourage dictatorial rule. In particular, the notion that China had just emerged from fengjian and had an unsophisticated population of "peasants" provided a poor framework for appreciating the full capacities and commitment of the Chinese people. In addition, since the Communists still found little or no value in Chinese history or philosophy, they compounded the problems of entering a new era and reconstructing the social system by separating themselves from the viewpoints most appropriate to their needs: China's own traditions and, in particular, the radical thought of the junxian age and the "socialist" theories embodied in the datong approach.

The overall result of this situation has been that from the vantage of both social justice and economic development, the People's Republic has made some progress on the tasks it faced forty years ago. At the same time, however, it has also experienced failures, many of great magnitude. Over time, policies have developed that have sometimes seemed to be more in harmony with Chinese possibilities and Chinese realities. However, the process has barely begun, and most observers would agree that today the Chinese government and the Communist Party find themselves in deep trouble.

EMULATING THE SOVIET UNION

The first five years of Communist rule in China were devoted primarily to establishing an effective political system. There were also considerable concern and comparative success in improving public welfare and beginning economic growth. It was an era in which China came under heavy Soviet influence and also fought the United States in Korea. Overall, these early years did much to establish the structure and set the tone for the subsequent history of the People's Republic.

In the Yenan years, Chinese communism had been comparatively free of foreign influences, if not in theory, at least to a considerable degree in practice. With the establishment of the People's Republic, however, Mao Zedong proclaimed a renewed dedication to the Soviet Union as China's "teacher" in socialism. At the same time, he said that the new government would "lean to one side" in international affairs in favor of Russia and the Eastern bloc. On the broadest level, the reason for this approach was that Russia was the most powerful nation in the world that proclaimed itself to be a Marxist-Leninist state. In the 1920s the Chinese Communists had copied Russian models because they suggested techniques for a successful revolution; now, Russia appeared to hold the clue on how to create and develop a socialist society.

More specifically, Soviet national practice stressed things that were particularly crucial in the early years of the Communist ascendancy: political order and economic development. At the same time, Russia, fresh from her victories in the Second World War, seemed to indicate how a socialist country could maintain her national security in a hostile world. Finally, direct Russian aid, both for economic development and as an ally in international affairs, required that China emulate the Soviet Union, for the latter, in the theocratic style of Marxism-Leninism, required Communist countries to follow and, indeed, to fawn over her political organization and socioeconomic theories.

Once in power, the Chinese Communists were able to reestablish a stable political system quickly and with comparative ease. This achievement was partly a tribute to their own political skills and sense of organization as well as to the long-standing Chinese traditions of political unity and to the thirst for order after several generations of chaos and war. The system that was established was, essentially, a highly centralized dictatorship of the Communist Party. This sort of rule was not, of course, in line with the datong ideals that had influenced the revolution in its pre-Communist phase and that aimed at enhancing democracy and replacing the excessive centralization of the junxian system with the decentralized benefits of fengjian. However, the system reflected both the immediate need for national order and the Soviet example. At the same time, it was in accord with the Marxist belief that the Chinese people were politically backward and needed to be led and, indeed, to some extent, forced into making social progress.

More precisely, in line with the Russian model, China established a dual structure of authority resting on the Communist Party and on the government. As in the Soviet Union, however, the two were closely intertwined, and ultimate power rested with the former. The party-government hierarchy moved in an orderly fashion from Peking down to the village level. This system meant that the direct control of the central authorities actually penetrated further into society than it had in the latter parts of the junxian age, when the lowest official unit of political life was the county.

By 1949, the Communist Party, the core of the system, had four to five million members. As usual, we do not have a good statistical study of the group's social composition. However, it seems to have included a fair representation of the broad coalition that had carried out the revolution. Party membership was considered to be a great honor and was avidly sought. Cadres were expected to keep a high tone of commitment and selfless devotion to society, and repeated "rectification campaigns'' and educational drives were carried out to insure that they would remain so.

Officially, the party was organized democratically through a series of elections from the lowest units up to the top, the Central Committee and its Standing Committee and, supreme over all, the Political Bureau (Politburo), a group of about ten people who stood at the zenith of the system. In practice, however, power and decision making moved from the top downward rather than from the bottom up. The Politburo and its undisputed head, Mao Zedong, ran things. Below them, orders and even slates of candidates came from one level to the one beneath. Those on a lower rung had precious little input into policy, and public criticism of those in control, in particular of the Politburo, was not permitted.

The Communist Party ran the government and society in much the same way as Mao Zedong and the Politburo ran the party; the official structure was democratic, but the practice was highly regimented. In theory, the government was made up of a coalition composed of a number of political parties, a system that aimed at giving expression to the broad support that the revolution had received. In Communist jargon, China was a ''Dictatorship of the People'' rather than a ''Dictatorship of the Proletariat'' as existed in Russia where only the Communist Party was permitted. At the same time, governmental power was supposed to pass upward through various levels to a parliament, the National People's Congress, which was established as the highest political organ of the state.

In reality, however, the Communist Party was completely dominant; all aspects of political life were under its control, and orders moved outward from it to the rest of society. People did not feel free to criticize party members, and no real opposition was permitted to exist. To cement the system and his own power, Mao Zedong established himself as chief of state as well as chairman of the party. During the Communists' rise to power something of a cult of personality had begun to develop around the chairman. Now this grew apace, and official propaganda rarely missed a chance to speak in glowing terms of Mao's leadership and of his pivotal role in Chinese life.

The average citizen was involved in the hierarchy of party and government through the so-called mass line. Originally begun in Yenan times, the mass line bore some testimony to the ideal of giving all people a political role. In reality, however, it generally functioned in a manipulative rather than a democratic fashion. Essentially, the line meant enrolling the population into large organizations that were said to represent its interests but were, for the most part, transmission belts for government power. The groups ranged from a Youth League and a Women's Federation to organizations based on labor and sports. By the early 1950s, at least half the people of China belonged to one group or another. In addition, the mass line included huge drives and campaigns meant to unite the citizenry behind a specific goal, such as increasing production or fighting corruption. In almost all cases, however, the emphasis was on mobilizing the people rather than granting them actual power.

For those suspected of posing a threat to the system or of being in serious opposition to it, punishment was extremely severe. In the late 1940s and early 1950s, many of the former elite in the rural areas were denounced and tried; many were executed. In the cities there were several campaigns aimed at ferreting out "counter-revolutionaries," and there was also much killing. We do not have figures on the total number of people who died, but Mao himself admitted to at least one million executions, and sober foreign estimates have run as high as five million.[1]

Those killed were generally accused of being local tyrants or of having collaborated with the Japanese during the war. Nonetheless, there is evidence that the average person was able to understand the crimes involved as products of the tragic and competitive atmosphere of the previous decades. As a result, party cadres, acting on orders from above, often had to stage manage trials and arouse people to mete out punishment.[2] In a sense, then, the mass killings of these early years were not only terrible in their own right, but also represent a further example of political manipulation, of the fear that the Chinese people were too unsophisticated to reeducate and assimilate those who disagreed or might disagree with the new society, however powerless they had become.

One thing that bolstered the dictatorial tendencies of the time and also China's reliance on the Soviet Union was the Korean War. The United States became involved in Korea in June 1950 and by the autumn of that year was beginning to carry the war to the northern, Communist portion of the divided nation, territory directly adjacent to China's Manchurian provinces. Peking, with its government barely in place and with memories of imperialism fresh in its consciousness, felt threatened and issued repeated warnings against further American moves toward the border. These went unheeded, however, and in October, China entered the conflict on the northern side. An unofficial but bloody war ensued, which lasted for three years and in which Russia gave considerable aid to China.

In America, it should be noted, the Korean War generated intense hostility toward the new government in China. The United States became the guardians of the Kuomintang regime on Taiwan and continued to recognize it rather than Peking as the legitimate government of China. At the same time, the United States worked to isolate Peking on the international scene and to make certain that Taiwan represented the country in the United Nations and in other international activities, such as the Olympics. Taiwan retained China's seat in the UN until 1971, and the United States did not began a rapprochement until the next year, finally recognizing the legitimacy of the People's Republic in 1979. American policy and China's exclusion from the world community were probably the most vivid and galling reminders of the imperialist era during the first decades of the People's Republic.

Once unity and order had been restored, the new government began to deal with China's other problems. The most striking advances were in the field of public welfare and in the status of women, areas where the injustices of the past had done much to fuel the revolution and where the reestablishment of effective government coupled with Communist ideology could achieve rapid but fundamental improvements.

The Communists made a concerted effort to alleviate the endemic want and misery that had plagued the nation for so long, to give people some security and a sense of possibility for the future. Most importantly, they worked effectively to insure that everyone had the basic necessities of life. As a result, though the nation remained extremely poor, the mass degradation of the previous century and a half became, for the most part, a thing of the past. In addition, the Communists worked to reestablish a broadly based system of schools and, thereby, began a major improvement in the educational levels of the average person for the first time since the eighteenth century. Finally, the government put much effort into medical care and initiated the foundations of a national system of public health.

At the same time, the new regime was deeply concerned to end discrimination against women. The role that women played in the Communist Party and in various mass organizations gave them a greater public power than they had ever enjoyed before. Soon new marriage laws began to work against injustices in private life. Needless to say, foot binding, which had been in decline since early in the century, came to a complete halt. On paper, then, women were set on the path of full parity with men. In many aspects of life this equality has remained rather theoretical, as it has in all societies, even those committed to the full emancipation of women. However, in China, achievements in women's rights have been immense, particularly in comparison to the junxian past, and the progress that has occurred may, in the number of people it has directly affected, be accounted the greatest improvement that the destruction of the old order has brought to society.

Despite their concern with improving public welfare, there was one major aspect of the task that the Communists chose to ignore, the question of population control. China's huge population was the product of the nation's extended and prosperous junxian age. The number of people had declined in times of chaos but had doubled during each era of dynastic stability, leaving a legacy of half a billion to the People's Republic.

The pressure of population against resources had, of course, been a prime factor in the decline of living standards in the previous 150 years and a crucial impetus to the revolution. Effective government and improved living standards could be expected to begin a new round of population growth, now from a higher base than ever before. The new government, however, not only did not advocate and work for demographic control but attacked the idea as reactionary and antisocialist. This surprising and inappropriate attitude, which meant that all improvements in national prosperity had to be divided up among an ever increasing number of people, was the result of Marxist tradition and Soviet practice.

The Marxist opposition to population control came to a significant degree from the fact that the ideology developed when the West was just entering the junxian age and so had no experience with the burst of population attendant on the system. Marx scorned thinkers like the Englishman Malthus who worried about a population explosion, accusing them of being conservatives who did not understand or opposed the unlimited capacities of industrial capitalism to insure progress and human happiness. At the same time, the Soviet Union suffered from underpopulation as a result of war and the fact that it had the largest territory in the world and, therefore, made opposition to population control a part of Communist dogma. For these reasons, Peking virtually ignored the issue of overpopulation until the 1970s. By then China had a billion people, and the resulting problems were felt in every area of life. In the long view, neglecting demographic pressures may prove to have been the most serious mistake in the early history of the People's Republic.

The basic advances in human welfare begun by the new government rested on good order, commitment, and utilizing China's existing economic base to the utmost. Sustained progress, particularly as the population continued to grow, however, required the introduction and application of contemporary industrial and scientific techniques to economic life. In the previous hundred years, all efforts at comprehensive and sustained development had failed. As a result, the hope that socialism would make modernization possible and, thereby, overcome the nation's poverty and military weakness was also a key factor in the revolution; from the beginning, the Communists considered it to be one of their prime tasks.

In 1949, the first step toward development was simply to restore the economy to prewar levels, for production in agriculture, industry, and commerce was below what it had been in the 1930s. In addition, society still had to deal with the inflation that had swept the nation in the late 1940s and helped to bring down the Nationalists. Through a combination of effective planning and sound fiscal policies the People's Republic carried out the not insubstantial task of restoration promptly and with great success. By 1952, the economy had regained earlier levels, and a sound currency system was in place. Then the push for development began.

In the past, the chief obstacles to modernization had been the lack of political order and the difficulty of accumulating capital for investment from a huge population living close to subsistence and, overall, with little surplus left for applying to growth. The problem of order had now been resolved, but the question of raising capital was as serious as ever. The Chinese leaders chose to deal with the issue in accord with their general policy of emulating the Soviet Union. This meant adopting what American scholars have come to call the "Stalinist Model of Development," the method used to get modernization going in the Soviet Union in the late 1920s and 1930s. At the same time China obtained some direct Russian aid and technical assistance and a considerable number of Soviet advisers.

In general, the Stalinist Model is a development plan that neglects the immediate needs of consumption and of agriculture in favor of rapid industrial growth. It involves the nationalization of all productive capacities of the country. This is then coupled with tight controls over economic planning, production, and distribution. Capital for growth is obtained from the agricultural sector and through tight reins on living standards. The money thus made available is invested in industry and primarily in heavy industry, so-called producer's durables, equipment needed for further industrial growth.

The plan is clearly a product of the Western socialist tradition as interpreted in the Soviet Union. It understands socialism as the complete nationalization of the economy and of tight central control, rather than in the datong manner as a blend of the best in fengjian and junxian, as a mixture of public and private, of centralization and decentralization. At the same time, it has a strong urban bias because it emphasizes heavy industry and because if any group is directly benefited, it is the industrial worker. Finally, of course, the Stalinist Model is unconcerned with questions of population pressure, which, if ignored, means that every increase in the gross national product (GNP, the total of goods and services produced in the nation) needs to be divided among every more people.

Nonetheless, the plan was appealing to China's leaders, overall, because they themselves continued to plan policy in terms of an unswerving commitment to Marxism-Leninism and Soviet practice and were expected to do so by Russia and the advisers who were supplied to China. At the same time, full nationalization and centralization reflected the new government's stress on order and were at least roughly compatible with ideals of the Great Community that said that society should have a far larger public sector and far more collective planning than had been the case in junxian times. Finally, industrial growth rather than agricultural development was understood to be the prerequisite for improving China's military capability and so defending the nation's newly won position of international equality.

In line with the Stalinist plan, the government quickly began to collectivize the economy and to establish control over it. In Soviet fashion, a five-year plan was promulgated to coordinate activities and set targets for growth. Industry and commerce were brought under Peking's direction. Many enterprises were nationalized. In others, the original owners continued in possession, though only on paper. In practice they became government employees, and all remnants of private enterprise were understood as temporary expedients, a compromise with socialism.

Similarly, agriculture also moved steadily toward collectivization to accord with socialist ideals as well as to increase production and to tax farmers more effectively. In Russia in the 1930s, collectivization had been a highly coercive and bloody process. Though there were problems in China, the process went far more smoothly. The chief reason seems to have been that the competitiveness, inequalities, and insecurity of the junxian land system, problems that had long fueled the opposition and that had contributed to the socialist thrust of the revolution, now made Chinese farmers more receptive to collective ownership than were those in Russia, with its recent fengjian past. In addition, despite their Marxist-Leninist prejudices, the Chinese Communists had far more powerful roots in a rural constituency than did their Russian counterparts.

The reorganization of agriculture began just before the establishment of the

People's Republic and continued immediately thereafter, when the Communists carried out a nationwide program of land reform and redistribution. Then from 1953 to 1956 collectivization developed in stages. First came Mutual Aid Teams and Cooperatives, production units in which the farmers kept title to their land but worked their fields together. Each village generally included several cooperatives.

Then came the establishment of collectives. A collective usually included a whole village, and the bulk of the land, the portion used for the production of grains, became public property. Families received a return depending on how much labor they contributed, but not on the amount of land that they held. Each family also retained a small plot of its own that was generally used for vegetables, fruits, and an animal or two. As in the case of the private sector in industry, these plots were seen as a compromise with the ideal of abolishing all private property.

Given the problems that China had experienced in recent centuries with economic development, the Stalinist Model was put into effect with considerable success. During the five-year plan, the national rate of savings, that is, the amount of money put aside for investment on a national basis, seems to have been comparable to the high rates that the Soviet Union achieved in the 1930s. This rate was particularly remarkable in view of the fact that China had a lower per capita income than had Russia, and so there was less surplus available for investment after the people's basic needs were met.

As the capital thus accumulated began to be used, China showed a rapid rise in the GNP. The major part of the rise, of course, came in industry and especially in heavy industry. Most of this was in the form of electric power for factories, the extraction and processing of minerals and petroleum, and the production of machinery. By 1958, China was a major industrial power in terms of total output (though not, of course, in per capita production), perhaps one of the top ten nations in the world.

Agriculture grew also, though, as one would expect given the development plan, far more slowly. Unlike industry, this rise did not come about through new investment, for which the five-year plan made few provisions. Rather it was basically a result of the greater sense of justice and security that the Communists brought to rural areas. In addition, it rested on increased efficiency in the coordination and application of labor power, both in the fields and for various large-scale projects, such as improvements in water control. The rise in agricultural production was, of course, central to the gains in industry. The farms provided not only much of the capital for growth but also food for the growing number of people in manufacturing. At the same time, the crucial imports of industrial equipment that China did not yet make were paid for through the export of agricultural goods.

THE TORTUOUS SEARCH FOR A CHINESE WAY

By the mid-fifties, then, the Chinese government, though dictatorial and dogmatic, seemed to be making significant headway in dealing with the nation's most pressing problems. At this time, however, Mao Zedong and the Communist leaders began to see difficulties in the way things were progressing and initiated changes in policy that were to signal a new era in the history of the People's Republic. Essentially, they began to move the nation away from Soviet models.

In the long run, as had been the case earlier at Yenan, this shift signaled the possibility of using China's own heritage and the good sense and commitment of its people as the basis of political life, economic growth, and the construction of socialism. In practice, however, the new approaches continued to be plagued by the deep alienation from the past and all its works that had originally inspired the May 4th generation, the group that still dominated the country. Similarly, the new policies still reflected the intolerant sectarianism of Marxism-Leninism and, in particular, the view that the average citizen of China, the heir of an irretrievably useless and backward past, was deeply prone to error unless properly led.

As a result, the innovations of the late fifties failed for the most part, leaving even greater problems in their wake. At the same time, they opened the way to an increase in the dictatorial authority of those who ruled the country; for if guidelines to action now came neither from Russian models nor from the Chinese past and if the Chinese people were not sophisticated and progressive but simply "poor and blank," as Mao Zedong said in these years, then success depended more than ever on the unique insights and wisdom of the Communist Party and, in particular, on Mao himself.

In 1956, the new atmosphere began to become evident in all areas of Chinese life. The most striking changes came in political affairs with the so-called Hundred Flowers Campaign of that year and in economic planning with the "Great Leap Forward" of 1958–1961. The basic reason for the shift was that a revolutionary process invariably returns, even if, as in this case, only tentatively and unconsciously, to the national traditions of the country involved. More concretely, the new strategies received their impetus from developments in the Soviet Union and her European satellites, as well as from a slowdown in economic growth at home.

Joseph Stalin died in 1953, and soon the repercussions were felt throughout the Soviet bloc. A wave of rebellion broke out against Russian control of Eastern Europe. By 1956, Nikita Khrushchev, Stalin's successor, had openly attacked the late ruler as a brutal tyrant. Among China's Communist leaders, who had been emulating the Soviet Union, it was a time to wonder if the problems of dictatorship, so clearly causing problems elsewhere, had not taken hold in their own country. At the same time, with Stalin's passing, Mao Zedong became senior to Moscow in the world Communist movement. This change seems to have increased his sense of independence and even encouraged him to the view that he was now the supreme arbiter of Marxist-Leninist doctrine.

Just as the Stalinist approach to politics began to come into question, so did the Stalinist model of development. The major problem with the plan was its industrial bias, a difficulty related, as we have noted, to the antirural thrust of Marxism and of the Western tradition as a whole. Under the plan, of course, only industry had received new investments, and the growth that had been achieved in farm production had come about through reorganization. In the long run, however, such changes were insufficient to make a permanent breakthrough in Chinese agriculture, which, overall, had already been very efficient in the past. What was needed to spur on a steady growth were new investments.

As a result, the rise in agricultural production began to slow. At the same time, given China's unchecked increase in population, even the progress already made was barely noticeable in terms of per capita income. Such problems, of course, not only were serious in their own right but also spelled trouble for advances in public welfare and, of even more immediate concern to the government, for industrialization itself; for the latter, of course, depended on a continuing surplus in agriculture for its own further success.

The first response to the new situation was the Hundred Flowers Campaign. The name Hundred Flowers comes from the great intellectual era of the late Zhou, the time of the Hundred Schools of Thought. Mao gave the movement its name with the motto "Let a Hundred Flowers Bloom, Let a Hundred Schools of Thought Contend," and its basic thrust was to permit more open discussion of national issues and policies than had been the case heretofore.

In particular, white-collar intellectuals and specialists in economic planning and production were urged to give their views on matters of national concern. As a result, the new approach responded to the crisis in Eastern Europe in a manner that hinted at bringing Chinese political practice into accord with the liberal possibilities in its own radical tradition, as well as the broad support that the revolution had achieved. At the same time, the campaign also represented a way of enlisting trained people in revitalizing economic growth.

In response to the weaknesses of the first years of the Communist regime, the elite produced a flood of criticism and a wealth of new ideas. Like most people in China, almost all of them had supported the revolution, and a not insignificant number had even returned from abroad in 1949 to help their nation in what they hoped would be its moment of rebirth. As a result, there were almost no attacks on the general goal of socialism nor calls for a return to old and discredited ways of doing things. Nonetheless, the suggestions for change were often broad and fundamental. The critics not only proposed alternatives to this or that particular policy, including suggestions for investment in agriculture and for a vigorous policy of birth control, but also attacked the dictatorial character of Communist rule.

At first, Mao and the Communist leadership seemed to go along with the campaign, and, concomitant with the new openness, a vigorous drive was begun to improve the party's "style of work" and to make it more amenable to popular opinion. However, the nation's rulers soon grew fearful of losing power, let alone the unquestioned authority that their theological approach to politics deemed necessary, and they quickly began to rein in the critics. Their worries were heightened by the last and greatest of the uprisings in Eastern Europe in Hungary in October 1956.

The fear that limited freedom of expression might open the door to a rebellion like Hungary's, of course, bore clear testimony to the lack of confidence that the Chinese Communists still had in their own revolution and their own people; for no critic of the regime seriously expected that real democracy could be achieved quickly, and there was little similarity between the situation in China and the rebellion in Hungary, which was, essentially, directed at Soviet occupation.

Nonetheless, Mao Zedong and the party leaders launched a sharp swing away from open discussion and disagreement. By 1957, what remained of the Hundred Flowers Movement was brought to a halt and replaced by a harsh and unjust "Anti-Rightist Campaign." Those who had made criticisms or suggested new policies were denounced as reactionary and antisocialist. Many were imprisoned, sent to labor camps, or suffered the loss of their jobs. Eventually, Mao made matters worse by claiming that he had started the Hundred Flowers Campaign only to uncover secret opponents of socialism, dangerous and poisonous weeds. Like Stalin before him, Mao, it seemed, would rather be thought a cynical tyrant than to admit that he had made errors in policy or in his estimation of the opposition to them.

The retreat from the Hundred Flowers Campaign proved to be the beginning of a great and sustained tragedy for the People's Republic that was to encompass much of the next twenty years. The end of liberalization began a series of sudden shifts in policy and, for the most part, increased repression, which became ever more serious as China's rulers continued to seek new directions, but only on the basis of their own unique insights. Thus, the regime began not only to abuse some of the most loyal, courageous, and useful people in the country but to squander thereby some of the vast support that it had enjoyed, for all of its problems, until that time.

While the failure of the Hundreds Flowers Campaign injured the elite in the first instance, the Great Leap Forward, which followed a year later, was to become a disaster for the whole of society. The basic purpose of the Leap was to redress the imbalance between agricultural and industrial growth and, in this sense, also marked a change from the stark urban bias of Soviet practice and hinted at the possibility of new policies more in line with Chinese realities and needs.

Like the Hundred Flowers Movement, however, the Great Leap also proved to be a confused and contradictory shift, for the new scheme still made no provision for using capital in the agricultural sector, where it was absolutely necessary if further growth was to be expected. Rather, it continued to rest on the vain hope that yet greater effectiveness in the utilization of labor, coupled with ideological fervor, could raise farm production by its own bootstraps as it continued to provide industry with as much investment as before.

The greater efficiency in agriculture was to come from the formation of People's Communes, the major organizational innovation of the Great Leap. The government created the first commune in 1958, and, within a few months, they had come into existence everywhere. The communes combined several collectives and their respective villages into a new administrative unit that averaged about twenty-five thousand people. Within each commune there was also a turn to extreme collectivization, which was further supposed to spur efficiency and to breed a commitment to the general welfare. Chinese agriculture was, of course, already collectivized. As a result, these further steps, reminiscent of the Taipings, represented an extreme by any standards, let alone the balanced economic ideals of the datong tradition.

In the collectives, farmers had received pay depending on how much work they and their families did, though not on the basis of how much land they held. Now they were not supposed to be paid at all but simply to be supplied with what they needed. The communes abolished the private plots of the past as a matter of course, and any sort of personal property became suspect. In many cases, everything from furniture to domestic animals became public property, and families often ceased to dine alone but were expected to eat in vast mess halls.

The entire atmosphere was also pervaded by a fanatic spirit that denigrated expertise in favor of boldness and ideological purity, ''redness,'' as it was known. All who doubted the justice or wisdom of what was happening were branded as cowardly and reactionary, and the political repression and imprisonments of the Anti-Rightist Campaign continued on a even greater scale than before. While we do not have good information on the number of people who have been sent to labor camps since the 1950s, figures in the tens of millions have been suggested.[3]

Further to assure that the Great Leap produced the desired rise in production, local cadres received no quotas or detailed suggestions on how they were to increase yields. Rather, in line with the drive for boldness and initiative, they were simply ordered to produce as much as possible. The methods were expected to include indoctrination, more intense cultivation, and new public works. In addition, the communes were urged to emphasize small-scale manufacturing that could supply local needs without putting a drain on heavy industry, which was still supposed to produce equipment for further industrial growth.

The direct impact of the new policies on the cities was less than on rural China. However, the latter did not remain unaffected. There were some moves toward creating urban communes. More importantly, the same emphasis developed on redness as opposed to expertise, on silencing all opposition and on using labor to the utmost in an atmosphere of ideological fervor. The government established an extremely unrealistic goal for industry: to overtake Great Britain within fifteen years; and the everlasting symbol of the Leap in urban areas became the one million backyard steel furnaces that city dwellers are said to have built.

As one might suppose, given the high efficiency of Chinese farmers prior to the establishment of the People's Republic, as well as the progress that had been achieved in the early fifties, the Leap failed to raise agricultural production. Indeed, it proved to be a disaster, and yields actually declined. One reason was simply that a further reorganization of rural life, coming on the heels of recent changes, caused problems in itself; things had just settled down after the process of collectivization and were then suddenly changed again.

More importantly, yields fell because the intense pressure from the government to increase production encouraged cadres to ignore local traditions and local wisdom in farming. Inappropriate crops were planted, and all sorts of wasteful and foolish projects were begun. It is said, for example, that in some places so many wells were dug that a disastrous drop in the water table resulted. Most crucially, however, the Leap collapsed because the pressure on the average farmer became unbearable. Always hardworking, he was now told to labor even harder, and, at the same time, he was robbed of all personal or familial incentives for increased production.

By the harvest of 1959, the errors of the Leap began to become evident, and some of its most extreme features began to be reversed. Overall, however, the movement continued. There were some difficulties with weather that year and for several years to come. But such natural problems paled into insignificance when compared to the ravages of the new policies in what soon began to be called the "Three Bad Years" from 1959 to 1961.

The harshness of commune life coupled with declining production drove many farmers to the cities, further reducing yields. Fields lay untended. Inevitably, food shortages developed, and with it came malnutrition and famine.[4] At the same time, the Leap halted the progress in education, medical care, and other aspects of public welfare, which had been making good strides until that point. Given Chinese political traditions, one suspects, rebellion was in the air.

The cities also suffered, although to a lesser degree. The general hysteria and the wasteful use of human and material resources quickly began to affect factories. By 1960 they started to close down. Then manufacturing suffered a further decline because of the problems in the countryside, for agriculture remained the major prop for industrial growth. In addition to the other disasters of the Leap, China, with falling production in all sectors of the economy and unused labor capacity, was in a depression.

Overall, the Great Leap left the average person with the same feeling of disillusionment that the elite had developed as a result of the Hundred Flowers. At the same time, China's first steps toward finding her own path to a just new society had met with failure. Nonetheless, it should be noted that from the point of view of this process, the late fifties did leave a small positive legacy. The Hundred Flowers Campaign had occurred, however briefly, holding out a hope of democracy, of the political freedom that could and should be possible in China. At the same time, the establishment of the communes began to dismantle the excessive administrative and economic centralization that had hitherto dominated the Chinese scene and to create the possibility of bringing political life into greater harmony with the fengjian ideals that had informed the revolution in its pre-Communist phase.

One further product of the late fifties involved foreign relations, for in these years and immediately afterward the momentous Sino-Soviet dispute began. The split was, in a sense, the inevitable result of China's search for new policies that did not emulate the Soviet Union and that, in turn, grew out of the differing histories and needs of the two nations. However, in the theological and monolithic atmosphere of the Communist movement, there was no room for amicable disagreement between two parties over major policies, foreign or domestic.

This was a question not simply of dogmatism, however, but also of power. If two parties were in dispute, there was clearly no unique truth at one time, no obvious guidelines to action that could be ascertained on the basis of the ''universal'' and ''scientific'' insights of Marxism-Leninism. As a result, if two parties agreed to disagree, each lost something of its claim to a special insight into the march of history that supported its dictatorship at home. If there could be differences between parties in different countries, why could not the citizens in each oppose their rulers?[5]

Once the inability to disagree led to an open dispute between Russia and China, relations grew steadily more acrimonious. From the Chinese point of view, one of the most provocative Russian acts was the withdrawal of Soviet economic advisers during the Great Leap, a peripheral reason for the problems of the Three Bad Years. Eventually, the two sides disputed everything, the issues ranging from the proper interpretation of Marx and Lenin to the correct analysis of international affairs, from border disputes to claims that each side was interfering in the other's internal affairs. Occasionally minor military skirmishes took place. The dispute continued at full blast for over twenty-five years and, even now, is only gradually ebbing.

As the Great Leap began to fail, Mao Zedong privately assumed some of the blame, though in the style of Communist dictatorships, this acknowledgment was not made public. In 1959 he stepped down as head of the Chinese state, though he continued to hold his position as chairman of the Communist Party, and his influence and prestige remained immense. In Mao's place, Liu Shaoqi took over the reins of government and the management of day-to-day affairs. Like Mao, Liu was from a farming background in Hunan Province. Born in 1900, he was a senior figure in the Communist Party who had been active in revolutionary affairs and administration for forty years, and it was assumed that he would eventually become Mao's successor.

In the early sixties, under Liu's direction, China moved away from many of the excesses of recent years and even made some progress in the search for an appropriate Chinese path to socialism. The main successes came in decentralization and economic affairs, and there were even some minor improvements in politics. In 1961, the Great Leap officially came to an end. Technological expertise resumed its proper place in agriculture and industry, and ideological fervor lost ground. Farmers again received pay on the basis of the amount of work they did, and private plots were reestablished. Other forms of extreme collectivization also disappeared.

The communes remained in place, though in a reorganized form. Many of their immediate functions in agricultural life were returned to the old collectives, which had been renamed Production Brigades, each roughly including one village; for many matters, indeed, decentralization went beyond what it had been prior to the Leap, with the revival in importance of still smaller units, the old Mutual Aid Teams, now called Production Teams. At the same time, the communes provided a suitably large local organization for major public works and for rural manufacturing.

The most striking development of the early sixties, however, was the decision finally to emphasize agriculture as a major priority in development and to provide it with some of the investment it desperately needed if it was to achieve real advances. The new investment came in the form of steel, cement, farm equipment, and chemical fertilizer. The commitment to produce the latter was a particularly clear sign of the new policies, for establishing an industry in chemical fertilizer requires heavy outlays of capital. The other new inputs were used directly in farming or for public works and local manufacturing. The growth in such industry also marked a departure from the past with its stress on large urban factories and, in addition, made production more amenable to local agricultural needs.

Though the new approach marked an important advance over the policies of the preceding years, problems still continued. Most importantly, Marxist ideology still prevented an effective program of demographic control, and population growth continued to eat away at all increases in the nation's wealth. In addition, despite the new priorities, the actual investment in agriculture was still on the low side as compared to industry. Nonetheless, the changes were striking, and most foreign economists were impressed with the realism that had entered Chinese planning and, though the government ceased to publish economic statistics after the Leap, by what seemed a steady and more healthy rise in farm production.

As in economic affairs, the early sixties brought a retreat from some of the worst political excesses of the Anti-Rightist Campaign and the Leap. People were again able to discuss issues more openly and sometimes to criticize public policy. Indeed, a limited Hundred Flowers Movement developed. Nonetheless, there was no basic change in direction as there was, to some degree, in economics, and criticism of the nation's rulers remained unacceptable. The country was still governed by a handful of people dictating to the Communist Party and by the party dictating to the rest of society.

It was Mao Zedong, who had played such a leading role in the construction of the existing order, who led the search for political renovation. The results were to prove as tragic as anything that had yet occurred in the People's Republic. Approaching his seventy-fifth year and in failing health, Mao became obsessed by the fact that the socialist society of which he had dreamed and for which he had fought was being permanently foreclosed by the formation of a new elite. Surprisingly, coming from him, he indicated that this elite was lodged in the Communist Party, indeed, that essentially it was the Communist Party. He decided that the party and its leaders were turning into a closed group whose only interest was maintaining itself in power and, perhaps, supplying some short-term economic gains.

Though Mao's concerns were, in many ways, more than justifiable, his response to them was still fraught with all the disrespect for Chinese history and with all the zeal and dogmatism that had influenced the thinking of his generation for so long. As a result he did not put his immense prestige and political skills behind a call for the genuine democracy that alone could permanently limit the power of the party, for he still mistrusted the Chinese people to create a good society in an atmosphere of calm and deliberation.

Rather, Mao used his power to initiate a bizarre replay of the May 4th Movement: The Great Proletarian Cultural Revolution. Thus, he decided to reconstruct China from the ground up once again. This time, however, the goal would be to free the culture not only from the evils of the Chinese past but also from the shortcomings that he had begun to sense, if only unconsciously, in Western outlooks and, in particular in Marxism-Leninism. Mao decided, further, to accomplish this goal, by utilizing the same group that had led the May 4th Movement: the youth.

He came to this decision because as he looked around, Mao also became concerned that the young people of the nation, who had never known the evils of the old society, were in danger of losing their revolutionary edge. If he could turn the younger generation against the party, he felt that he could kill two birds with one stone. The young would obtain revolutionary experience, and the domination of China's rulers would be dismantled.

As the Cultural Revolution developed, it came to involve many other issues, including the succession to Mao, conflicts between the army and the party, and continuing tensions between rural and urban China. Among other things, Mao's wife, Jiang Qing, began to amass immense power as a spokesperson for her husband, a function that was a perverse reflection of the role that women had played in the May 4th Movement and that was reminiscent, too, of the authority that the empresses of old had sometimes enjoyed.

The first sign of the Cultural Revolution was a "Socialist Education Campaign," which began in 1964. The new movement emerged in full force in the summer of 1965, when Mao encouraged high school youth, college students, and other young people to organize Red Guards. Red Guard units were supposed to attack and depose "all those in command taking the capitalist path," a group that, in practice, meant Communist cadres and, more broadly, all authority figures over the age of thirty. The creation of the Red Guards also represented a move in favor of the army against the party, for the new groups often had connections to the former, as well as a paramilitary flavor.

Since the ideology behind the Cultural Revolution saw no strengths in Chinese tradition and precious few in the practice of Marxism-Leninism, its only basis could be the thought of Mao Zedong himself. As a result, to stimulate the Red Guards to action, Mao encouraged an unprecedented cult of personality centered on himself and his infallible wisdom. The most famous symbol of the cult became the *Selected Quotations from Mao Zedong*, the so-called Little Red Book, which was printed and distributed in over a billion copies and became a talisman for overcoming all obstacles.

Once goaded on by such authority, the youth proved zealous. In addition to the propaganda urging them forward, they were also stimulated by the fact that the educational advances of the previous decade had left a larger group of talented and trained young people than could be accommodated by China's still relatively backward economy. At the same time, schools closed down. Shutting the schools was tied to the fact that they were, for the most part, under party control and also said to be unfairly biased toward the elite. However, the basic reason they were closed, aside from freeing the young for political activism, was to promote the idea that there was nothing worth teaching, either in China's long-term past or in her recent Communist heritage.

In this nihilistic atmosphere the youth and the older people who decided to go along with them, either out of fear or self-interest, began attacks on everything from music to the organization of factories. Cultural treasures, buildings, and artworks were defaced and sometimes destroyed. Industrial production declined. Most seriously, however, the followers of the Cultural Revolution began widespread abuse of party members, intellectuals, and social leaders of all sorts.

It was a time of humiliation, beatings, killings, and suicides, and those who died may have numbered up to half a million.[6] Ever more people were sent to prisons and work camps. The most famous figure to suffer was Liu Shaoqi himself. He became a symbol of the party and its failings. Stripped of all his positions, he disappeared from public view, eventually dying under mysterious circumstances. In Liu's place, Marshal Lin Biao, the minister of defense and an avid supporter of the Cultural Revolution, began to assume the role of Mao's successor.

Much of what went on in the Cultural Revolution did not immediately affect rural China, probably because the Great Leap Forward had shown how farmers would react to excessive zeal and the immediate economic disaster that could ensue. In any case, the progress of the early sixties seems to have continued for a time, and rural people may even have benefited from the movement. The average farmer seems to have dealt with his local cadres more forthrightly than ever before, and in this era the paramedical "barefoot doctors" began to complete the work of providing medical care to all. Eventually, however, the chaos and fervor of the campaign affected the countryside also. Schools closed down or became useless, and agricultural production began to decline once more or, at least, ceased to grow.

By the late sixties, with the cities in chaos and rural China beginning to suffer, it was obvious that the Cultural Revolution was a fiasco. Under the leadership of Zhou Enlai, party members began to reassert their authority, and the army cooperated. However, the movement went on officially, partly through its own momentum and partly because so many powerful people, including Mao, his wife, and their immediate followers, had now staked their political fortunes on its continuance.

There were still terror among thinking people and attacks on all deviations from the revolutionary line. Many schools remained shut, and those that did reopen taught little. And now, too, the search for scapegoats began. Mao and Jiang Qing turned on Lin Biao, who, perhaps planning a coup, fled the country. Lin may have died in a plane crash while making his escape. More tragically, millions of young people, former Red Guards, joined their victims in jail and on prison farms.

This terrible and confused atmosphere, as well as economic stagnation, continued until 1976. Early in that year Zhou Enlai died. His death became an opportunity for massive demonstrations against the remaining power of the Cultural Revolution group. In September, Mao himself passed away. Shortly thereafter, party leaders brought the Cultural Revolution to a definitive close by arresting Jiang Qing and her closest allies, the so-called Gang of Four.

CHINA TODAY

After the death of Mao Zedong and the end of the Cultural Revolution, the Communist Party resumed control of China and in the succeeding years has continued the general tendency begun in the late 1950s to find an appropriately Chinese approach to national affairs. As compared to the previous twenty years, there has been some progress. But, overall, the results remain extremely mixed, and China still seems far from having found her own way to a successful and healthy society.[7]

On the positive side, there was a retreat from the fanaticism of the Great Leap and the nihilism of the Cultural Revolution in favor of calmer and more pragmatic policies, particularly in economics. As a result, the so-called reforms of the 1980s often proved more appropriate to the needs and possibilities of Chinese society and in some ways even opened the way to policies that, albeit unconsciously, seemed to reflect the values that had informed the Chinese revolution prior to the ascendancy of communism.

On the other hand, the broader problems that have marked the search to rediscover China's own way have remained evident. Most importantly, the Communists have been unable and, indeed, unwilling to legitimize the People's Republic in terms of Chinese tradition. So while commitment to the Stalinist model and, indeed, to Marxism-Leninism has continued to decline, there has been no serious effort to revive or consciously to utilize China's own legacy of ethical, political, and socioeconomic theory.

As a result, the nation now finds itself in a moral and intellectual limbo, somewhat beyond the May 4th era with its faith in the transcendent possibilities of Western thought but not yet in touch with China's own past and, in particular, with the attitudes that would seem most relevant to her current needs and moment in history, the progressive views of the junxian age. More concretely, dictatorship is still in place, economic success has proven limited, and there is widespread corruption. Society, in turn, has grown cynical, and there is almost universal disillusionment with the government and the Communist Party.

As might be expected, given Chinese tradition, this situation has stimulated the formation of an active opposition movement. The most recent and the greatest manifestation of this movement, the massive drive for democracy in the spring of 1989, was brutally crushed. Repression, however, has done nothing to resolve the nation's problems but only served to heighten the anger and tensions within Chinese society.

In 1976, power first passed into the hands of Hua Guofeng, a vice-premier and minister of public security. It was under Hua, who ran the government for about two years, that China began to retreat from some of the extremes of previous years. Education once again became regularized, and economic planning emphasized the so-called Four Modernizations, in agriculture, industry, science and technology, and national defense. At the same time the cult that surrounded Mao began to be dismantled, and criticisms of him and of mistaken policies in the past were increasingly heard. Victims of government vilification going back to the 1950s were rehabilitated, and, as far as we know, many of the victims still in jail were freed. By the end of 1978, however, Hua lost power to Deng Xiaoping, who has been in control since.

Deng was born in Sichuan Province in 1904 into a prosperous farming family. He was caught up in the May 4th Movement as a high school student and then went to France, where he became a Communist. He studied briefly in the Soviet Union before returning home and from the late twenties onward took an active role in Communist affairs. He was on the Long March and eventually became one of the leading figures of Chinese communism. By the 1960s he had held leading positions in the party, the army, and the government and was one of the prime targets of the Cultural Revolution. In the 1980s, it was Deng who was most associated with the image of pragmatism, and the more open economic policies of the decade are often linked with his name as the so-called Deng Xiaoping reforms. Nonetheless, as perhaps the last Chinese leader who will come from the May 4th era, Deng, for all his vaunted pragmatism, retained the negative view of Chinese history and thought that so marked his generation.

Partly for this reason and partly because the Communists were simply unwilling to share power, there was relatively little improvement in political life under his leadership. In addition, what change did occur often seemed an unwilling response on the part of the party to twenty years of failure and to the ever growing disillusionment with Marxism-Leninism. As a result, though, there was some relaxation of the most extreme forms of control, China retained a system where, as in the past, a small group ran the Communist Party, and the party lorded it over the rest of society. This system, in turn, affected all other matters, including economics.

In some ways the greatest moment of freedom occurred in the late 1970s, when Deng Xiaoping was competing for power with Hua Guofeng. This was the time of the so-called Democracy Wall in Peking, where people could put up wall posters that were critical of the government and its policies. A permanent product of this era was the decision not to reappoint a state chairman, the extremely powerful position from which Mao had ruled both the party and government. In practice, though, Deng continued to do just that.

Once he stabilized control, the absolute power of the party was reaffirmed. By 1980 Democracy Wall was closed, and the so-called Four Freedoms—to speak out freely, to air one's views fully, to engage in great debates, and to write wall posters—were deleted from the constitution. In their place Deng stressed the ''Four Fundamental Principles'': socialism, the dictatorship of the proletariat, the leadership of the Communist Party, and adherence to Marxism-Leninism and the thought of Mao Zedong.

Within these limitations, however, some improvement did take place. Perhaps the most significant was what might be called a relative depoliticization of life in China, the fact that the authorities simply could not or did not care to extend as much control over society as in the past. The party line no longer gave a specific point of view on every aspect of life, nor did every piece of literature, history, and philosophy agree on everything. Much was still forbidden, both personally and intellectually, but more was allowed.

In addition, there was some broadening of decision making in rural administration, though perhaps at the expense of local solidarity vis-à-vis the power of higher authorities. Thus, communes, brigades, and work teams were supposed to limit themselves to economic matters, and new political organs were created on the local scene: the *xiang*, or township at the level of the commune and the *cun*, or village at the level of the production brigade. Finally, the eighties saw some intermittent experiments with multicandidate elections for party and governmental positions and, occasionally, relatively freer debate in the National People's Congress and various public forums.

On the other hand, on fundamental matters, political and intellectual control remained as tough as ever. Most importantly, even prior to 1989, all serious movements for democracy were crushed, and those involved were punished with imprisonment or the loss of employment. A far smaller but not insignificant example of the degree to which control was maintained was that even in what might be considered to be the relatively minor area of historiography, scholars were still forced to call prerevolutionary China fengjian. This bizarre distortion of the past, of course, simply served to keep society from knowing where it stood historically and, what was most important to the Communists, utterly cut it off from the nation's liberal tradition.

While political change was extremely limited in the eighties, as we have noted, there was some genuine progress in economic life. Most importantly, Deng Xiaoping moved the People's Republic further than ever before from extremes of collectivity and central planning. At the same time, his reforms showed particular concern for the rural economy and for the comparative welfare of farmers. In addition, the government worked to improve the quality of life by emphasizing the development of light industries producing consumer goods such as clothing, bicycles, and radios. Finally, it put a serious and long overdue emphasis on population control.

In all areas from the concern for rural life to the stress on birth control, these changes marked a further move away from Soviet practice and toward policies more appropriate to China's needs. Most strikingly, the revitalization of private activity brought the nation ever closer to an updated version of Mencius's economic ideals, which sought to blend the strengths of fengjian and junxian by combining public ownership of what might be called the basic means of production with free trade.[8] On the other hand, the impact of tradition was, at best, unconscious or very indirect, and policy was made and defended almost entirely in terms of pragmatism. This situation coupled with the lack of political change created endless difficulties for the reforms and by the end of the decade robbed them of almost all momentum.

In the countryside, the centerpiece of the new policies was and remains the so-called responsibility system. Under this plan land remains in public hands; however, it is leased and then managed privately, almost always by an individual family, though villages often work as a unit for things like buying fertilizer and harvesting. The length of the leases varies but is generally for at least fifteen years and, where land is poor and requires improvement, can extend to thirty years or more. In return for the land, farmers must pay taxes and sell a fixed quota of produce to the government, generally in the form of grain. What remains can be sold on the open market. Overall, the prices paid for the government's quota are higher than in earlier years, and what farmers can get for produce sold on the market is higher still.

In addition to the responsibility system the new rural policies encouraged families to undertake sideline production and to develop so-called specialized households. The latter can concentrate on anything from forestry, animal husbandry, or raising vegetables to repair work and transportation. At the same time the government has continued to encourage small-scale rural industry within the public sector for things like foodstuffs, clothing, agricultural machinery, cement, and fertilizer. This industry, in turn, has led to one of the most striking results of the reforms: the prominence of small towns; their importance, indeed, gives some promise of alleviating the urban-rural dichotomy that grew out of the Western impact and of restoring the suburban atmosphere that marked so much of China at the end of the eighteenth century.

Economic reform also began in the cities, though far more slowly than in agriculture. The most important changes have gone under the name of "profit contracting" and "profit retention" and aim at limiting centralized planning and bringing decisions on production and marketing to the level of individual enterprises. Thus, interconnections among companies, banks, and sales outlets are now supposed to resemble market mechanisms, and accounting is to be done in terms of the profitability of an activity. In addition, managers and workers can benefit directly from greater productivity by keeping what remains after a certain percentage of production or of taxes has been paid to the government. Though most urban dwellers still work for public enterprises, additional reforms have also encouraged small-scale private businesses in things like restaurants, repair shops, and small stores.

Finally, the eighties were also marked by an effort to end the relative autarky of Chinese economic life. As a result, there have been a rise in foreign trade and even a noteworthy amount of foreign investment in China. At the same time tens of thousands of students have gone overseas to study, including upward of forty thousand in the United States.

To help insure that future increases in population did not eat away at economic growth, one of the most important developments of the eighties was a long overdue program of birth control. This effort was clearly in accord with Chinese needs and marked an important departure from the earlier and disastrous policies that, because of the imperatives of Marxist theory and Soviet practice, ignored population pressures. The new approach began in the early 1970s with a call for later marriage and the wider spacing of children. By the 1980s official government policy was to limit each family to a single child. The goal was to keep the population, already a staggering one billion, from growing by more than two hundred million over the next several decades.

In accord with the new policy the pill and various birth control devices are widely distributed, and abortion is commonly used. At the same time there are social and economic rewards for those who obey the new rules and penalties for those who do not. The enforcement of the latter can vary from the comparatively lenient view that "one child is perfect, two are acceptable, but never three" to draconic measures, including forced abortions. The latter bear testimony not only to continued dictatorship and an unethical atmosphere but also to the grave errors that the government made by encouraging population growth for so long.

Overall the economic reforms have had many successes. The greater fairness shown to farmers coupled with the incentives attendant on private management and profit seems to have resulted in a solid rise in agricultural production through the middle of the eighties. In addition, a quarter of Chinese industry is now located outside of large cities, and at least half the output of villages and small towns is in various forms of nonagricultural production. The result has been a substantial and striking improvement in the living standard of the nation's farmers and of rural people in general.

Similarly, despite their more limited scope, the urban reforms have also made a contribution to the general opening and vigor of the economy. Many more goods and services have become available, and in towns throughout the country there has been a vigorous spurt in construction work. It is difficult to know precisely how effective the new policies have been in controlling population growth. Nonetheless, most observers feel that the government's efforts, while open to severe criticism as to the manner in which they have been enforced, have resulted in a marked decline in China's birthrate.

Despite these not inconsiderable successes, however, the economic reforms have also encountered very great problems. As a result, increases in the production of agricultural staples stopped in 1985, and by the end of the decade the economy, as a whole, was running into serious difficulties.

As usual, a major reason for these problems has been the lack of any theoretical framework for change; this lack has not only created a moral vacuum but also caused endless confusion precisely in those areas of policy where traditional thought would be most useful: the relationship between public and private activity and between central and local authority. At the same time, dictatorship and the continued power of the party have caused sudden swings in policy while leaving in place entrenched interests not eager for change. Finally, both these problems have combined to encourage widespread corruption and an atmosphere where the very line between the legal and the illegal has often disappeared.

The impact of these factors was evident from the beginning of the reforms when the power of Communist cadres resulted in serious injustices in the allocation of land and the opportunities for specialized production. At the same time, the general decline in governmental activity often left agricultural investment to individual decisions that, in some cases, proved insufficient for sustained, long-term growth. In addition, social services that were handled by the commune structure, such as education and health care, began to suffer. Among other things, this problem caused contradictions in the system of birth control, for the responsibility system put some premium on the number of people in a family and also left the care of parents and other social services in familial rather than public hands.

More recently, two issues, in particular, have served to focus the limitations of the reforms. The first has been the so-called policy of dual pricing, which was established in order to find a balance between planning and the marketplace. The other is inflation, which has been caused primarily by confusions in the relationship between central and local power.

Dual pricing means, essentially, that Peking has maintained fixed prices for a percentage of important goods. In agriculture these include grain and other staples, such as cotton, sugar, and edible oils; in industry they include things like steel, cement, coal, and electricity. Beyond what the government takes as its quota, these controlled items can be sold at market prices, as can products that are not controlled, such as nonstaple foods, industrial equipment, and consumer goods. As a result of the system, the price of about 50 percent of China's output is still controlled administratively rather than through the market.

In the abstract, the dual price system might be an effective way of gradually decontrolling prices, limiting inflation, and getting some sense of what the market requires. In practice, it has caused endless difficulties. One key problem is that political disputes at the highest levels of the Communist Party often center on the size and character of the public sector. This problem has meant that as different groups have held power, the economy has experienced sudden shifts in policy with little concern for the needs of society.

In addition, people simply do not want to produce things that have to be sold to the government at artificially low prices, and this attitude has caused a drop in output in the very goods that are most essential to the economy. In particular, many of the key products that are needed for agriculture, such as fertilizer and fuel, have been in short supply and made the production of the staples that must be sold to the government all the more unattractive. This situation is accounted as the prime reason why agricultural growth ran into difficulty in the second half of the 1980s.

Finally, the system has probably provided the major arena for corruption. Communist cadres and other bureaucrats, who still dominate the economy, siphon off goods obtained at low administrative prices and sell them on the open market, obtaining large and illicit profits either for themselves or for their units. At the same time producers use whatever means possible to avoid selling products to the government, and all concerned resort to speculation, bureaucratic deals, and payoffs.

By hurting production, the dual pricing policy itself has contributed to the nation's other major problem, inflation. At the same time the intensely political character of economic planning has pushed up prices, sometimes directly and sometimes by sowing anxiety over the future.

More importantly, however, decentralization has meant that Peking has been less able to raise revenue. To meet the problem, it has increased the supply of money and so, of course, has contributed to inflation. Similarly, credit institutions at all levels of society, backed and even pressured by various political forces, have created an excessive and unwarranted rise in credit and buying power, which has led to the same result. Of course, inflation has further stimulated corruption, particularly as it has hurt the income of the huge government establishment and of all others on fixed incomes.

In the face of such growing confusion and the general decline in respect for law and order, all efforts at economic austerity failed. In 1987 the inflation rate reached 18 percent. Then, in 1988, partly for political reasons and partly in order to meet the problems of dual pricing, Peking launched a major effort to decontrol more goods. This simply produced mass chaos and a sharp rise in prices, and within months controls were reimposed. As a result, the existing problems continued, while inflation for the year reached 27 percent.

Though dual pricing and inflation have highlighted the most obvious problems of the reforms, other difficulties have also developed. Efforts to end lifetime employment with no clear consensus on how to do it or, indeed, whether it is a good policy, have caused unemployment and dissatisfaction. Decentralization has sometimes resulted in economic fragmentation where different regions unnecessarily compete with one another and where large groups of people, particularly farmers, have become vagabonds searching for better opportunities. Finally, because of the relatively large amounts of money involved and the many opportunities for misappropriating it, the opening to the West has spawned widespread corruption. Similarly, the right to study abroad has sometimes been unfairly monopolized by the children of the powerful. In addition, very few of the students who have gone overseas, of whatever background, have returned home; this development, of course, has robbed China of some of her finest and best educated young people.

Because of the troubles that have continued to plague the People's Republic, an active opposition movement has steadily been gaining strength. In the face of a dictatorial government, this movement has been unable to organize publicly, and so it is difficult fully to gauge its power. To date, its most public manifestation has been a steady drumbeat of criticism by intellectuals and a series of demonstrations by students. However, at one time or other, every group in Chinese society has joined in, and by all accounts hostility to the regime is extremely widespread. The situation has, of course, been made all the worse by the brutal suppression of the Democracy Movement of 1989.

In general, the opposition has basically drawn its most direct inspiration from the Western liberal tradition. In addition, it has been encouraged by developments in the Communist world and, in particular, the policy of liberalization initiated in the Soviet Union by Mikhail Gorbachev. Finally, it has even rested to some degree on the anti-Communist and populist sentiments that the Cultural Revolution, for all of its nihilism, left as one of its legacies.

On the other hand, the movement has not drawn openly on China's own intellectual and political heritage. In fact, its most vocal elements, the students and intellectuals, have tended to be very critical of Chinese tradition and to view the Communist dictatorship as simply the latest manifestation of an irremediably evil past. This view, in turn, has limited the influence of the opposition and even allowed the government to make the bizarre charge that it is somehow unpatriotic or "un-Chinese." In fact, of course, such weaknesses simply reflect the very alienation from the Chinese past that the Communists themselves have worked so hard to foster.

Nonetheless, like the reforms of the eighties, the opposition has also been unconsciously informed by Chinese thought, in this case the deeply held belief that tyranny and bad government are ultimately illegitimate and that upright people have a responsibility to oppose them. In addition, the activities of intellectuals and students have been directly influenced by the May 4th Movement, which was itself partly a manifestation of China's age-old tradition of political activism by these same groups.

The drive for democracy of recent years began with the demonstrations attendant on the death of Zhou Enlai in 1976. It continued with the Democracy Wall movement of the late 1970s, which was so harshly put down when Deng Xiaoping assumed power. Thereafter, activism and repression continued on a regular and almost continuous basis. For example, in 1983 in response to widespread suggestions that Chinese society was suffused with personal alienation, the government launched a so-called Spiritual Pollution Campaign aimed at suppressing the idea and at restricting Western influences. The campaign, however, never really got off the ground, partly because it was too out of accord with the mood of economic openness and, as a result, left Deng Xiaoping himself open to criticism. More importantly, the campaign probably failed because the actual degree of alienation in China was simply too great.

Then, in 1984 and in 1986 the opposition was again active, and there were major student movements critical of the government. Deng responded with harsh crackdowns, particularly in 1986, and early the next year Hu Yaobang was ousted from his position as secretary general of the Communist Party because he was judged to be too accommodating to the students. He was replaced by Zhao Ziyang, who was soon to meet a similar fate himself.

At the end of the decade, opposition reached a crescendo as all the nation's problems seemed to come to a head. In rural China, farmers increasingly refused to hand over the required goods to the government, and the latter found it harder and harder to pay for what was taken. By the harvest of 1988 Peking actually had to issue IOUs, which, of course, met with considerable resistance, and force and violence were used on both sides. This development not only produced a very tense situation but also meant that in the spring of 1989 some farmers did not have the necessary funds to begin planting.

In urban areas, where people had to buy more of what they used, inflation was taking a particularly serious toll. At the same time, there were said to be tens of millions of rural people in various cities and towns looking for work. The result was a sharp rise in protests, strikes, and demonstrations. Early in 1989, intellectuals began to organize to use the upcoming meeting of the National People's Congress as a forum for opposing the government.

Overall, the "social mood" in the country became very tense.[9] There was a spurt in the crime rate and a corresponding wave of executions, not only for violent actions like train robbery but also for economic crimes such as bribery, embezzlement, fraud, and smuggling. However, the atmosphere of pervasive corruption continued, heightening dissatisfaction in all parts of society. All serious belief in Marxism-Leninism seemed to be dead, and, needless to say, there was no letup in dictatorship.

In April, things came to a head with the death of Hu Yaobang, who had become something of a hero to the opposition after his ouster two years earlier. Demonstrations openly calling for more democracy began among university students in Peking. By May, these demonstrations had support from people in all walks of life, including blue-collar workers, and began to number over a million people. Soldiers sent to control the situation often seemed sympathetic. In the meantime, similar movements developed in other towns and cities across the nation, sometimes supported by unemployed farmers who found themselves in urban areas.

In general the Democracy Movement was remarkably peaceful and calm. In turn, it received some support from those in power, most notably from Zhao Ziyang himself. However, Deng Xiaoping and the elders of the party opposed any compromise and were able to muster the necessary support from the armed forces to maintain control. In May Zhao fell from power and was replaced by the ultra-hard-liner, Li Peng.

Then on June 3 and 4 troops moved with brutal ferocity against the movement. Hundreds, perhaps thousands, of people were killed in Peking in what has come to be known as the Tiananmen Massacre, and uncounted more were killed in other cities.

In the time since, more people have been arrested, brutualized, and sometimes executed. Dictatorship has been strengthened, and there has been an across-the-board retreat from reform. Such actions have, of course, simply exacerbated the nation's troubles and left no really strong support for the government within Chinese society.

The opposition has again been forced underground. However, despite the regime's willingness to use ruthlessness and repression, it seems limited in what it can do. Many activists in the democracy movement have been able to evade detection, testimony to the sympathy that their cause has aroused in the population at large. Others have escaped, and Chinese living overseas have been almost unanimous in their condemnation of events at home. There have even been occasional signs of open dissent not only on campuses but in rural areas and in the army. At the same time, the collapse of the Communist regimes in Central Europe has put the government on warning and heartened the opposition. The Chinese Communist Party and the People's Republic are clearly in deep trouble.

If we conclude, then, by taking a very long view and by evaluating China today in terms of the datong tradition and the ideals that impelled the revolution, we find an uneven picture. One can note that the bases for a decentralized political system are, to some extent, in place, and even the possibility for creating the "meritocratic-aristocracy," for which Gu Yanwu called, is perhaps there. Similarly, the economic system has shown some possibility of reaching a balance between public and private, and China is safer militarily than she has been in hundreds of years. There is an active opposition movement on the scene.

On the other hand, the People's Republic has had absolutely no success in creating an effective ideology for the post-junxian era. Ultimately, the reason for this failure has been the deep alienation from the past that has marked China's revolutionary process and that has been immeasurably heightened by the notion of transcendent change embedded in Marxism. As a Confucian might predict, the result has been a mutually reinforcing combination of unsatisfactory government and moral and intellectual chaos. This situation, in turn, has prevented real progress toward the ideals of community and democracy of which traditional revolutionaries dreamed and, indeed, has blocked truly effective thought about any issue from economic organization to China's proper relationship to the Western world. At the moment, it has even limited the effectiveness of the opposition.

Under these circumstances one hesitates to predict the future. What does seem evident at this writing, however, is that many in China believe that the present era feels much more like the end of a dynasty than the beginning. There is, therefore, every possibility that the Communist government will prove to be yet another powerful, unifying regime on the order of the Qin and Sui, which was unable to maintain control for more than a generation. However, one must also note that because of the ideological problems that the opposition shares with the government, there is still a chance that the People's Republic may yet have time to reform itself.

Whatever the short-term uncertainties, however, it is difficult to believe that the great traditions of social theory and political idealism within Confucianism can remain stilled for long. Nor can one doubt that the good sense of the Chinese people, with their vast store of historical experience, will find a way of handling this new and challenging moment in their national life.

Notes

PREFACE

1. Charles O. Hucker, *China's Imperial Past: An Introduction to Chinese History and Culture* (Stanford, 1975).

2. For an analysis of these terms see Ch. 1, note 1.

3. Named for the Japanese scholar Naito Konan. For a recent discussion of his work see Joshua A. Fogel, *Politics and Sinology: The Case of Naito Konan (1866–1934)* (Cambridge, Mass., 1984), particularly the Preface and Ch. 5.

4. For a fuller discussion of the term, see Ch. 1, section on ''Other Philosophies; The Concept of Datong'' and Ch. 1, note 41.

5. This is also the generation that influenced Naito (see note 3, above). For a discussion of how these terms were applied in the 1890s see the recent collection of essays by Min Tu-ki, *National Polity and Local Power: The Transformation of Late Imperial China*, ed. Philip A. Kuhn and Timothy Brook (Cambridge, Mass., and London, 1989).

6. Quoted in *The Pattern of Chinese History*, ed. John Meskill (Boston, 1965), pp. 98ff.

CHAPTER 1

The basic information in this chapter is in accord with such standard texts as E. O. Reischauer and J. K. Fairbank, *East Asia: The Great Tradition* (Boston, 1960) and Charles O. Hucker, *China's Imperial Past* (Stanford, 1975). An excellent general history of the period which has proven particularly helpful is Hsu Cho-yun, *Ancient China in Transition* (Stanford, 1965). The biggest difference between my presentation and the standard one is that I make systematic use of the traditional concepts of fengjian and junxian (see note 1, below).

The chapter includes a long and unabashedly sympathetic treatment of Confucianism. Though the value of the philosophy is debated among historians of the revolutionary era of the 20th century, my presentation is in accord with the views of most specialists on the subject and those who study the traditional period. These include the two basic introductions to Chinese thought available in English: Fung Yu-lan, *A History of Chinese Philosophy*, tr. Derk Bodde, 2 Vols. (Princeton, 1952) and Hsiao Kung-chuan, *A History of Chinese Political Thought*, tr. F. W. Mote, Vol. 1 (Princeton, 1979).

My emphasis on what might be called the democratic or liberal possibilities within the philosophy has been particularly influenced by a classic work, H. G. Creel, *Confucius and the Chinese Way* (New York, 1960). A more recent and interesting study with a similar theme is William Theodore de Bary, *The Liberal Tradition in China* (Hong Kong, 1983).

1. The etymology of fengjian relates to a sacrificial mound, presumably set up to mark the enfeoffment of a vassal, and came to mean decentralized rule through fiefs and a hereditary aristocracy. Junxian is made up of two terms, *jun* and *xian*, which designate administrative subunits and came to mean government through a centralized bureaucracy of nonhereditary officials. Fengjian is closely associated with the Three Dynasties and junxian with the breakdown of the Zhou, with Legalist philosophy, and with the reunification of China under the first junxian dynasty, Qin, in 221 B.C.

The words fengjian and junxian were not used until the transition from one system to the other was underway and perhaps not until after the Qin. Fengjian in its later usage appeared first, in the historical commentary known as the *Zuo Zhuan* (a text variously dated from the fifth to the third century B.C.). Junxian makes its earliest appearance in the second century B.C., in the *Shi Ji* of Sima Qian, the first general history of the ancient period.

The association of fengjian and junxian with a market and nonmarket economy, respectively, comes from the fact that the Three Dynasties had a feudal mode of land tenure, idealized as the so-called well-field system. For example, the important commentator on the fengjian system, Wu Lai (A.D. 1297–1340) wrote that "well-fields were small enfeoffment, enfeoffment was large well-fields" and that the two institutions were interdependent; quoted in Yang Lien-sheng, "Ming Local Government," in Charles O. Hucker, ed., *Chinese Government in Ming Times* (New York, 1969).

On the other hand, Shang Yang (d. 338 B.C.), the Legalist minister to the king of Qin, is said to have established the junxian system there at the same time as he abolished the well-fields and allowed the private ownership and sale of land. The Legalists, in general, and the great synthesizer of the philosophy, Han Feizi, in particular, established the conceptual link between junxian and capitalist economic forms by consistently opposing the fengjian system and supporting both a centralized political system and a competitive market economy; see Fung Yu-lan, *History of Chinese Philosophy*, Vol. 1, Ch. 13.

It should be noted, however, that these early Legalists, despite their call for an economic system based on private property, often advocated government monopolies in key commodities. The powerful laissez-faire implications of junxian were not evident until the system was finally established beginning in the late Tang and Song dynasties. From then on, such monopolies gradually disappeared until, by the eighteenth century, there was only one important one left (see Hucker, *China's Imperial Past*, p. 351).

The association of fengjian with military values and junxian with civilian values comes from the link between warrior aristocrats and the former and the link between civilian bureaucrats and the latter. This connection was made at least as early as Li Si, the Legalist adviser to the first emperor of Qin; see his opposition to fengjian in William de Bary, Wing-tsit Chan, and Burton Watson, comps., *Sources of Chinese Tradition*, 2 Vols.

(New York, 1960), I, p. 140. The distinction became a common theme in discussions of the two systems thereafter; see Yang Lien-sheng, "Ming Local Government."

Religion was associated with the fengjian system because of the spiritual power and cohesion of the Three Dynasties, while junxian was related to secularism because of the decline of such values in the late Zhou and because of the antireligious rationalism of the Legalist philosophers. Thus, Liu Congyuan (A.D. 773–819), the late Tang Dynasty proponent of junxian and a fervent religious skeptic, found it necessary to begin his essay "Fengjian Lun" ("On Fengjian") with a critique of the belief that there was anything particularly sacred about the ancient system; see J. Mason Gentzler, "A Literary Biography of Liu Tsung-yuan," Ph.D. diss., Columbia University, 1966, Ch. 7. On the other hand, Gu Yanwu (A.D. 1613–1682), who advocated reviving the spirit of fengjian to supplement what he considered to be the excessively junxian character of his own time, contrasted the two systems by writing, "The sages of antiquity used a public spirit to serve all under Heaven by reverently granting land as fiefs, the rulers of today simply take all within the four seas as their personal jun and xian [prefectures and districts]"; see Gu Yanwu, "Junxian Lun" ("Essays on Junxian"), Essay 1 in Tang Jinggao, ed., *Gu Yanwu Wen* (*Selected Writings of Gu Yanwu*; Shanghai, 1928).

It should be noted that fengjian is often translated as "feudalism." There is no generally accepted translation for junxian, though it is sometimes called the "prefectural system." "Capitalism," in its most general sense of postfeudal society and "modern times" and thus of centralized bureaucratic government, a market economy, and civilian and secular values, perhaps gives the feel. The comparatively recent transition of the West from fengjian to junxian may explain why we have not developed a generally accepted word for the latter. For more on this issue see Ch. 2, note 9, and Ch. 3, section on "The West."

2. *Analects*, Bk. 11, Sec. 11. The translation is from Arthur Waley, *The Analects of Confucius* (London, 1938; reprinted New York, paper ed., no date), p. 155.

3. *Analects*, Bk. 7, Sec. 20; Waley, p. 127. Waley uses "disorders" rather than "portents," but his gloss indicates that what is meant is natural portents.

4. *Analects*, Bk. 6, Sec. 20. The translation is from de Bary, *Sources*, Vol. 1, p. 29. I have substituted translations from this anthology for others when, as is often the case, they seem particularly felicitous and to the point.

5. *Analects*, Bk. 20, Sec. 3; Waley, p. 233. Here and elsewhere Waley uses "gentleman" to translate junzi. I prefer "virtuous person," which seems both broader and more precise.

6. *Analects*, Bk. 7, Sec. 22; Waley, p. 127.

7. This and the following quote are from *Mencius*, Bk. 1A, Sec. 3. The translation is from D. C. Lau, tr., *Mencius* (London, 1970), p. 51.

8. The definition is that of Professor Stanley Kelley, Jr., of Princeton University.

9. *Analects*, Bk. 8, Sec. 10; Waley, p. 174.

10. The first quote is from *Analects*, Bk. 1, Sec. 2; Waley, p. 83. Waley translates *luan*, chaos, as "revolution"; this, I think, gives too conservative a tone. The second quote is from Bk. 9, Sec. 17; Waley, p. 142.

11. *Mencius*, Bk. 1B, Sec. 8; Lau, p. 68.

12. The first quote is from *Mencius*, Bk. 4, Sec. 7; Lau, p. 120, and the second quote is from Bk. 5A, Sec. 7; Lau, p. 146.

13. Hsu Cho-yun, *Ancient China*, pp. 158ff.

14. *Analects*, Bk. 17, Sec. 6; de Bary, *Sources*, Vol. 1, p. 26. On pp. 30–33 there is a selection of other quotes from the *Analects* that characterize the virtuous person.
15. *Analects*, Bk. 15, Sec. 23; de Bary, *Sources*, Vol. 1, p. 25.
16. *Mencius*, Bk. 4A, Sec. 5; Lau, p. 120.
17. *Analects*, Bk. 12, Sec. 11; Waley, p. 166.
18. *Mencius*, Bk. 1A, Sec. 7; de Bary, *Sources*, Vol. 1, p. 93.
19. *Mencius*, Bk. 3A, Sec. 3; de Bary, *Sources*, Vol. 1, p. 94.
20. *Analects*, Bk. 13, Sec. 9; Waley, p. 173.
21. *Analects*, Bk. 17, Sec. 1; de Bary, *Sources*, Vol. 1, p. 23 (the information about the UN is also given here).
22. *Analects*, Bk. 17, Sec. 7; Waley, p. 124.
23. *Mencius*, Bk. 6B, Sec. 2; Lau, p. 172.
24. This quote is from *Analects*, Bk. 7, Sec. 19; Waley, p. 127. The following two are from Bk. 3, Sec. 14; Waley, p. 97 and Bk. 2, Sec. 23; Waley, p. 93.
25. These and other selections on teaching from the *Analects* are in de Bary, *Sources*, Vol. 1, pp. 23–27. In order, the quotes are from Bk. 7, Sec. 17; Bk. 8, Sec. 8; and Bk. 7, Sec. 24.
26. *Analects*, Bk. 2, Sec. 13; Waley, p. 90.
27. *Analects*, Bk. 2, Sec. 4; de Bary, *Sources*, Vol. 1, p. 22.
28. The first quote is from *Analects*, Bk. 14, Sec. 45; Waley, p. 191, and the second is from Bk. 7, Sec. 32; Waley, p. 130.
29. *Mencius*, Bk. 2A, Sec. 5; Lau, p. 82.
30. *Mencius*, Bk. 4B, Sec. 5; Lau, p. 129.
31. *Analects*, Bk. 15, Sec. 24; Waley, p. 198.
32. *Analects*, Bk. 2, Sec. 3; Waley, p. 88.
33. *Analects*, Bk. 15, Sec. 4; Waley, p. 193. I have translated the famous concept of wuwei, ''inactivity,'' as ''laissez-faire'' in order to bring out its political and economic aspect. This is how it was often understood in such contexts; see, for example, de Bary, *Sources*, Vol. 1, p. 50. As we shall see in Ch. 3, the physiocrats, who popularized the idea of laissez-faire economics in the eighteenth-century West, admired the Confucian China of their time.
34. The first quote is from *Mencius*, Bk. 3A, Sec. 3; Lau, p. 97, and the second is from Bk. 2A, Sec. 5; Lau, p. 82.
35. *Mencius*, Bk. 4A, Sec. 14; Lau, p. 124.
36. The first quote is from *Analects*, Bk. 13, Sec. 29; Waley, p. 178, and the second is from Bk. 15, Sec. 1; Waley, p. 193.
37. *Xunzi* (*Hsun Tzu*), tr. Burton Watson, *Basic Writings of Mo Tzu, Hsun Tzu, and Han Fei Tzu* (New York, 1967), p. 120.
38. *Mencius*, Bk. 5A, Sec. 5; Lau, p. 143.
39. The first quote is from *Mencius*, Bk. 4A, Sec. 9; Lau, p. 121, and the second is from Bk. 7B, Sec. 14; Lau, p. 196.
40. See note 1, above.
41. There are no books on the datong tradition in English and no standard way of translating the term. My understanding of the concept has been particularly informed by two important works in Chinese: Hou Wailu, ed., *Zhongguo lidai datong lixiang* (*The Datong Ideal through the Course of Chinese History*; Peking, 1959); and its companion volume, *Zhongguo datong sixiang ziliao (Materials on Datong Thought)*, comp. Department of Philosophy of the Chinese Academy of Sciences (Peking, 1959). Among the

English works that deal with the idea are Fung Yu-lan, *History of Chinese Philosophy*; Hsiao Kung-chuan, *A History of Chinese Political Thought*; Laurence G. Thompson, tr., *Ta T'ung Shu: The One-World Philosophy of K'ang Yu-wei* (London, 1958); Martin Bernal, *Chinese Socialism to 1907* (Ithaca, N.Y., 1976); and Wolfgang Bauer, *China and the Search for Happiness* (New York, 1976); Frederic Wakeman, *History and Will* (Berkeley, 1973).

The term datong first appears in a passage on divination in the *Book of History* and even the aristocratic atmosphere of the early Zhou seems to allude to a broad sense of political community: "Now you consent . . . the tortoise consents, the milfoil consents, the dignitaries and noblemen consent, the common people consent; that is called the datong" (Thompson, *Ta T'ung Shu*, p. 35). In his introduction, Thompson cites thirteen ways that the term has been translated (p. 29). These include, among others, "The same social ideal as in Western communism or anarchism," "The Great Commonwealth," "The Great Communion," and the "Era of 'world brotherhood.' " "Great Community" is used by Mote in his translation of Hsiao Kung-chuan. It seems to me to get across the Chinese ideal very nicely, from the local, national, and international perspective.

42. The two quotes from the *Rites* are from Fung Yu-lan, *A History of Chinese Philosophy*, Vol. 1, p. 377. I have changed the translation of datong from Great Unity to Great Community.

43. See, for example, *Mencius*, Bk. 3A, Sec. 3 and Bk. 2A, Sec. 5; Lau, pp. 99 and 82.

44. Cited in Vincent Y. C. Shih, *The Taiping Ideology* (Seattle, 1967), p. 230.

45. *Analects*, Bk. 8, Sec. 9; Waley, p. 134. In the original, "follow the Way" reads "follow it," but Waley makes clear that "the Way" is what is meant.

46. This and the following quotes on Xu Xing are from *Mencius*, Bk. 3A, Sec. 4; Lau, p. 100.

47. Quoted in de Bary, *Sources*, Vol. 1, p. 140.

48. Quoted in Shih, *The Taiping Ideology*, p. 331.

CHAPTER 2

Basic information in this chapter continues to be in accord with standard texts such as Hucker, *China's Imperial Past* and Reischauer and Fairbank, *East Asia: The Great Tradition*. I have also cited specific works where they have proven particularly helpful. I should also note an important new book dealing with social history: Susan Naquin and Evelyn S. Rawski, *Chinese Society in the Eighteenth Century* (New Haven and London, 1987). Their approach is heavily influenced by Western social science and recent trends in Western historiography, both of which are often inclined to debunk traditional Chinese thought and society. What seems particularly significant, therefore, is that, despite some differences, their carefully researched work supports the traditional picture presented in Hucker.

As in Chapter 1, I have continued to analyze the story in Chinese terms (most importantly, fengjian, junxian, and datong) and to make the necessary changes in terminology. In addition, since the major purpose of my study is to link the revolutionary history of the nineteenth and twentieth centuries with the past, I have paid particular attention to the opposition tradition.

1. Yang Lien-sheng, *Studies in Chinese Institutional History* (Cambridge, Mass., 1963), p. 90.

2. The change is noted in Burton Watson, *Ssu-ma Ch'ien: Grand Historian of China* (New York, 1958), p. 147. The description of Chen She is from the celebrated essay "The Faults of Qin" by the early Han poet and statesman Jia Yi, which is translated in de Bary, *Sources*, Vol. 1, p. 152. The description of Liu Bang is from the *Shi Ji* and is quoted by Watson, p. 147.

3. Quoted in Fung Yu-lan, *History of Chinese Philosophy*, Vol. 2, p. 129.

4. de Bary, *Sources*, Vol. 1, p. 376.

5. These figures come from Hucker, *China's Imperial Past*, pp. 272, 292, and 301.

6. F. W. Mote, "The Transformation of Nanking," in G. William Skinner, ed., *The City in Late Imperial China* (Stanford, Calif., 1977).

7. The first quote is from Hucker, *China's Imperial Past*, p. 105; and the second is given in Mote, "The Transformation of Nanking," p. 105.

8. Reischauer and Fairbank, *East Asia: The Great Tradition*, p. 290.

9. A good description of China's social structure in the junxian age can be found in Hucker, *China's Imperial Past*, pp. 329ff.

In his discussion of the social structure of the Ming and Qing, Hucker does not explicitly use Mencius's distinction between *laoxinzhe* (those who labor with their minds) and *laolizhe* (those who labor with their hands). However, these categories fit his description and provide, I think, a nice example of how things fit together if one consciously applies traditional Chinese categories of analysis.

Hucker emphasizes that it is difficult to come up with English words to characterize this social situation. One reason may be that our society has entered the junxian age only in the last two hundred years or so. As a result, our vocabulary is deficient in junxian terms. Thus, for example, we have a reasonable translation for fengjian, "feudalism," but none that is generally agreed upon for junxian. Similarly, we have a precise word for the elite of a fengjian society, "aristocracy," but none for that of junxian; and we have a word for the average person in the former system, "commoner," but none for that of the latter.

Furthermore, the words we do associate with a junxian system often have a strong fengjian bias, implying overly sharp class lines, or a cultural bias, implying sharp distinctions between urban and rural people. For example, those who worked with their hands in junxian society are best described as manual workers, but these words imply work in an urban setting, a situation even more true, of course, for such terms as "blue-collar" or "proletariat."

Like Hucker (and Naquin and Rawski), I consciously reject the word "gentry" to describe the elite. The term is still commonly employed, but it has several serious problems. The first is that, once again, it has an overly fengjian ring, an excessive implication of hereditary status. In addition, it is used ambiguously to mean both those who passed the imperial exams and those who only had aspirations in that direction or, indeed, were simply wealthy. Most serious, though, is the fact that the concept of "gentry" excludes the majority of the elite, who may not have been involved in the examination system at all and, as Hucker points out, "in its lower echelons . . . included a broad range of shopkeepers, small-scale manufacturers," and others (p. 339).

Hucker suggests "managerial class" or simply "some innocuous term such as the 'social elite' " (p. 338), and I simply use the word "elite." For the rest of society, I have also used "innocuous" words like "the common man," "the average citizen," and, where it is not ambiguous to the fact that it includes farmers, ''workers'' or ''manual workers.'' In addition, when they can be employed without sounding exotic, I have also used ''long-gowned'' for the elite and ''short-jacketed'' for the average person (see the following note).

10. This distinction in dress between the *duanyi* (short-jacketed) and the *changshan* (long-gowned) is first evident in the Song at the beginning of the junxian age. See Jacques Gernet, *Daily Life in China on the Eve of the Mongol Invasion, 1250–1276* (New York, 1962), pp. 129–130. It was still used to distinguish the elite and the average person in the twentieth century; see, for example, the famous short story of Lu Xun, ''Kong Yiji,'' in Lu Xun, *Lu Xun Quanji* (*The Complete Works of Lu Xun*), Vol. 1 (Peking: 1956), p. 20. I discuss this story in Chapter 6.

11. One book has suggested that ''professional'' might, in fact, be the appropriate word to describe the Confucian establishment of the Ming and Qing, a group that essentially consisted of the degree-holders. See John W. Dardess, *Confucianism and Autocracy: Professional Elites in the Founding of the Ming Dynasty* (Berkeley, 1983).

12. A nice feel for the flavor of society in this respect can be found in the great early Qing novel, *Ru Lin Waishi* (*Unofficial History of the Literati*, or, as it is best known in English, *The Scholars*). See Wu Jungzi, *The Scholars*, tr. Yang Hsien-yi and Gladys Yang (Peking, 1973).

13. Quoted in Evelyn S. Rawski, *Education and Popular Literacy in Ch'ing China* (Ann Arbor, 1979), p. 2.

14. Rawski, *Education and Popular Literacy*, pp. 8ff for figures. On the spread of popular literature see pp. 111ff.

15. Hucker, *China's Imperial Past*, p. 341.

16. A book that gives a sense of the relationship between the emperor and the bureaucracy is Ray Huang, *1587, A Year of No Significance: The Ming Dynasty in Decline* (New Haven, 1981).

17. This is the general conclusion of Robert Marsh, *The Mandarins: The Circulation of Elites in China, 1600–1900* (Glencoe, 1961).

18. G. William Skinner, ed., *The City in Late Imperial China*, p. 19.

19. Yang Lien-sheng, ''Ming Local Government,'' p. 10.

20. Hucker, *China's Imperial Past*, p. 351.

21. For example, a recent study that shows governmental activism in revitalizing an area is Peter Perdue, *Exhausting the Earth: State and Peasant in Hunan, 1500–1850* (Cambridge, Mass., 1987). The book also shows how such activism declined as problems were solved and, one might add, in the face of the laissez-faire tendencies of the age.

22. A book that emphasizes the tremendous pressures that Neo-Confucians faced precisely because they believed that the good society could really be established is Thomas Metzgar, *Escape from Predicament: Neo-Confucianism and China's Evolving Political Culture* (New York, 1977).

23. de Bary, *Sources*, Vol. 1, p. 473.

24. de Bary, *Sources*, Vol. 1, p. 404.

25. de Bary, *Sources*, Vol. 1, p. 469.

26. Quoted in Hucker, *China's Imperial Past*, p. 371.

27. My picture of the tradition of popular opposition comes from Yuji Muramatsu, ''Some Themes in Chinese Rebel Ideologies'' in Arthur F. Wright, ed., *The Confucian Persuasion* (Stanford, Calif., 1960); Shih, *The Taiping Ideology* (see especially Ch. 8–

11); Hou, *Zhongguo lidai datong lixiang*; Department of Philosophy of the Chinese Academy of Sciences, *Zhongguo datong sixiang ziliao*.

Muramatsu does not use the term datong or its equivalent, taiping (Great Peace), but his excellent overview is compatible with other works that do, providing, I think, another nice example of how traditional terms can help to integrate information.

On taiping as a common synonym for datong see *Zhongguo datong sixiang ziliao*, Sec. 2 and 3, especially, p. 15, and a number of discussions in Shih (for example, pp. 48 and 236). The latter translates datong as "World of Great Harmony."

28. Quoted in Shih, *The Taiping Ideology*, p. 331.

29. Quoted in Muramatsu, "Some Themes in Chinese Rebel Ideologies," p. 256.

30. Shih, *The Taiping Ideology*, p. 338.

31. On this process see Dardess, *Confucianism and Autocracy*.

32. The information on Wang and his followers comes from Wang Yangming, *Instructions for Practical Living and Other Neo-Confucian Writings*, tr. with notes and commentaries, by Chang Wing-tsit (New York, 1963); William de Bary, "Individualism and Humanitarianism in Late Ming Thought," in de Bary, ed., *Self and Society in Ming Thought* (New York, 1970); Julia Ch'ing, *To Acquire Wisdom: The Way of Wang Yangming* (New York, 1976); Tu Wei-ming, *Neo-Confucian Thought in Action: Wang Yangming's Youth, 1472–1509* (Berkeley, 1976).

33. Wang Yangming, *Instructions for Practical Living*, p. 118.

34. Wang Yangming, *Instructions for Practical Living*, p. 10.

35. Wang Yangming, *Instructions for Practical Living*, p. 273. I have changed the translation of qin min from "loving the people" to "intimacy" or "closeness" to the people. It provides, I think, a more precise rendering of *qin* in a sociopolitical context and am grateful to Professor Tu Wei-ming for concurring in this emendation.

36. Quoted in Ch'ing, *To Acquire Wisdom*, p. 34.

37. Quoted in Tadao Sakai, "Confucianism and Popular Educational Works," in de Bary, ed., *Self and Society in Ming Thought* (New York, 1970), p. 339.

38. Yuji Muramatsu, "Some Themes in Chinese Rebel Ideologies," p. 262.

39. William de Bary, "*A Plan for the Prince: The Ming-i tai-fang lu of Huang Tsung-hsi*," Ph.D. diss., Columbia University, 1953, pp. 101ff.

40. de Bary, *Sources*, Vol. 1, p. 536.

41. de Bary, *Sources*, Vol. 1, p. 535. I have used the Chinese text to get the precise translation when fengjian and junxian are used. This can be found in Huang Zongxi, *Mingyi Daifang Lu (A Plan for the Prince)*, Commercial Press Edition (Shanghai, 1937), p. 4.

42. Quoted in Tang Jinggao, ed., *Gu Yanwu Wen* (*Selected Writings of Gu Yanwu*), Preface, p. 16.

43. See note 27, above.

44. This and the quote that follows are from Gu Yanwu, "Junxian Lun" ("Essays on Junxian"), Essay 1 in *Gu Yanwu Wen*, pp. 1–2. The translation is based on de Bary, *Sources*, Vol. 1, pp. 556ff.

45. It is interesting to note that the word *luan*, which I have taken in the usual sense of "chaos" has, in fact, been translated as "revolution." See Waley's rendering of the word in *Analects*, Bk. 1, Sec. 2; Waley, p. 83. It is also worth pointing out that Gu's word for "people's livelihood," *minsheng*, is the same one used three hundred years later by Sun Yat-sen in his celebrated Three People's Principles and is often taken as the center of the latter's own understanding of datong.

46. One must say "on the surface." Despite the apolitical reputation of the approach, a close study from within the Confucian tradition of what texts were worked on and what the implications were for politics may show otherwise. Suggestive along these lines is Benjamin Elman, *From Philosophy to Philology: Intellectual and Social Aspects of Change in Late Imperial China* (Cambridge, Mass., 1984).

CHAPTER 3

The general information that follows on Chinese foreign relations remains in accord with standard texts supplemented by the specific works cited. In addition to the continued use of Chinese terminology, my most significant change has been in employing the word "nationalism" to designate one of the Chinese attitudes toward foreigners; for a discussion of this change see note 2.

1. Reischauer and Fairbank, *East Asia: The Great Tradition*, Ch. 7, provides a particularly excellent account of the northern peoples. Behind it lies the classic Owen Lattimore, *Inner Asian Frontiers of China* (New York, 1940), which is still worth reading for its colorful and sympathetic detailing of life beyond the Wall.

2. In using the word nationalist to designate one of the Chinese approaches described below I have departed from general usage. Thus, Reischauer and Fairbank use the rather negative words "ethnocentrism" or "xenophobia" (see pp. 291ff.) while Hucker uses a positive word "patriotism" (see pp. 399ff.). One obvious advantage of "nationalism" is that it is relatively value-free.

There are, however, theoretical reasons why it has been avoided. These are summarized in Reischauer and Fairbank, *East Asia: The Great Tradition*, p. 292. Nationalism, they write, is bound up with a feeling of cultural "insecurity or even inferiority," and the Chinese did not have this feeling. It seems to me that while nationalism may have such origins, belief in one's own cultural superiority is also compatible with the general understanding of the term. Furthermore, they agree that Chinese ethnocentrism did arise as a response to the foreign pressures and occupations of the junxian age, which would mean that there was some insecurity involved in its development in China also.

The other theoretical issue, they suggest, is that the "strength" of nationalism depends on "the identification of the individual with the national political unit," and the individual in China "commonly felt no particular identification with the state." This point, it seems to me, is a matter of degree and, furthermore, is contravened by the attitudes I discuss below, particularly in the opposition tradition, and by the strand Hucker describes as patriotic. Reischauer and Fairbank suggest the word "culturalism" for China. It is an excellent term, and I employ it for one of the Chinese positions. However, it does not cover the full panoply of views and, as I suggest, is, indeed, compatible with nationalism.

Other reasons why the term nationalist has been avoided are historical. First of all, the Qing, the dynasty in power when Western imperialism came on the scene, was foreign. Therefore, as we shall see, it emphasized the culturalist point of view and denigrated and even repressed nationalist feelings. This situation has made a full appreciation of the latter approach more difficult. Second, by the end of the nineteenth century, virtually all agree that there was a vast upsurge of nationalism. Like many phenomena of the revolutionary era, the prominence of nationalism, indeed, its very existence, has been attributed to the coming of the West. However, when one relates the revolution to Chinese tradition, it soon becomes evident that it was precisely in times when the opposition was on the rise and when there were foreign pressures that an efflorescence of nationalism was to be expected.

I should note that some writers have, in fact, used, or at least considered using, the term nationalism in reference to junxian China. Thus, de Bary, *Sources*, Vol. 1, p. 543, speaks of the ''intense nationalism'' of Wang Fuzhi, the early Qing opponent of the Manchus. Similarly, Ssu-yu Teng and John Fairbank, *China's Response to the West* (Cambridge, Mass., 1954), p. 7, describes such radicals as Huang Zongxi and Gu Yanwu as nationalists, though it puts the terms ''nationalist'' and ''nationalistic'' in quotes.

3. See Yuji Muramatsu, ''Some Themes in Chinese Rebel Ideologies,'' pp. 264ff.; and Shih, *The Taiping Ideology*, Ch. 11. It should be reiterated that these authors do not use the word nationalist but rather such terms as ''racialist'' or ''the ethnic issue.''

4. Reischauer and Fairbank, *East Asia: The Great Tradition*, p. 267.

5. Miyazaki Ichisada, ''Yosei Shuhi Yushi Mondai'' (''The Yungzheng Emperor's Vermilion Instructions'') in *Toyoshi Kenkyu* (*The Journal of Oriental Research*) 15:4 (March 1957): 3.

6. de Bary *Sources*, Vol. 1, p. 373.

7. Shih, *The Taiping Ideology*, p. 353.

8. Quoted in Reischauer and Fairbank, *East Asia: The Great Tradition*, p. 275.

9. Both this and the quote from Zhu that follows are from Shih, *The Taiping Ideology*, p. 367.

10. Julia Ch'ing, *To Acquire Wisdom: The Way of Wang Yang-ming*, p. 44.

11. de Bary, *Sources*, Vol. 1, p. 547.

12. Quoted in Teng and Fairbank, *China's Response to the West*, p. 9.

13. Silas H. L. Wu, *Passage to Power: Kang Hsi and His Heir Apparent, 1661–1722* (Cambridge, Mass., 1979), p. 126.

14. The basic information that follows on China and the West through 1800 can be found in Derk Bodde, *China's Cultural Tradition: What and Whither?* (New York, 1957); G. F. Hudson, *Europe and China* (Boston, 1961); Lewis Maverick, *China: A Model for Europe* (San Antonio, 1946); and Adolf Reichwein, *China and Europe* (orig. pub. 1925, repub. Taipei, 1967). The framework of analysis, however, which stresses science, the transition from fengjian to junxian, and the notion of transcendent progress, is, essentially, my own.

15. Hudson, *Europe and China*, p. 68.

16. The term reve chinois is alluded to in Maverick, *China: A Model for Europe*, p. 60.

17. Bodde, *China's Cultural Tradition*, p. 7.

18. Hudson, *Europe and China*, p. 313.

19. Bodde, *China's Cultural Tradition*, p. 15.

20. Maverick, *China: A Model for Europe*, p. 209.

21. Hudson, *Europe and China*, p. 320.

22. This and the following quotes from Voltaire are from Reichwein, *China and Europe*, p. 89.

23. This and the following quote are from Charles Montesquieu, *The Spirit of the Laws*, tr. Thomas Nugent (New York, 1949), p. 124.

24. Maverick, *China: A Model for Europe*, p. 209.

25. This quote and the two that follow on military attitudes can be found in Hudson, *Europe and China*, pp. 320–321.

26. Bodde, *China's Cultural Tradition*, p. 8.

27. See F. W. Mote, "The Transformation of Nanking" in Skinner, ed., *The City in Late Imperial China*. It is also well to remember that our very word for civilization comes from the Latin word for city and that in the fengjian order of the West the serf or peasant ranked at the bottom of society, an attitude that probably continued to affect views as the junxian order developed (in China they ranked just below the aristocrats). The urban bias of the West is one reason that words designating rural people, from "boor" through "peasant," have consistently degenerated in meaning.

28. The contrast to China has been commented upon in Benjamin Schwartz, *The World of Thought in Ancient China* (Cambridge, Mass., 1985), p. 65.

CHAPTER 4

The chapters on the revolutionary era cover my academic specialty, and the material comes from a wide variety of sources. For the most part, however, the basic information can still be found in texts such as John K. Fairbank, E. Reischauer, and A. Craig, *East Asia: The Modern Transformation* (Boston, 1965) and Immanuel C. Y. Hsu, *The Rise of Modern China* (New York, 1983). At the beginning of each topic I have also cited a few of the specialized works that have been particularly important to my presentation.

However, as opposed to earlier chapters where, except in emphasis and terminology, my presentation has worked to follow the standard interpretation, what follows is more original. First of all, in line with the general purpose of this study (linking the Chinese revolution to the past) I have stressed the internal, Chinese dynamics of the story rather than the impact of the West. This emphasis has become an increasingly common approach in American scholarship but one that has, until very recently, been only weakly reflected in general works. For a discussion of the issue see Paul A. Cohen, *Discovering History in China* (New York, 1984). More important, I have, I hope, sharpened this approach by using concepts and modes of analysis derived from Chinese tradition rather than from Western theories, which tend to distort the historical setting by suggesting a prerevolutionary China akin to the ancien regime, feudal or traditional in a basic sense, and so to vitiate the effort to understand internal causation.

Second, when the West comes on the scene, I have analyzed its influence in terms of the Chinese story rather than the other way around. In particular, I have stressed that the Chinese revolution took place in a decaying junxian society while the West has been in a transition from fengjian to junxian. This approach again reiterates that in sociopolitical terms the West has not been more modern than China and so enables us to understand that it was the fengjian side of the Occident that, in addition to science and the notion of transcendent progress, proved particularly influential.

1. Fairbank, Reischauer, and Craig, *East Asia: The Modern Transformation*, pp. 89ff. The works that have been particularly helpful on the problems of the early nineteenth century are Susan Mann Jones and Philip A. Kuhn, "Dynastic Decline and the Roots of Rebellion" in Fairbank, ed., *The Cambridge History of China*, Vol. 10; Hsaio Kung-chuan, *Rural China: Imperial Control in the Nineteenth Century* (Seattle, 1960); and Susan Naquin, *Millenarian Rebellion in China: The Eight Trigrams Uprising of 1813* (New Haven, 1976).

2. Reischauer and Fairbank, *East Asia: The Great Tradition*, p. 392.

3. James Polachek, "Literati Groups and Literati Politics in Early Nineteenth-Century China," Ph.D. diss., University of California, Berkeley, 1974.

4. Gong Zizhen, for example; see Department of Philosophy of the Chinese Academy of Sciences, *Zhongguo datong sixiang ziliao*, p. 52.

5. The following works have been especially useful in discussing relations with the West in the early nineteenth century: Chang Hsin-pao, *Commissioner Lin and the Opium War* (Cambridge, Mass., 1964); John K. Fairbank, *Trade and Diplomacy on the China Coast* (Cambridge, Mass., 1953); and Frederic Wakeman, Jr., "The Canton Trade and the Opium War" in Fairbank, ed., *The Cambridge History*, Vol. 10.

6. This and the quote that follows are from Fairbank, *Trade and Diplomacy*, p. 173.

7. Fairbank, *Trade and Diplomacy*, p. 73.

8. Fairbank, *Trade and Diplomacy*, p. 69.

9. Fairbank, Reischauer, and Craig, *East Asia: The Modern Transformation*, p. 135.

10. Teng and Fairbank, *China's Response to the West*, p. 25.

11. Most useful on the Taiping Rebellion have been Eugene Boardman, *Christian Influence upon the Taiping Rebellion* (Madison, 1952); Philip A. Kuhn, "The Taiping Rebellion" in Fairbank, ed., *The Cambridge History*, Vol. 10; Franz Michael with Chang Chung-li, *The Taiping Rebellion: History and Documents*, Vol. 1, *History* (Seattle, 1966); and Shih, *The Taiping Ideology*.

12. This quote and the quote that follows are from Shih, *Taiping Ideology*, pp. 5 and 14.

13. Shih, *Taiping Ideology*, p. 6.

14. Shih, *Taiping Ideology*, p. 41.

15. Shih, *Taiping Ideology*, p. 43.

16. de Bary, *Sources*, Vol. 2, p. 37.

17. Shih, *Taiping Ideology*, p. 50.

18. Shih, *Taiping Ideology*, p. 47.

19. Quoted in Shih, *Taiping Ideology*, p. 61.

20. Quoted in Shih, *Taiping Ideology*, p. 63.

21. Mary C. Wright, *The Last Stand of Chinese Conservatism* (Stanford, 1957). In addition to Wright, Kwang-ching Liu, "The Ch'ing Restoration," in Fairbank, ed., *The Cambridge History*, Vol. 10, has been especially helpful in writing about the Restoration.

22. Wright, *Last Stand*, p. 73.

23. K. C. Liu, "Ch'ing Restoration," p. 411.

24. This quote and the following quotes are from Liu, "Ch'ing Restoration," pp. 415, 443, and 438.

CHAPTER 5

For a general introduction to the notes of this chapter, see the introduction to the notes of Ch. 4

1. On the Self-strengthening Movement I have relied most heavily on Albert Feuerwerker, *China's Early Industrialization: Sheng Hsuan-huai and Mandarin Enterprise* (Cambridge, Mass., 1958); Ting-yee Kuo and Kwang-ching Liu, "Self-strengthening: The Pursuit of Western Technology" in Fairbank, ed., *The Cambridge History of China*, Vol. 10; and Yen-p'ing Hao and Erh-min Wang, "Changing Chinese Views of Western Relations," in J. K. Fairbank and Kwang-ching Liu, ed., *The Cambridge History of China*, Vol. 11.

2. Quoted in Hao and Wang, ''Changing Chinese Views of Western Relations,'' p. 160.

3. de Bary, *Sources*, Vol. 2, p. 53.

4. Teng and Fairbank, *China's Response to the West*, p. 109.

5. Hao and Wang, ''Changing Chinese Views of Western Relations,'' p. 159.

6. On the qingyi, most useful have been Lloyd Eastman, *Throne and Mandarins: China's Search for a Policy during the Sino-French Controversy, 1880–1885* (Cambridge, Mass., 1967); Min Tu-ki, ''Musul pyonpop undong ui paegyong e taehayo t'ukhi ch'ongnyup'a wa yangmup'a rul chungsim uro'' (''On the Background of the Reform Movement of 1898 with Special Reference to the Qingliu pai and the Yangwu pai''), *Tongyang sahek yon'gu*, No. 5 (1971): 101; and John Schrecker, ''The Reform Movement of 1898 and the Ch'ing-i: Reform as Opposition,'' in Paul Cohen and John Schrecker, eds., *Reform in Nineteenth-Century China* (Cambridge, Mass., 1976).

7. Fairbank, Reischauer, and Craig, *East Asia: The Modern Transformation*, p. 330.

8. Quoted in Benjamin Schwartz, *In Search of Wealth and Power: Yen Fu and the West* (Cambridge, Mass., 1964), p. 16.

9. Quoted in Schwartz, *In Search of Wealth and Power*, p. 16.

10. Kang Youwei, *Chronological Autobiography*, tr. Jung-pang Lo in Jung-pang Lo, ed., *K'ang Yu-wei, A Biography and a Symposium* (Tucson, 1967), p. 50.

11. My understanding of the Reform Movement has been especially shaped by Hsiao Kung-chuan, *A Modern China and a New World: K'ang Yu-wei, Reformer and Utopian, 1858–1927* (Seattle, 1975); Jung-pang Lo, ed., *K'ang Yu-wei, A Biography and a Symposium*; John Schrecker, ''The Reform Movement of 1898 and the Ch'ing-i''; Schwartz, *In Search of Wealth and Power*; and the many works of Min Tu-ki, of which the most comprehensive on the Reform Movement is *Chungguk kundae hyongmyong undong ui yon'gu: Kang Yu-i chungsim ui 1898-nyon kaehyok undong* (*An Investigation of the Movement for Reform in Modern China: The Reform Movement of 1898 Which Centered on Kang Youwei*) (Seoul, 1985).

12. This and the following quote are from Kang Youwei, *Chronological Autobiography*, tr. Jung-pang Lo, p. 33.

13. Kang Youwei, *Chronological Autobiography*, p. 36.

14. Quoted in Hsiao, *A Modern China and a New World*, p. 62.

15. In this period of his life Kang Youwei generally remained within the Chinese cultural tradition and did not absorb the Western concept of transcendent progress, of a complete break with the Chinese past (See Hsiao, *A Modern China and a New World*, pp. 41ff and p. 436). This observation is not, however, the case in a book that is difficult to date but that is probably Kang's most famous work, the *Datong Shu* (*On the Great Community*).

Here he describes a utopian society that, though in many ways compatible with traditional datong ideas, blends things Chinese with ''the finest and best of the ancient wisdom of India, Greece, Persia, Rome, and of present-day England, France, Germany, and America'' (Quoted in Hsiao, p. 439). The work leaves all history behind. Among other things, it describes a world without national boundaries and calls for an end to private property, the family, and all gender distinctions. It ends with a vision of mankind living in a mystical unity with the universe.

Kang seems to have begun the *Datong Shu* by the 1890s; however, it was not completed until he went into exile after the failure of the Reform Movement in 1898. For a long while he refused to publish the work. The first third did not appear in print until 1913, and the bulk did not come out until 1935, ten years after Kang's death.

Overall, the *Datong Shu* is a most interesting addition to the literature of utopias and also a good example of the transcendent outlook that overtook the Chinese revolution in the twentieth century and resulted, among other things, in the adoption of Marxism. The entire work has been ably translated: see Laurence G. Thomspon, tr., *Ta T'ung Shu: The One-World Philosophy of K'ang Yu-wei*.

16. Quoted in Fung Yu-lan, *History of Chinese Philosophy*, Vol. 2, p. 679.

17. Fung Yu-lan, *History of Chinese Philosophy*, Vol. 2, p. 681.

18. Quoted in Fung Yu-lan, *History of Chinese Philosophy*, Vol. 2, p. 675.

19. For the quote and a discussion of the issue see Hsiao, *A Modern China and a New World*, p. 120.

20. Quoted in Alfred Forke, *Geschichte der neueren chinesischen Philosophie* (*History of Modern Chinese Philosophy*) (Hamburg, 1938), p. 580.

21. Kang Youwei, *Chronological Autobiography*, p. 65.

22. Quoted in John Schrecker, "The Pao-kuo Hui: A Reform Society of 1898," *Papers on China*, Vol. 14, p. 51.

23. This and the following quote from Liang are in Schrecker, "The Pao-kuo Hui," pp. 51 and 53. Checking the originals, I have retranslated a few words.

24. The list of names is from Jian Bozan et al., eds., *Wuxu Bianfa* (*The Reform Movement of 1898*) (Shanghai, 1953), Vol. 4, p. 395.

25. Jian, ed., *Wuxu Bianfa*, Vol. 3, p. 25.

26. These and the following are quoted in Hsiao, *A Modern China and a New World*, p. 421.

27. The quotes from Tan are all from de Bary, *Sources*, Vol. 2, p. 89.

28. This is most powerfully evident in the work of the great translator of liberal thought, Yen Fu. Yen turned even the most individualistic Western outlooks (as that of Herbert Spenser, for example) into arguments for collective values. See Schwartz, *In Search of Wealth and Power*.

29. See William Theodore de Bary, *The Liberal Tradition in China* (Hong Kong and New York, 1983) and also my discussion of Huang and Gu in Chapter 2, section on "The Opposition Tradition."

30. Teng and Fairbank, *China's Response to the West*, p. 161.

31. Kang Youwei (pseud. Ming Yi), "Gongmin Zizhi Pian" ("On Self-Government by the Citizenry") in the *Xinmin Congbao* (*The New People's Miscellany*), No. 7, p. 28. Kang's pseudonym here actually seems to allude to the *Mingyi Daifang Lu*, the most famous work of Huang Zongxi, who, of course, advocated a fengjian revival (see note 29, above).

For a discussion of this article and its authorship by Kang see Philip A. Kuhn, "Local Self-Government under the Republic," in Frederic Wakeman, Jr., and Carolyn Grant, eds., *Conflict and Control in Late Imperial China* (Berkeley, 1975), p. 272.

32. Quoted in John Schrecker, *Imperialism and Chinese Nationalism* (Cambridge, Mass., 1971), p. 54.

33. It has been commonly said that the initial motto of the movement was "Overthrow the Qing and expel the foreigners." However, there has always been some doubt on the matter, which has been made explicit in a recent work: Joseph W. Esherick, *The Origins of the Boxer Uprising* (Berkeley, 1987).

34. The most useful works on the last decade of the Qing have been Martin Bernal,

Chinese Socialism to 1907 (Ithaca, N.Y., 1976); Roger Des Forges, *Hsi-liang and the Chinese National Revolution* (New Haven, 1973); Michael Gasster, "The Republican Revolutionary Movement," in Fairbank and Liu, eds., *The Cambridge History*, Vol. 11; Li Yu-ning, *The Introduction of Socialism into China* (New York, 1971); Harold Schiffrin, *Sun Yat-sen and the Origins of the Chinese Revolution* (Berkeley, 1968); Schrecker, *Imperialism and Chinese Nationalism*; Mary C. Wright, ed., *China in Revolution: The First Phase, 1900–1913* (New Haven, 1968).

35. *Xiang Bao Leizuan* (*Selections from the Hunan Journal*) (1902; reprinted, Taipei, 1968), Vol. 1, p. 311.

36. For a discussion of Japan's industrialization see Kazushi Ohkawa and Henry Rosovsky, "A Century of Japanese Economic Growth," in William W. Lockwood, ed., *The State and Economic Enterprise in Japan: Essays in the Political Economy of Growth* (Princeton, 1965).

37. See Ch. 6, section on "Marxism," for a discussion of the relationship between the two terms.

38. Quoted in Gasster, "The Republican Revolutionary Movement," p. 491.

39. Quoted in Fairbank, Reischauer, and Craig, *East Asia: The Modern Transformation*, p. 641.

CHAPTER 6

For a general introduction to the notes of this chapter, see the introduction to the notes of Ch. 4. In addition to the materials mentioned there, a good general overview of the period is James E. Sheridan, *China in Disintegration: The Republican Era in Chinese History, 1912–1949* (New York, 1975). The sections on this era in John K. Fairbank, *The United States and China* (Cambridge, Mass., 1983) are also particularly fine. Similarly, Vols. 12 and 13 of the *Cambridge History* are available and contain much relevant material. The story as presented in the *Cambridge History* is summarized in Fairbank's more recent *The Great Chinese Revolution 1800–1985* (New York, 1986).

1. On the era of disunity the most useful books have been Edward Friedman, *Backward toward Revolution: The Chinese Revolutionary Party* (Berkeley, 1974); and Ernest P. Young, *The Presidency of Yuan Shih-k'ai: Liberalism and Dictatorship in Early Republican China* (Ann Arbor, 1977).

2. Most helpful on the May 4th Movement have been Guy S. Alitto, *The Last Confucian: Liang Shu-ming and the Chinese Dilemma of Modernity* (Berkeley, 1979); Chow Tse-tsung, *The May Fourth Movement* (Cambridge, Mass., 1960); Lin Yu-sheng, *The Crisis of Chinese Consciousness: Radical Antitraditionalism in the May Fourth Era* (Madison, 1979); Maurice Meisner, *Li Ta-chao and the Origins of Chinese Marxism* (Cambridge, Mass., 1967); Benjamin Schwartz, *Chinese Communism and the Rise of Mao* (Cambridge, Mass., 1951); and Benjamin Schwartz, ed., *Reflections on the May 4th Movement: A Symposium* (Cambridge, Mass., 1972).

3. Quoted in Lin Yu-sheng, *The Crisis of Chinese Consciousness*, p. 65.

4. This and the following are from de Bary, *Sources*, Vol. 2, p. 153.

5. Quoted in Lin Yu-sheng, *The Crisis of Chinese Consciousness*, p. 96.

6. Lu Xun, *Selected Works of Lu Hsun*, tr. Yang Hsien-yi and Gladys Yang (Peking, 1956), Vol. 1, p. 12.

7. Lu Xun, *Selected Works*, Vol. 1, p. 27.

8. Marx first heard of the Taipings through the writings of the German missionary Gutzlaff. Through a combination of overpopulation and foreign economic competition, Marx wrote in 1850 that China had

> reached the brink of ruin and is already threatened with a mighty revolution. But worse was to come. Among the rebellious plebs individuals appeared who pointed to the poverty of some and to the wealth of others, and who demanded, and are still demanding a different distribution of private property. When Herr Gutzlaff came among civilized people and Europeans again after an absence of twenty years, he heard talk of socialism and asked what this might be. When it had been explained to him he cried out in horror: "Shall I then nowhere escape this pernicious doctrine? For some time now many of the mob have been preaching exactly the same thing in China!"
>
> Now Chinese socialism may admittedly be the same in relation to European socialism as Chinese philosophy in relation to Hegelian philosophy. Nevertheless . . . when our European reactionaries . . . finally come to the Great Wall of China, to the gates leading to the stronghold of arch-reaction and arch-conservatism, who knows if they may not read the following inscription upon them: "République Chinoise, Liberté, Égalité, Fraternité."

See Karl Marx and Frederick Engels, *Collected Works* (New York, 1978), Vol. 10, p. 266.

Some of Marx's writings on China have been collected in *Marx on China, 1851–1860, Articles from The New York Daily Tribune*, ed. with Introduction and Notes by Dona Torr (London, 1951). The Introduction also quotes much of the above.

It is interesting to note that the greatest contradiction in Marx may be his belief that capitalism came into its own only with the French Revolution but that by the late 1840s and 1850s, it was already near its doom, for this time is amazingly short for what, in Marx's view, was the most radical event in Western history to represent reaction. Therefore, while it is probably coincidental, it is worth pointing out that the Chinese Revolution, in general, and the Taiping Rebellion, in particular, massive datong movements directed against against an overripe junxian system, were underway at the time. Marx's sense of the problem may be evident here, for example, when he associates a Taiping victory ("socialism") with "Liberté, Égalité, and Fraternité," the slogans of the French Revolution (his quintessential capitalist event).

9. Quoted in Benjamin Schwartz, *Chinese Communism and the Rise of Mao*, p. 215.

10. Teng and Fairbank, *China's Response to the West*, p. 248.

11. Teng and Fairbank, *China's Response*, p. 250.

12. Teng and Fairbank, *China's Response*, p. 265.

13. Of the many books on the Nationalist era and the rise of the Communists the most useful have been Conrad Brandt, Benjamin Schwartz, and J. K. Fairbank, eds., *A Documentary History of Chinese Communism* (Cambridge, Mass., 1952); Lloyd Eastman, *The Abortive Revolution: China under Nationalist Rule, 1927–1937* (Cambridge, Mass., 1974); Chalmers A. Johnson, *Peasant Nationalism and Communist Power: The Emergence of Revolutionary China, 1937–1945* (Stanford, 1962); Schwartz, *Chinese Communism and the Rise of Mao*; Mark Selden, *The Yenan Way in Revolutionary China* (Cambridge, Mass., 1971); and James C. Thompson, Jr., *While China Faced West: American Reformers in Nationalist China, 1928–1937* (Cambridge, Mass., 1969).

14. de Bary, *Sources*, Vol. 2, p. 205.

CHAPTER 7

The study of the People's Republic is a field in itself, and perhaps as much has been written about it in the West as on all the rest of Chinese history combined. The basic information in this chapter can be found in works such as Fairbank, *The United States and China* and *The Great Chinese Revolution 1800–1985* and Craig Dietrich, *People's China: A Brief History* (New York, 1986). Vol. 14 of the *Cambridge History*, the first of two on the People's Republic, is also available. I have continued to cite specific works where they have been particularly useful, though the analysis in terms of traditional Chinese categories remains my own, of course.

1. Fairbank, *The United States and China*, p. 373.

2. This comes through, I think, in William Hinton, *Fanshen: A Documentary of Revolution in a Chinese Village* (New York, 1966), especially Part 2; and Isabel Crook and David Crook, *Ten Mile Inn: Mass Mobilization in a Chinese Village* (New York, 1979), Ch. 3–6.

3. See Richard Walker, *The Human Cost of Communism in China*, printed for the Committee on the Judiciary, U.S. Senate, 92d Congress, 1st Session (Washington, D.C., 1971), p. 16.

4. Though there is no question that the Great Leap was a catastrophe, it should be noted that one is left with some uncertainty about the number of people who died. At the time, and for many years thereafter, most Western scholars, including some with access to intelligence information, said there was malnutrition but not famine. These were the views, for example, that were commonly expressed in the objective and highly respected journal *The China Quarterly*; see the citations under "Great Leap" in Michael Dillon, comp., *The China Quarterly Index* to Nos. 1–80 (1960–1979), 2 Vols. (London, 1983).

There was, however, an article, written in 1962, that said that the Leap was causing malnutrition and might result in famine if the bad harvests of previous years continued. See Joseph Alsop, "On China's Descending Spiral," *The China Quarterly* 11 (July–Sept. 1962), p. 21. In the following issue there was a symposium devoted to Alsop's article, "On China's Descending Spiral," 12 (Oct.–Dec. 1962), p. 19. The contributors responded with a variety of views. One writer who was sympathetic to Alsop, though to some degree questioning his sources, was Richard Walker. As things turned out, the harvest of 1962 proved relatively successful.

When Walker later published his own forthrightly anti-Communist study, *The Human Cost of Communism in China* (see above note), he gave figures for famine that ranged from a minimum of one million dead to the possibility of two million.

Then, in the early 1980s, China released demographic data that suggested that abnormal deaths between 1958 and 1962 ranged from fifteen million to upward of thirty million. Later the government sent out investigative teams, which reported over forty million dead. These grim figures are difficult to evaluate, however, for when Peking began its economic reforms, it launched a campaign against the policies of the previous twenty years, including the Leap. It should be noted, however, that most foreign specialists accept the figures. In my opinion, more precise judgment on the matter must await further study and, perhaps, greater historical perspective.

5. For an excellent discussion of the dispute in these terms see Benjamin I. Schwartz, "Sino-Soviet Relations: The Question of Authority," in his *Communism in China: Ideology in Flux* (Cambridge, Mass., 1968).

6. See Fairbank, *The Great Chinese Revolution*, p. 320; and Walker, *The Human Cost of Communism in China*, p. 16. Though it seems difficult to imagine exaggerating the

evils of the Cultural Revolution, it should again be noted that, since the late 1970s there has been a major campaign against it (see note 4).

7. In addition to the general works cited above, the following have been particularly helpful on the story of the past fifteen years: Birthe Arendrup, Carsten Thogersen, and Anne Wedell-Wedellsborg, eds., *China in the 1980s and Beyond* (London, 1986); Per Fischer, "China's Leaders: Loss of Credibility," *Aussenpolitik* 14 (1989); Kathleen Hartford, "The Political Economy behind Beijing Spring," forthcoming; Immanuel C. Y. Hsu, *China without Mao: The Search for a New Order* (New York, 1983); Elizabeth Perry and Christine Wong, eds., *The Political Economy of Reform in Post-Mao China* (Cambridge, Mass., 1985), in particular, Kathleen Hartford, "Socialist Agriculture is Dead; Long Live Socialist Agriculture! Organizational Transformations in Rural China"; John Schrecker, "Racism and Confusion in China," *The Brandeisian* 2:3 (March 1989), p. 8; Tang Tsou, *The Cultural Revolution and Post-Mao Reforms* (Chicago, 1986); David Zweig, "Peasants and Politics," *World Policy Journal* (Fall 1989); and the successive volumes in the excellent series put out yearly by different editors for the China Council of the Asia Society, *China Briefing*, and, in particular, Andrew J. Nathan, "Politics: Reform at the Crossroad" and Bruce L. Reynolds, "The Chinese Economy in 1988," both in the volume for 1989.

8. See Ch. 1, section on "Other Philosophies; the Concept of Datong." Mencius, of course, spoke not of heavy industry but only of land. However, it seems reasonable to construe his views in this way. It should be stressed, though, that this analysis is based on my own understanding of the tradition rather than on the way things are put in China today, at least publicly. It is also worth noting that the responsibility system of land tenure (see below) also has considerable similarity to the equal-field system of the Tang. The latter was, of course, influenced by Mencian ideals and afterward was often considered to be a particularly just approach to the allocation of land (see Ch. 2, section on "The Sui and Tang . . . ").

An interesting book that shows some of the economic ideals of the Confucian radicals of the late Qing is Chen Huan-chang, *The Economic Principles of Confucius and His School* (New York, 1974), 2 Vols. This is a reprint of a Ph.D. dissertation (Columbia University, 1911) written by a Chinese scholar who in 1904 passed the highest level of the examinations, the *jinshi*.

9. This excellent term is introduced in Nathan, "Politics: Reform at the Crossroads," and the following paragraph essentially quotes from his article, pp. 18ff.

Guide to Pronunciation

In this book I have used the so-called *pinyin* system for romanizing Chinese. I have, however, used traditional spellings for certain names that have a well-established anglicized form (such as Canton, Peking, and Yangtze) or are especially well known in other forms of romanization (such as Sun Yat-sen or Chiang Kai-shek). In addition, I have not changed the romanization that appears in the names and titles cited in the notes and bibliography.

In pinyin the values of the letters that differ from English are pronounced roughly as follows:

1. At the beginning of syllables:

    c as the *ts* in ca*ts*up

    q as the *ch* in *ch*eese

    x as the *sh* in *sh*erry

    z as the *dz* in a*dz*

    zh as the *j* in *j*am

2. At the beginning or middle of syllables:

    a as the *a* in m*a*rgin

    e as the *u* in d*u*ck

3. At the end of syllables:

    ai as the *ie* in l*ie*

    ao as the *ow* in c*ow*

    hi as the *er* in *er*mine

    i as the *ea* in s*ea*

ian as the word *yen*
iu as the *ow* in l*ow*
o as the *o* in c*o*ffee
ou as the *ow* in l*ow*
o in *ong* as the *u* in p*u*dding
u as the *oo* in m*oo*n
un as the *oo* in w*oo*d

4. The syllable:

yi is pronounced as the *ea* in s*ea*
yan is pronounced like *yen*
zi is pronounced like the *dz* in a*dz*

Glossary of Chinese Terms

baojia 保甲
changshan 長衫
datong 大同
duanyi 短衣
fu min 富民
geming 革命
hao tie bu zuo ding 好鐵不作釘
hao ren bu zuo bing 好人不作兵
huangdi 皇帝
jinshi 進士
jun tian 均田
junxian 郡縣
junzi 君子
kaozheng 考證
laolizhe 勞力者
laoxinzhe 勞心者
li 理
li min 利民
liu junzi 六君子
luan 亂
minquan 民權
minsheng 民生
minzu 民族
nei luan wai huan 內亂外患
qi 氣
qin min 親民
qingyi 清議
ren chi ren 人吃人
ru xue 儒學
san gang 三綱
San Dai 三代
shehuizhuyi 社會主義
sheng quan fa cai 升官發財
shi 士
shifeng 士風
su feng 素封
taiji 太極

taiping 太平
tianming 天命
tu jun 土均
wang 王
wuwei 無爲
xiaoren 小人
xin min 新民
yan lu 言路
yin, yang 陰陽
zheng ming 正名
zhongxing 中興

Bibliography of Materials Cited

Alitto, Guy S. *The Last Confucian: Liang Shu-ming and the Chinese Dilemma of Modernity*. Berkeley: University of California Press, 1979.

Alsop, Joseph. "On China's Descending Spiral." *The China Quarterly*, 11 (July-Sept. 1962), 21–37.

Arendrup, Birthe, Carsten Thogersen, and Anne Wedell-Wedellsborg, eds. *China in the 1980s and Beyond*. Scandinavian Institute of Asian Studies. London: Curzon Press, 1986.

Bauer, Wolfgang. *China and the Search for Happiness*. New York: Seabury Press, 1976.

Bernal, Martin. *Chinese Socialism to 1907*. Ithaca, N.Y.: Cornell University Press, 1976.

Boardman, Eugene. *Christian Influence upon the Taiping Rebellion*. Madison: University of Wisconsin Press, 1952.

Bodde, Derk. *China's Cultural Tradition: What and Whither?* New York: Rinehart, 1957.

Brandt, Conrad, Benjamin Schwartz, and J. K. Fairbank, eds. *A Documentary History of Chinese Communism*. Cambridge, Mass.: Harvard University Press, 1952.

Chang Hsin-pao. *Commissioner Lin and the Opium War*. Cambridge, Mass.: Harvard University Press, 1964.

Chen Huan-Chang. *The Economic Principles of Confucius and His School*. Ph.D. diss., Columbia University, 1911. Originally published as Nos. 112–113 of *Studies in History, Economics, and Public Law*; reprinted, 2 Vols., New York: Gordon Press, 1974.

China Briefing. Edited variously by Robert Oxnam, Richard Bush, Steven Goldstein, John Major, and Anthony J. Kane for the China Council of the Asia Society. Boulder, Colo.: Westview Press, 1981–89.

Ch'ing, Julia. *To Acquire Wisdom: The Way of Wang Yang-ming*. New York: Columbia University Press, 1976.

Cohen, Paul A. *Discovering History in China*. New York: Columbia University Press, 1984.

Cohen, Paul A., and John Schrecker, eds. *Reform in Nineteenth-Century China*. Cambridge, Mass.: Harvard University Press, 1976.

Chow Tse-tsung. *The May Fourth Movement*. Cambridge, Mass.: Harvard University Press, 1960.

Creel, H. G. *Confucius and the Chinese Way*. New York: Harper and Row, 1960.

Crook, Isabel, and David Crook. *Ten Mile Inn: Mass Mobilization in a Chinese Village*. New York: Pantheon Books, 1979.

Dardess, John W. *Confucianism and Autocracy: Professional Elites in the Founding of the Ming Dynasty*. Berkeley: University of California Press, 1983.

de Bary, William Theodore. "Individualism and Humanitarianism in Late Ming Thought." In *Self and Society in Ming Thought*, ed. by William Theodore de Bary. New York: Columbia University Press, 1970.

———. *The Liberal Tradition in China*. Hong Kong: Chinese University Press, 1983.

———. "A Plan for the Prince: The Ming-i tai-fang lu of Huang Tsung-hsi." Ph.D. diss., Columbia University, 1953.

———, ed. *Self and Society in Ming Thought*. New York: Columbia University Press, 1970.

de Bary, William Theodore, Wing-tsit Chan, and Burton Watson, comps. *Sources of Chinese Tradition*. 2 Vols. New York: Columbia University Press, 1960.

Des Forges, Roger. *Hsi-liang and the Chinese National Revolution*. New Haven: Yale University Press, 1973.

Dietrich, Craig. *People's China: A Brief History*. New York: Oxford University Press, 1986.

Dillon, Michael, comp. *The China Quarterly Index* to Nos. 1–80 (1960–1979), 2 Vols. London: Contemporary China Institute, School of Oriental and African Studies, 1983.

Eastman, Lloyd. *The Abortive Revolution: China under Nationalist Rule, 1927–1937*. Cambridge, Mass.: Harvard University Press, 1974.

———. *Throne and Mandarins: China's Search for a Policy During the Sino-French Controversy, 1880–1885*. Cambridge, Mass.: Harvard University Press, 1967.

Elman, Benjamin. *From Philosophy to Philology: Intellectual and Social Aspects of Change in Late Imperial China*. Cambridge, Mass.: Harvard University Press, 1984.

Esherick, Joseph W. *The Origins of the Boxer Uprising*. Berkeley: University of California Press, 1987.

Fairbank, John K. *The Great Chinese Revolution 1800–1985*. New York: Harper and Row, 1986.

———. *Trade and Diplomacy on the China Coast*. Cambridge, Mass.: Harvard University Press, 1953.

———. *The United States and China*. Cambridge, Mass.: Harvard University Press, 1983.

Fairbank, John K., A. Feuerwerker, K. C. Liu, and R. MacFarquhar, eds. *The Cambridge History of China*, Vols. 10–14. Cambridge, Eng.: Cambridge University Press, 1978–1987.

Fairbank, John K., E. Reischauer, and A. Craig. *East Asia: The Modern Transformation*. Boston: Houghton Mifflin, 1965.

Feuerwerker, Albert. *China's Early Industrialization: Sheng Hsuan-huai and Mandarin Enterprise*. Cambridge, Mass.: Harvard University Press, 1958.

Fischer, Per. "China's Leaders: Loss of Credibility." *Aussenpolitik* 14 (1989), 309–320.

Fogel, Joshua A. *Politics and Sinology: The Case of Naito Konan (1866–1934)*. Cambridge, Mass.: Harvard University Press, 1984.

Forke, Alfred. *Geschichte der neueren chinesischen philosophie* (History of Modern Chinese Philosophy). Hamburg: De Gruyter, 1938.

Friedman, Edward. *Backward toward Revolution: The Chinese Revolutionary Party*. Berkeley: University of California Press, 1974.

Fung Yu-Lan. *A History of Chinese Philosophy*. Tr. by Derk Bodde. 2 Vols. Princeton: Princeton University Press, 1952.

Gasster, Michael. "The Republican Revolutionary Movement." In *The Cambridge History of China*, Vol. 11, ed. by J. K. Fairbank and K. C. Liu. Cambridge, Eng.: Cambridge University Press, 1978–1987.

Gentzler, J. Mason. "A Literary Biography of Liu Tsung-yuan." Ph.D. diss., Columbia University, 1966.

Gernet, Jacques. *Daily Life in China on the Eve of the Mongol Invasion, 1250–1276*. New York: Macmillan, 1962.

Hao Yen-p'ing, and Wang Erh-min. "Changing Chinese Views of Western Relations." In *The Cambridge History of China*. Vol. 11, ed. by John K. Fairbank and K. C. Liu. Cambridge, Eng.: Cambridge University Press, 1978–1987.

Hartford, Kathleen. "The Political Economy behind Beijing Spring." Forthcoming.

———. "Socialist Agriculture Is Dead; Long Live Socialist Agriculture! Organizational Transformations in Rural China." In *The Political Economy of Reform in Post-Mao China*, ed. by Elizabeth Perry and Christine Wong. Cambridge, Mass.: Harvard University Press, 1985.

Hinton, William. *Fanshen: A Documentary of Revolution in a Chinese Village*. New York: Monthly Review Press, 1966.

Hou Wailu 侯外廬, ed. *Zhongguo lidai datong lixiang* 中國歷代大同理想 *(The Datong Ideal through the Course of Chinese History)*. Peking: Kexue (Science), 1959.

Hsiao Kung-chuan. *A History of Chinese Political Thought*. Tr. by F. W. Mote, Vol. 1 Princeton: Princeton University Press, 1979.

———. *A Modern China and a New World: K'ang Yu-wei, Reformer and Utopian, 1858–1927*. Seattle: University of Washington Press, 1975.

———. *Rural China: Imperial Control in the Nineteenth Century*. Seattle: University of Washington Press, 1960.

Hsu Cho-Yun. *Ancient China in Transition*. Stanford: Stanford University Press, 1965.

Hsu, Immanuel C. Y. *China without Mao: The Search for a New Order*. New York: Oxford University Press, 1983.

———. *The Rise of Modern China*. New York: Oxford University Press, 1983.

Huang, Ray. *1587, A Year of No Significance: The Ming Dynasty in Decline*. New Haven: Yale University Press, 1981.

Huang Zongxi 黃宗羲 . *Mingyi Daifang Lu* 明夷待訪錄 (A Plan for the Prince). Shanghai: Commercial Press, 1937.

Hucker, Charles O. *China's Imperial Past: An Introduction to Chinese History and Culture*. Stanford: Stanford University Press, 1975.

———, ed. *Chinese Government in Ming Times*. New York: Columbia University Press, 1969.

Hudson, G. F. *Europe and China*. Boston: Beacon Press, 1961.

Jian Bozan 翦伯贊 et al., eds. *Wuxu Bianfa* 戊戌變法 (*The Reform Movement of 1898*). 4 Vols. Modern Chinese Historical Series, No. 8: Shanghai: Shenzhou Guoguang, 1953.

Johnson, Chalmers A. *Peasant Nationalism and Communist Power: The Emergence of Revolutionary China, 1937–1945*. Stanford: Stanford University Press, 1962.

Jones, Susan Mann, and Philip A. Kuhn. "Dynastic Decline and the Roots of Rebellion." In *The Cambridge History of China*, Vol. 10, ed. by John K. Fairbank. Cambridge, Eng.: Cambridge University Press, 1978–1987.

Kang Youwei 康有爲 (pseud. Ming Yi 明夷), "Gongmin Zizhi Pian" 公民自治篇 ("On Self-Government by the Citizenry") in the *Xinmin Congbao* 新民叢報 (*The New People's Miscellany*), No. 7 (1902), 27–38.

Kuhn, Philip A. "Local Self-Government under the Republic." In *Conflict and Control in Late Imperial China*, ed. by Frederic Wakeman, Jr., and Carolyn Grant. Berkeley: University of California Press, 1975.

———. "The Taiping Rebellion." In *The Cambridge History of China*, Vol. 10, ed. by John K. Fairbank. Cambridge, Eng.: Cambridge University Press, 1978–1987.

Kuo Ting-yee, and K. C. Liu. "Self-strengthening: The Pursuit of Western Technology." In *The Cambridge History of China*, Vol. 10, ed. by John K. Fairbank. Cambridge, Eng.: Cambridge University Press, 1978–1987.

Lattimore, Owen. *Inner Asian Frontiers of China*. New York: American Geographical Society, 1940.

Lau, D. C., tr. *Mencius*. London: Penguin Classics, 1970.

Li Yu-ning. *The Introduction of Socialism into China*. New York: Columbia University Press, 1971.

Lin Yu-Sheng. *The Crisis of Chinese Consciousness: Radical Antitraditionalism in the May Fourth Era*. Madison: University of Wisconsin Press, 1979.

Liu Kwang-ching, "The Ch'ing Restoration." In *The Cambridge History of China*, Vol. 10, ed. by John K. Fairbank. Cambridge, Eng.: Cambridge University Press, 1978–1987.

Lockwood, William W., ed. *The State and Economic Enterprise in Japan: Essays in the Political Economy of Growth*. Princeton: Princeton University Press, 1965.

Lo Jung-Pang, ed. *K'ang Yu-wei, A Biography and a Symposium*. Tucson: University of Arizona Press. 1967.

Lu Xun (Lu Hsun). 鲁迅 . *Lu Xun Quanji* 鲁迅全集 (*The Complete Works of Lu Xun*). Vol. 1. Peking: Renmin Wenxue, 1956.

———. *Selected Works of Lu Hsun*. Tr. by Yang Hsien-yi and Gladys Yang. Vol. I. Peking: Foreign Languages Press, 1956.

Marsh, Robert. *The Mandarins: The Circulation of Elites in China, 1600–1900*. Glencoe: Free Press, 1961.

Marx, Karl, and Frederick Engels. *Collected Works*. Vol. 10. New York: International, 1978.

Maverick, Lewis. *China: A Model for Europe*. San Antonio: Paul Anderson, 1946.

Meisner, Maurice. *Li Ta-chao and the Origins of Chinese Marxism*. Cambridge, Mass.: Harvard University Press, 1967.

Meskill, John, ed. *The Pattern of Chinese History*. Boston: D. C. Heath, 1965.

Metzgar, Thomas. *Escape from Predicament: Neo-Confucianism and China's Evolving Political Culture*. New York: Columbia University Press, 1977.

Michael, Franz, with Chang Chung-li. *The Taiping Rebellion: History and Documents*. Vol. 1, *History*. Seattle: University of Washington Press, 1966.

Min Tu-Ki 閔斗基. *Chungguk kundae kaehyok undong ui yon'gu: Kang Yu-i chungsim ui 1898-nyon kaehyok undong* 中國近代改革運動의 研究 — 康有爲中心의 1898改革運動 (*An Investigation of the Movement for Reform in Modern China: The Reform Movement of 1898 Which Centered on Kang Youwei*). Seoul: Ilchogak, 1985.

———. ''Musul pyonpop undong ui paegyong e taehayo t'ukhi ch'ongnyup'a wa yangmup'a rul chungsim uro'' 戊戌變法運動의 背景에 대하여—特히 清流派와 洋務派를 中心으로— (''On the Background of the Reform Movement of 1898 with Special Reference to the Qingliu pai and the Yangwu pai''), *Tongyang sahek yon'gu (Journal of Asian Historical Studies)* No. 5 (1971), 101–151.

———. *National Polity and Local Power: The Transformation of Late Imperial China*, ed. by Philip A. Kuhn and Timothy Brook. Cambridge, Mass.: Harvard University Press, 1989.

Miyazaki Ichisada 宮崎市定. ''Yosei Shuhi Yushi Kaidai'' 雍正硃批諭旨解題 (''The Yungzheng Emperor's Vermilion Instructions''), *Toyoshi Kenkyu (The Journal of Oriental Research)* 15:4 (March 1957), 1–32.

Montesquieu, Charles. *The Spirit of the Laws*. Tr. by Thomas Nugent. New York: Hafner, 1949.

Mote, F. W. ''The Transformation of Nanking.'' In *The City in Late Imperial China*, ed. by G. William Skinner. Stanford, Calif.: Stanford University Press, 1977.

Muramatsu Yuji. ''Some Themes in Chinese Rebel Ideologies.'' In *The Confucian Persuasian*, ed. by Arthur F. Wright. Stanford, Calif.: Stanford University Press, 1960.

Naquin, Susan. *Millenarian Rebellion in China: The Eight Trigrams Uprising of 1813*. New Haven: Yale University Press, 1976.

Naquin, Susan, and Evelyn S. Rawski. *Chinese Society in the Eighteenth Century*. New Haven: Yale University Press, 1987.

Nathan, Andrew J. ''Politics: Reform at the Crossroad'' In the *China Briefing* for 1989, ed. by Anthony J. Kane. Boulder, Colo.: Westview Press.

Ohkawa, Kazushi, and Henry Rosovsky. ''A Century of Japanese Economic Growth.''

In *The State and Economic Enterprise in Japan: Essays in the Political Economy of Growth*, ed. by William W. Lockwood. Princeton: Princeton University Press, 1965.

"On China's Descending Spiral." Several contributors. *The China Quarterly* 12 (Oct.-Dec., 1962), 19–53.

Perdue, Peter. *Exhausting the Earth: State and Peasant in Hunan, 1500–1850*. Cambridge, Mass.: Harvard University Press, 1987.

Perry, Elizabeth, and Christine Wong, eds. *The Political Economy of Reform in Post-Mao China*. Cambridge, Mass.: Harvard University Press, 1985.

Polachek, James. *Literati Groups and Literati Politics in Early Nineteenth-Century China*. Ph.D. diss., University of California, 1974.

Rawski, Evelyn S. *Education and Popular Literacy in Ch'ing China*. Ann Arbor: University of Michigan Press, 1979.

Reichwein, Adolf. *China and Europe*. Orig. pub. 1925; repub. Taipei: Ch'eng-wen Publishing Company, 1967.

Reischauer, E. O., and J. K. Fairbank. *East Asia: The Great Tradition*. Boston: Houghton Mifflin, 1960.

Reynolds, Bruce L. "The Chinese Economy in 1988" In the *China Briefing* for 1989, ed. by Anthony J. Kane. Boulder, Colo.: Westview Press.

Sakai, Tadao. "Confucianism and Popular Educational Works." In *Self and Society in Ming Thought*, ed. by William Theodore de Bary. New York: Columbia University Press, 1970.

Schiffrin, Harold. *Sun Yat-sen and the Origins of the Chinese Revolution*. Berkeley: University of California Press, 1968.

Schrecker, John. *Imperialism and Chinese Nationalism*. Cambridge, Mass.: Harvard University Press, 1971.

———. "The Pao-kuo Hui: A Reform Society of 1898." *Papers on China*, Vol. 14 (1960), 50–69.

———. "Racism and Confusion in China." *The Brandeisian* 2:3 (March 1989), 8, 14.

———. "The Reform Movement of 1898 and the Ch'ing-i: Reform as Opposition." In *Reform in Nineteenth-Century China*, ed. by Paul Cohen and John Schrecker. Cambridge, Mass.: Harvard University Press, 1976.

Schwartz, Benjamin. *Chinese Communism and the Rise of Mao*. Cambridge, Mass.: Harvard University Press, 1951.

———. *Communism in China: Ideology in Flux*. Cambridge, Mass.: Harvard University Press, 1968.

———. *In Search of Wealth and Power: Yen Fu and the West*. Cambridge, Mass.: Harvard University Press, 1964.

———. *The World of Thought in Ancient China*. Cambridge, Mass.: Harvard University Press, 1985.

———, ed. *Reflections on the May 4th Movement: A Symposium*. Cambridge, Mass.: Harvard University Press, 1972.

Selden, Mark. *The Yenan Way in Revolutionary China*. Cambridge, Mass.: Harvard University Press, 1971.

Sheridan, James E. *China in Disintegration: The Republican Era in Chinese History, 1912–1949*. New York: Free Press. 1975.

Shih, Vincent Y. C. *The Taiping Ideology*. Seattle: University of Washington Press, 1967.

Skinner, G. William, ed. *The City in Late Imperial China*. Stanford, Calif.: Stanford University Press, 1977.

Tang Jinggao 唐敬杲, ed. *Gu Yanwu Wen* 顧炎武文 (*Selected Writings of Gu Yanwu*). Shanghai: Commercial Press, 1928.

Teng Ssu-yu, and John Fairbank. *China's Response to the West*. Cambridge, Mass.: Harvard University Press, 1954.

Thompson, James C., Jr. *While China Faced West: American Reformers in Nationalist China, 1928–1937*. Cambridge, Mass.: Harvard University Press, 1969.

Thompson, Laurence G., tr. *Ta T'ung Shu: The One-World Philosophy of K'ang Yu-wei*. London: Allen and Unwin, 1958.

Torr, Dona, ed., with Introduction and Notes. *Marx on China, 1853–1860, Articles from The New York Daily Tribune*. London: Lawrence and Wishart, 1951.

Tsou Tang. *The Cultural Revolution and Post-Mao Reforms*. Chicago: University of Chicago Press, 1986.

Tu Wei-ming. *Neo-Confucian Thought in Action: Wang Yang-ming's Youth, 1472–1509*. Berkeley: University of California Press, 1976.

Wakeman, Frederic, Jr. "The Canton Trade and the Opium War." In *The Cambridge History of China*, Vol. 10, ed. by John K. Fairbank. Cambridge, Eng.: Cambridge University Press, 1978–1987.

Wakeman, Frederic, Jr., and Carolyn Grant, eds. *Conflict and Control in Late Imperial China*. Berkeley: University of California Press, 1975.

———. *History and Will*. Berkeley: University of California Press, 1973.

Waley, Arthur, tr. *The Analects of Confucius*. London: 1938; reprinted New York: Vintage Books, no date.

Walker, Richard. *The Human Cost of Communism in China*. Printed for the Committee on the Judiciary, U.S. Senate, 92d Congress, lst Session. Washington, D.C.: GPO, 1971.

Wang Yangming. *Instructions for Practical Living and Other Neo-Confucian Writings*. Tr. with notes and commentaries by Chang Wing-tsit. New York: Columbia University Press, 1963.

Watson, Burton, tr. *Basic Writings of Mo Tzu, Hsun Tzu, and Han Fei Tzu*. New York: Columbia University Press, 1967.

———. *Ssu-ma Ch'ien: Grand Historian of China*. New York: Columbia University Press, 1958.

Wright, Arthur F., ed. *The Confucian Persuasion*. Stanford, Calif.: Stanford University Press, 1960.

Wright, Mary C., ed. *China in Revolution: The First Phase, 1900–1913*. New Haven: Yale University Press, 1968.

———. *The Last Stand of Chinese Conservatism*. Stanford: Stanford University Press, 1957.

Wu Jungzi, *Ru Lin Waishi (Unofficial History of the Literati)*. Tr. by Yang Hsien-yi and Gladys Yang as *The Scholars*. Peking: Foreign Languages Press, 1973.

Wu, Silas H. L. *Passage to Power: Kang Hsi and His Heir Apparent, 1661–1722*. Cambridge, Mass.: Harvard University Press, 1979.

Xiang Bao Leizuan 湘報類纂 (*Selections from the Hunan Journal*). 1902; reprinted, Taipei, 1968.

Yang Lien-sheng. ''Ming Local Government.'' In *Chinese Government in Ming Times*, ed. by Charles O. Hucker. New York: Columbia University Press, 1969.

———. *Studies in Chinese Institutional History*. Cambridge, Mass.: Harvard University Press, 1963.

Young, Ernest P. *The Presidency of Yuan Shih-k'ai: Liberalism and Dictatorship in Early Republican China*. Ann Arbor: University of Michigan Press, 1977.

Zhongguo datong sixiang ziliao 中國大同思想資料 *(Materials on Datong Thought)* comp. Department of Philosophy of the Chinese Academy of Sciences. Peking: Zhonghua Shuju, 1959.

Zweig, David. ''Peasants and Politics.'' *World Policy Journal* (Fall 1989), 633–645.

INDEX

About the Author

JOHN E. SCHRECKER teaches at Brandeis University and is a member of the Fairbank Center for East Asian Research at Harvard. Among other works, he is the author of *Imperialism and Chinese Nationalism* and the co-author of *Mrs. Chiang's Szechwan Cookbook*. In addition to Chinese studies, his particular interest is intercultural and comparative history.